Entangled is a profound meditation on how the inhabitants of Kachemak Bay—human and nonhuman alike—have reckoned with the ebb and surge of cultural and ecological changes through time. With the curiosity of a biologist, the doggedness of a detective, and the eloquence of a poet, Marilyn Sigman beautifully deciphers a landscape marked by abundance and scarcity, stability and disruption, loss and resilience, memory and story. The fascinating result is a scientific whodunit, a natural and cultural history, a deep map, an elegy, and, above all, a love letter.

> —*Sherry Simpson, author of* Dominion of Bears, *winner of the 2015 John Burroughs Medal for Distinguished Natural History Book*

Marilyn Sigman unites her "science brain" with her naturalist's heart and an insatiable curiosity to bring us a beautifully written account of human and ecological connections. Part memoir, part natural history, part quest into understanding the nature of change—*Entangled* will delight not just readers intrigued with Alaska's resource and cultural history but all those concerned with what it means to know and honor a home place.

> —*Nancy Lord, former Alaska Writer Laureate, author of* Fishcamp *and* Beluga Days

Like creatures in an ephemeral tide pool, our lives are shaped by forces both within and beyond our control. In *Entangled*, Marilyn Sigman shows us that life is messy, shift happens, and riding the waves of change is best done with a steady kayak, muck boots, and an inner compass.

> — *Amy Gulick, photographer and author of* Salmon in the Trees: Life in Alaska's Tongass Rain Forest

In these pages Marilyn Sigman sweeps us along a path of personal discovery. This memoir is steeped in fast-moving, wondrously descriptive stories centered on the biology and archeology of the Kachemak Bay region of Alaska within the context of her personal and family history. Whether it be the investigation of the sea otter and the bidarki's role in shaping shoreline ecology, or the chain of environmental fallout precipitated by a recent ocean warming event (the "Blob"), or her telling of the spiritual and environmental story of the Kachemak people and their sudden mysterious disappearance, Sigman constructs a far-reaching picture of sometimes sudden historic and current environmental change. With great detail and the personal insight that comes from looking closely at the world around her, she draws us into the story behind the changes and their larger implications. Sigman has crafted a must-read for both local and visitor.

—*Craig Matkin, marine mammal scientist and director of the North Gulf Oceanographic Society*

ENTANGLED

People and Ecological Change
in Alaska's Kachemak Bay

"Raven's-Eye View of Kachemak Bay," by Mike Sirl.

ENTANGLED

People and Ecological Change
in Alaska's Kachemak Bay

MARILYN SIGMAN

Text © 2018 University of Alaska Press

Published by
University of Alaska Press
P.O. Box 756240
Fairbanks, AK 99775-6240

Cover and interior design by 590 Design.

Image credits:
Part 1: "Bidarki" (aka katy chiton) by Conrad Field
Part 2: "Kachemak lamp" by Kim McNett
Part 3: "Halibut" by Conrad Field
Part 4: "Otter carving" by Kim McNett

Cover art by Conrad Field.
Text by Weeden and Steinbeck printed with permission.

Library of Congress Cataloging in Publication Data

Names: Sigman, Marilyn, author.
Title: Entangled : people and ecological change in Alaska's Kachemak Bay /
    by Marilyn Sigman.
Description: Fairbanks : University of Alaska Press, [2018] | Includes index.
    | Identifiers: LCCN 2017031753 (print) | LCCN 2017048212 (ebook) |
    ISBN 9781602233492 (ebook) | ISBN 9781602233485 (pbk. : alk. paper)
Subjects: LCSH: Climatic changes | Alaska | Kachemak Bay Region.
    | Ecology | Alaska | Kachemak Bay Region. | Kachemak Bay (Alaska)
Classification: LCC QC903.2.A37 (ebook) | LCC QC903.2.A37 S54 2018 (print)
    | DDC 577.27/6097983dc23
LC record available at https://lccn.loc.gov/2017031753

Dedicated to the memory of my father,
Leo Sigman,
who took me fishing

All Alaskans must come to terms with the central problem of how a contemporary society can function harmoniously within arctic and subarctic environments. Harmonious function implies a deep and true knowledge of those environments and human interactions with them.

—Robert B. Weeden, *Messages from the Earth: Nature and Human Prospect in Alaska*

Table of Contents

Part I
Shifting Baselines

Arriving

I sit beside a roaring stream of water that pours through a gully toward the lip of a waterfall and plunges to the beach below. The water clatters with rocks, so loud it fills my mind. I feel its flow from the top of my head to my toes. Remaining stationary requires resistance to the seaward pull that carries torrents of soil, leaves, needles, blossoms, branches, and whole trees downward.

How could I ever hope to find peace and stillness in this place that is always in motion? This place could sweep me away in a seismic moment or wear me down slowly, drop by drop. The physical forces of the world move me just as surely as they move rocks and water. In this long rushing moment, I can barely stand firm and resist becoming part of the flow.

Kachemak Bay is an edgy place. It straddles the edges of lands scarred by glaciers. The cooled ash of volcanoes is interwoven with the leavings of streams that meandered the landscape for millions of years. Glaciers and streams wrote their chapters into this land. The volcanoes provided punctuation, and an entire book lies beneath the rubble, written huge by the patterned, heaving rhythm of the world's tectonic heart. Beyond a southern horizon of peaks, the Pacific Plate nudges the North American Plate in the many-fathomed Aleutian Trench. The plates lock up and then bolt into earthquakes. The Pacific Plate dives down and bubbles back up as fiery lava.

The name *Kachemak* is derived from Native words *ka*, "water"; *chek*, "cliff"; and *mak*, meaning "large, high, or great." It was Highcliff Bay on the earliest American maps and charts until Kachemak Bay stuck in 1896. One persistent local legend is that the word translates as "smoky bay," for the place where fires burned and smoldered in coal seams for decades. Homer, its largest town now, lies on the north shore with cliffs above the beach in either direction. Coal miners and fishermen, homesteaders and tourists, scientists and artists, Russian Old Believers and Methodists have all called it home—and Homer. No poet, Homer Pennock founded the town in the best tradition of Alaska conmen, leaving with the dough to die penniless in New York after one scheme too many. Now, the cabin hippies chop firewood, haul water, and homeschool their children. An advancing front of retirees shares the million-dollar views. Here the road ends.

The water shape-shifts, from bay to fog and cloud and back to the bay again as rain or snow. Currents and tides arrive from the south and depart to the north in a great counterclockwise gyre spun up by the moon and the revolving planet. The tides, with a range that is among the most extreme on Earth, are two enormous in-and-out breaths every day. The land recedes in trickles and sudden slips. During the melt season, the bare slopes of the bluff are strewn at their gully knickpoints with eighty-foot-tall spruce trees. They point down toward enormous piles of rocks and soil covered with vegetation that traveled so quickly that fireweed remains in bloom.

The boundary of land and beach and water shifts, changing slowly—tide by tide, storm by storm—or suddenly. The 1964 earthquake caused the bottom of the bay to drop by six feet in ten minutes, and the entire planet rang like a gong. It was only a minor setback for land that has been rising for thousands of years as the great weight of the glaciers is dissolved by the sun's warmth.

"We are all living for the halibut," we say in Homer. It's our made-for-tourists joke in the town the chamber of commerce claims, without credible challenge, to be the Halibut Fishing Capital of the World. "We are here because we're not all there," our bumper stickers proclaim. We've been dubbed one of America's One Hundred Best Small Art Towns (presumably because the town is small, not the art). Our artists weave fish skin and kelp into baskets, throw and bake beach clay into pots, turn moose antlers into coat racks, and burn a massive and communal basket of remembrance every year on the beach.

We have the "coolest zip code" in America among the Top Ten Dream Towns chosen by *Outside* magazine. According to *Men's Journal*, we're one of the Fifty Best Places to Live, "the capital of the subsistence lifestyle, where people move so they can eat what they kill." *Coastal Living* magazine has touted Homer as a "So you want to live in" kind of place, "a place where artists, entrepreneurs, and adventure seekers find nirvana on the shores of Alaska's Kenai Peninsula." A "funky enclave," it's one of Fifty Fabulous Places to Retire in America, one of Fifty Top (Wilderness) Places to Live and Play according to *National Geographic Adventure*, and one of the Top Ten Coolest Small Towns according to *Frommer's Budget Travel*. We're the town at the end of the road, not as impressive a distinction in largely roadless Alaska as it might be elsewhere. We're "the cosmic hamlet by the sea," so-named by our own patron saint, Brother Asaiah, who settled here in the short-lived Barefooters' commune and spent his elder years proclaiming peace and love at every city council meeting.

No one compiles a list of the one hundred best science towns in America, but Homer could certainly be a contender, with its combination of a State Critical Habitat Area, a National Estuarine Research Reserve, and an ice-free harbor that's the winter home port for a National Wildlife Refuge research vessel that ranges all the way out along the Aleutian Islands. At any given time, traps, divers, or sensing devices are somewhere within the bay. A marine lab on the south shore is thronged by scientists from NOAA (National Oceanic and Atmospheric Administration) and the University of Alaska. They roam and scour the bay, count the fish, measure the currents, and poke and prod the wildlife. They detect molecules from Chinese smokestacks in the fat of harbor seals that have sustained Alaska Native cultures for ten thousand years.

For eleven years, I was a naturalist in Homer and manager of the Center for Alaskan Coastal Studies, a nonprofit organization dedicated to guided field trips, hikes, and ecotours on beaches and through the forest. For six weeks between mid-April and late May, it was schoolchildren nearly every day. They emptied out Alaska classrooms to go on their beach field trips during the most extreme tides of the year. From Memorial Day to Labor Day, it was a combination of locals and tourists of all ages learning about not only the beach creatures but also the ecology of the forest and meadows, edible plants, and pioneer history with a smattering of archaeology thrown in. When I began working for the center in 1998, the organization based their trips and tours out of the Peterson Bay Field Station on the south shore, perched on an isthmus between Peterson and China Poot Bays and accessible only by boat. On the bluff above Homer, we provided even more educational hikes and programs at the 125-acre Wynn Nature Center. By the time I left the job, we had added acres, buildings, and yurts in both places; purchased a building in downtown Homer for our headquarters; and extended our yurt empire to Homer Spit to book tours among the halibut charter offices.

I couldn't have imagined a better job if I had conjured it up, even with the daily vexations of volunteer-engineered plumbing, obsequious fund-raising, and lost-and-found rain gear and socks. Being the logistical maven of errant naturalists, boats, food, and building supplies occupied most of my waking hours from April to October, but I was a naturalist at heart. I led tours whenever I was needed to fill in. Other days, I found a reason, however flimsy, to spend the day across the bay or several hours at the nature center. After adjusting the plumbing or declaring it intractable and soothing hurt feelings with my best supervisory empathy, I went for walks along the trails. I justified it as necessary to being both teacher and model for my much younger naturalist staff, but I always felt a little guilty that I was paid to do exactly what I loved.

I walked the beaches, attuning my meanderings to the tidal cycles. The rocks lurking beneath the water were exposed by the ebbing tide, and they teemed with life in glistening swaths. The many-legged and shelled creatures clung to their crevices and the last drops of moisture until the tide returned. I walked the forest trails when the plants emerged, green-legged, and the flowers shifted from violets in spring to a panoply of blossoms during summer and later as bursts of red and yellow marked their dying back under the spruce trees. I watched the sun rise in the sky higher and longer before descending into its short winter arc. During the winters, in the midst of writing grants and endless thank-you letters, I read everything I could find about the natural history of the boreal and coastal forests and the marine ecology of the North Pacific Ocean of which Kachemak Bay is a part.

I like to think of this as my Victorian naturalist period, in the sense of giving full rein as passionate amateur interested in all aspects of nature. It was lore I was after, the stories as well as the careful scientific observations that followed hypotheses and someone else's numbingly repetitive scientific methods and clever data analyses. Like the Victorian naturalists, I became a collector of the remains of living things and the facts of their natural histories. Unlike the Victorians, however, I had no curio cabinet or parlor to show off my finds. I didn't even have separate rooms for living and for entertaining guests. Shells, rocks, and artifacts—selected for their striking patterns and my quest for the stories that shaped them—slowly settled as sediment on my window ledges and bookshelves.

But the pace of change in the world overtook me. Over and above the daily cycles of tides and the stately march of seasons, things altered in the bay in ways I hadn't anticipated. I arrived during what turned out to be a spruce bark beetle epidemic, which spread on both sides of the bay. I recognized the extent of the infestation when I stood on my porch one winter day and heard loud crunching emanating from beneath the bark of my stack of firewood. Dead trees girdled by beetles soon crashed down into a jumble of pick-up sticks across our trails. Over the course of several summers, the glacier in the bay to the west of the field station galloped backward. More and more silt swirled into the tidal current and was deposited around our dock, grounding it more and more frequently. A new species of sea star that no one had seen in two decades of beach walks began showing up alive in massive windrows on the beaches at the same time that nearly a dozen species of sea stars that we saw regularly on low tides shrank to just a handful.

We adapted. A chainsaw brigade of volunteers opened up the trails blocked by dead spruce windfall each spring. Our forest hikes became quieter every year as the flute notes of thrushes and the scolding chirps of red squirrels became rarer. Hikes became less and less mysterious in the absence of the density and enclosure of live trees. Even the woodpecker's rat-a-tatting through dead wood for insects disappeared. I used my tidal math and my woeful physics to schedule pickups and drop-offs at the field station at times when the dock could be counted on to float. We drew fewer lines between different types of sea stars and their prey in our food web diagrams of who eats whom.

The pace of change accelerated. The environment shifted, veering in directions that my personal stash of lore and scientific information couldn't quite map. I reluctantly tuned into the science of climate change and the soon-raging debate. Which changes were natural and "normal"? Which were occurring in cycles that took place over decades or centuries, to which everything that lived in the bay, including myself, could surely learn to adapt? Which were caused by my own species at accelerating rates that would change the ecosystem irreparably? Was the future to be one of more and more change and loss of what I had come to see as intricate patterns of life, as givens?

Scientists amassed evidence of global climate change, which hit Alaska near the North Pole at nearly twice the rate of the planet's more temperate places. In addition to shorter cycles for insects like the spruce bark beetles, our ponds and lakes began evaporating and going dry during warmer summers. Animals—even sea turtles—moved northward from more tropical waters to now warmer Alaska seas. In the far north of Alaska, sea ice and permafrost melted more each year. Although the popular argument over climate change seemed to be one about belief, among scientists it was a matter of theory backed up by large amounts of evidence. The changes—the dead trees, the monster storms more intense than anyone could remember, even the temperature of the ocean measured by our scientists—became the stuff of everyday conversation in Homer.

The idea that the weather could change globally and in a direction that might be unstoppable does have the ring of a conspiracy theory, of the type a number of Homerites are prone to recite. It seemed to shake people up in the way that the theory of evolution must have shaken Victorian society and its naturalists. The country parsons who botanized to find evidence of the glory of God's creation and the budding agnostic scientists had been forced to take sides on the question of the true relations of the species, only one of which was considered to be made in the image of God. Just as the theory of evolution pointed backward to origins, climate change pointed backward to the smokestacks in London around the time Darwin published his theory. Both theories pointed forward as well to consequences, many of which some claim God would never allow to happen unless they signaled the prophesied end of the sinful world.

It was obvious to me that I would take the side of the scientists. Yet I felt compelled to understand the nature of the impacts that would be wrought in my own home. Could I teach anything that could forestall the end of the natural world as I had come to know it? Did human nature make drastic change inevitable? And if it did, how could I adapt to a vanishing world?

I began my search for some place to start, for a baseline. But I immediately realized there were problems with baselines. My sense of change, and of place, was based on my own personal baseline. I compared the rate and direction of changes in the bay to the only timeline I really knew: that of my own life.

Like everyone, I have trouble thinking about places except in terms of memories of more perfect, or more miserable, times. Some memories from my childhood feel solid and burnished, like the days I spent with my father fishing on small streams that meandered over Montana's sprawling ranchlands. As he drove farther away from the highway on narrow dirt tracks overgrown with grass that scraped the bottom of our station wagon, he told stories about his childhood and the driving trips he took into the same country with his parents. I was impatient at the time, and his stories barely registered. It took me years to figure out that going fishing was his way of remembering the land and waters of his childhood.

Catching trout for dinner mattered, but not nearly as much as memory. He often left me alone on the bank of the stream with a can of worms and a fishing pole as he fly-fished the holes farther and farther away until he was out of sight. I was particularly inept at learning to fly-fish, which may have been the reason for being left behind, but I think now that it was also his own desire for solitude in the places he remembered. In the end, he bequeathed me that same solitude and memories of an enduring Montana baseline, a place where wild animals and wild beauty, wheat crops, cattle, deer, and elk all thrived together on land threaded with the vibrant streams that we fished.

When I was ten and sitting on the bank of that Montana creek, my father, moving out of sight around the bend, was forty-five and remembering his own baseline of a place he had visited with his father thirty-five years before that. The Alaska I arrived to at the age of twenty-three and the Kachemak Bay I moved to at forty-seven are not the same places that anyone arrives to at a different time. Places change as does the nature of abundance. New people are born or arrive in new places all the time. Baselines and ecosystems shift.

Scientists recognize the phenomenon of shifting baselines. In 1995 Daniel Pauly, a fisheries biologist, published a paper titled "Anecdotes and the Shifting Baseline Syndrome in Fisheries Management." He chided fisheries managers for failing to identify the correct baseline for the size of a population of fish under "natural" conditions, before people began harvesting them or exploiting them as resources and extracting them from the ocean. The baseline that the managers begin with, Pauly suggests, is a personal one, based on the state of the world and fisheries at the start of their careers. If no one pays attention to historical data, if it even exists, before paying attention to populations of fish already being exploited, it's possible to make a terrible mistake. The managers, in effect, reset the baseline at a much lower level than it once was, just as I reset my baseline for a much tamer Montana than the one my father sustained in his memory. This matters, Pauly says, because long but slow declines of fish populations over extended periods of time would never be detected. It was widespread throughout fisheries management; it was a syndrome. What's lost in the process, Pauly concluded, is the "perception of change," when each generation redefines what's natural.

Alaska has certainly changed from the place I perceived when I arrived in 1974. But then I'm not the same person who arrived in Fairbanks to become a graduate student in the University of Alaska's Department of Wildlife Management. I knew absolutely nothing about wildlife management and little about the moose who were to become my study animals or the Kenai Peninsula that harbored the Moose Research Center. I thought then that I was entering a grand and pristine place, like Montana squared or cubed. I thought the environmental movement had just triumphed in the creation of a great sweep of legislation—the trio of the Clean Water Act, the National Environmental Policy Act, and the Wilderness Act—that would right so many environmental wrongs. For me, Alaska was the last stand for some of the largest and fiercest beasts in the world. I was thrilled that I would be paid a $400 monthly stipend and have opportunities to experience it.

What I didn't know was that I had arrived during a time of change in the field of wildlife management—the beginning of a glacial shift, not yet completed, from thinking of game animals like moose as crops to the dawning realization about the implications of ecological science. Mine was the second class of graduate students in Alaska who'd spent their undergraduate years at liberal universities—my own at Stanford, and the others at UC Santa Cruz, Cornell, and Antioch. We came directly from the tail end of the Vietnam War protests that segued into the first Earth Day. Some of us were women in a field that was overwhelmingly male. The guys who arrived as graduate students when I did had long hair and wore overalls ironically. Most of us had never hunted, unlike the graduate students who came before us who chose the field because they did. We practiced yoga and meditated. Although we threw ourselves enthusiastically into log cabin life—hauling water and chopping wood for heat, which was all we could afford—it was an adventure, not a commitment to becoming a real Alaskan. We spent the extra-long nights eating vegetarian meals and drinking the best wine we could afford instead of beer. We read Edward Abbey, Aldo Leopold (the essays, not his textbook, *Game Management*), and Gary Snyder by candlelight and Coleman lanterns.

We were dying to see wolves but arrived in the middle of debates about wolf control. In Alaska, you either hated wolves as evil, rapacious predators or you loved them as near mythical beasts or symbols of wilderness. We loved our fieldwork as extended sojourns in the wilds of Alaska (with the added benefit of transportation, equipment, and food paid for by grants), but we landed smack dab in the politics of the Alaska National Interest Lands Conservation Act, a virtual war over federal protection of capital-W Wilderness and wildlands. That debate also hardened into two opposing sides: you were either against the "lock-up" of lands from development and access for hunting and fishing or you were for the total protection of wilderness and habitat on the ecosystem scale. One side focused on the land, the environment, and secondarily on some stretches of the coastline and the other on the people in the foreground, moving across the ground without constraint to take and use or subsisting on the lands of their ancestors.

Our small group of graduate students were on the side of wilderness and what we understood to be the environment—the side for which our college days during the turbulent early 1970s had prepared us.

It was in the field that I found my Alaska. The best times in those early years were the seasons I followed moose around for my master's work and my seasonal fish and wildlife tech jobs. During my first winter in Alaska, I snowshoed after radio-collared moose to observe the elusive behaviors of cows and calves that kept them bonded. The question I was supposed to answer was whether or not cow moose were good mothers. The answer that the Alaska Department of Fish and Game biologists hoped for was no, so they could encourage hunters to shoot them in the fall to relieve their frustrations at being unable to find and shoot the much smaller numbers of bull moose in some places.

The Moose Research Center was forty miles by road from the town of Soldotna on the Kenai Peninsula, but I only went to town to buy groceries, do laundry, get my mail, and eat a few restaurant meals, against Edward Abbey's advice, at a place called Mom's. I was given a free place to lay down my sleeping bag in the loft in the Fish and Game boat shed, but I paid for it by being kept awake by the raucous poker games of the Fish and Game guys on Saturday night below me in the boat shed, games to which I was, of course, never invited.

The moose tolerated me much better than the Fish and Game biologists. When they did talk to me, they had a number of ways of poking fun at me with the expectation I would join in good naturedly. They told me endless moose hunting stories perhaps because they knew I wasn't a hunter. The moose were more companionable as I spent my days watching them and collecting data about their behavior. They were nonchalant about their flashy plastic ear tags and the huge radio collars they wore around their necks as they ate and ruminated and rested in patterns that defied what little I knew about statistical analysis.

I first visited Homer that winter, one that set records throughout Alaska for cold temperatures and deep snow. Most of the moose calves died and the cows became gaunt. One weekend in March, Tom, one of the fisheries biologists in Soldotna, invited me on a road trip. We drove south to Homer, which was only seventy miles away, but after months of meandering after diminishing numbers of moose, it felt like we were going to the far side of the universe. Tom was overjoyed to go somewhere that wasn't Soldotna, which he thought was as dull as I did. I recall very little about that trip except the snow—a long drive between huge white mounds on either side of the road, as if passing through a wormhole in the universe between the two towns. Homer was very quiet in the winter back then, and very few people appeared to live there. Tom's friends were literally holed up in a log cabin with stores of grains, frozen chunks of moose meat and salmon, and books, along with a healthy stash of dope. The whole weekend seemed like a winter dream.

The summers of 1975–80, I was dropped off by small planes or boats in remote places for months at a time. All types of wildlife needed to be surveyed and counted—moose, Arctic foxes, birds nesting in the Arctic, seabirds in their breeding colonies all along the Alaska coast, mountain goats on the Kenai Peninsula, salmon running up streams from Bristol Bay, Arctic char in the rivers of the Arctic National Wildlife Refuge.

One spring I spent three weeks on a ship on the southern edge of the sea ice that stretched from the North Pole to south of the Pribilof Islands. I fell asleep in my narrow bunk to the sounds of ice scraping the ship's sides as we ran for open water when the wind shifted and threatened to imprison us. The crew chipped away as ice encased the decks and lines. A helicopter whirred on and off the ship daily, bearing scientists and massive augers to drill through the sea ice and guns loaded with tranquilizer darts intended for walrus and seals. I counted something that I couldn't even see except under a microscope, pouring water in shades of green and brown sampled from just below the ice into tubes to be analyzed for the amount and types of teeming phytoplankton.

These were the glorious days B.T. (before technology), which arrived in the form of satellite phones that destroyed the remoteness of field camps. In those days, in addition to wall tents, boxes of food, datasheets, and a just-in-case bear gun, we were sent out with long poles that required "some assembly" into a single sideband radio tower. The antenna mounted on top of the tower could only transmit in a straight line of sight under clear weather conditions. We were technically required to call in from the field every night and verify that we had survived the last twenty-four hours and accomplished some work, but the radios worked intermittently at best. I was rarely dropped off alone, but the one time I was, it was to count mountain goats on an alpine bench. The pilot biologist crashed his plane on another alpine bench, one that didn't appear on any flight plan. Luckily he was found, and eventually so was I, a few days later than anticipated. I heard stories, never verified, about biologists dropped off in the spring and forgotten by fall.

On those long spring and summer days, we had observations and counts to make and long hikes to widely scattered sampling sites, but we also had plenty of time to just be wherever we had landed. I learned the plants and the birds in every region of the state and in every habitat. I watched gatherings and migrations of caribou and geese and salmon that lasted for days. We were establishing baselines. In the field, we could completely ignore the fact that much of our work was funded as the "before" studies bolstering plans for oil and gas development. I was falling in love with Alaska, wild Alaska, which I fervently believed would never be tamed. But although I didn't know it, the Alaska I had just begun to explore was already ending.

Fieldwork in Alaska's remote places, when it still felt remote, immersed me in the natural world in a way I found hard to recapture later in life. My work and life were intertwined with the lives of plants and animals and landscapes that filled my mind and dreams in a way that a human-dominated social world could never equal. It began to change when I eventually got a "real" job with benefits as a habitat biologist, a step closer to the human activities that were unraveling parts of Alaska's ecosystems. Still, I went to the field, but now I drove north from Fairbanks and slept in tents in gravel pits.

Our job was to survey a corridor for a proposed gas pipeline that would follow the Haul Road built for the construction of the oil pipeline that slices through five hundred miles of boreal forest, through the foothills and peaks of the Brook Range on the north through the tundra to the Arctic Ocean. The road and pipeline route crossed more than eight hundred rivers and streams that drained the vast area.

We counted and measured, but the baseline we documented was established after the oil pipeline had been built and the environmental damage somewhat crudely "repaired" and before the additional damage that building a gas pipeline would potentially inflict. We clambered down from the massive gravel mound of the Haul Road to measure water flowing through culverts that could block the migration of grayling, fish that weren't strong swimmers, to their upstream spawning areas. We walked the streams, sometimes far from the roads that crossed them, measuring their widths and depth and currents. As we scanned pools and undercut banks through polarized sunglasses, camouflaged fish appeared suddenly like optical illusions. We cataloged plants, birds, mammals, and fish in the corridor where the pipeline would be buried and the places that might yield the tonnage of gravel needed for roads and pads to insulate the permafrost from thaw.

Every day, as I swam up into wakefulness, I compared what I had seen and duly recorded the day before to a catalog of future scenarios of development, imagining how each piece of habitat could be disturbed, how places could be made less than whole. It was my job to figure out how to mitigate the damage, or restore the habitat to functionality, if not to its original form.

The next time I visited Homer, it was 1989. I visited twice that year, once in January and again in June. In January, on a frigid winter day, I found myself on a beach field trip that was part of the conference I was attending.

My visit in June was an escape from Valdez, where I was spending the summer trying to help monitor the cleanup of the *Exxon Valdez* oil spill. I dreamed about oil choking the barnacles and mussels with each incoming tide. I awakened each morning to the after-the-oil-spill world that oil companies had proclaimed would never happen in Alaska. I walked mucky beaches and found birds and sea otters covered in tar along the high tide line. We were told there was no real "before," no scientific baseline that would convince judges any harm had been done. My own baseline had been one of the patterns of life on the beach before the smothering blanket of oil rolled in. In Homer, I met people who, like me, had put the rest of their lives on hold to join the oil spill cleanup. Most of the oil stayed on the beaches beyond the bay, but tar balls and oily mousse rolled onto the beaches with each tide. My baseline shifted again, from the notion of the pristine nature of Alaska to that of a place vulnerable to human disaster that had turned the tides to poison.

Almost ten years to the day after the oil spill, I stood at the turnout above Kachemak Bay. This time I was moving to Homer, ready to settle like a barnacle that had been swirling around in whirlpools of plankton much too long. I breathed in that view of the bay and its snowy mountains and breathed out a long sigh, hoping I was on the threshold of another baseline.

Yet the bay was changing then, as it had been forever, and so was I. I had learned something by then about the dynamics of mountains and glaciers, rivers and beaches, and I had already seen declines in the abundance of fish and wildlife and of natural beauty and quiet in Alaska. I had been shaped, as surely as the land, by all that I had experienced before. But I hadn't heard even a whisper about the changes happening at the scale of the North Pacific Ocean's marine ecosystems or the planetary climate system. I didn't have a clue that these changes would ripple onto the shores of Kachemak Bay. I couldn't have imagined how they would ripple through my mind and my heart.

But what does it really matter if baselines are gradually shifting? If I tell you that my good old days of fly-fishing on Montana streams and working as a field biologist in Alaska were better than those of everyone born after me, just like every other old codger on the planet, could we ever reconstruct them? Can we at least sustain ecosystems in ways that serve up other species to meet some baseline of our uses and desires? The assumption that we

16

can lies at the base of the science-based resource management I was trained in and practiced.

Daniel Pauly's paper about shifting baselines went off like a small precision nuclear device in my mind, igniting arguments about the nature of "pristine" environments and "unexploited" populations of fish and the impact of selective human harvests that target the maximum and the largest. Jeremy Jackson, an ecologist at the Scripps Institute of Oceanography, held a conference in 2003 about shifting baselines to call attention to what he framed as a global fisheries crisis and failures to detect the collapse of entire marine ecosystems. Scientists at the conference pointed out a historical pattern in fisheries that first targeted large, slow-growing fish species. As their populations declined under intense fishing pressure, fisheries became uneconomic and ended. The majority of the stocks never recovered. Over time, the focus of exploitation shifted to smaller and faster-growing species but so slowly that fisheries managers with their short personal baselines and few centuries of scientific data never detected the entire pattern.

How long, the ecologists asked, can the yields we desire from other species be sustained at a maximum rate if we ignore this pattern? How can we know what we are managing *for* and what goal we are managing *toward* without looking backward to before humans dominated the food webs? Can ecosystems even recover, particularly in a world where the climate and the ocean are changing more rapidly than ever before in recorded history? "Recognizing shifting baselines," according to Jackson, "is the first step toward creating new ways of thinking that reintegrate past, present, and future."

But how do we begin to think in this new way? To consider that our perceptions of abundance or stability are all time bound? My baseline is always shifting—from the time I first become aware of something in a particular state of abundance or decline to the vagaries of my memory. How can I and the managers of what we view as our natural resources take responsibility for the sustainability of anything at all? What do we choose as our targets for healthy ecosystems and sustainable yields of fish and wildlife?

In fish and wildlife management, we like quantitative baselines, like population size, because we want to be reassured that the trends are going upward, in the right direction. Yet without access to an accurate measure of abundance in the distant past, we are incapable of fathoming the long-term magnitude, and rate, of change. How do we cope with changes that appear to be going in the wrong direction—dying forests, invasive species, increasing global temperatures, increasing acidity of the ocean, shrinking polar sea ice? If we let recent patterns become the "new normal," we're at risk of historical amnesia. How can we understand the importance of what has been lost if we literally can't perceive or account for what has gone missing? Lacking much ability to measure change that takes place over several generations, each generation will accept the slow disappearances and shrinkages of species and populations and the diminishment of the abundant wild and what we consider to be natural or normal.

After I had been living in Homer for ten years, the potential impacts of climate change became increasingly alarming. I wondered how I might journey back in time to learn from the distant past of Kachemak Bay, to begin to trace the long trajectory of abundance in this one particular place. But where to start? No one seemed to think much about the bay as an ecosystem until the early 1970s. The most quantitative and scientific data for fish and wildlife populations went back only to the late 1800s, and the most reliable data were a thin layer that went back only a few decades. But there were older numbers: the cases of salmon shipped from the bay in the late 1800s and the sea otter furs shipped from the Russian fur trading posts in the late 1700s. The logs and diaries kept by European explorers push the written record back to 1778 when Captain Cook rounded the cape he named after Princess Elizabeth and dropped anchor at the mouth of the bay. Beyond that, the unwritten record is archaeological and spotty, but it goes back eight thousand years in the carbon dates from the campsite of the first people known to have set foot on the shore of Kachemak Bay. Although the evidence is scant, some archaeologists believe it goes back even farther, to ten thousand years ago after the glaciers had receded.

In Alaska, I have learned, there is always another deeper baseline, the Distant Time of indigenous stories. It exists in that hazy frame of time immemorial, one that slides into view and vanishes again and again, like "ghost ecosystems" that scientists try to reconstruct. In the area around Kachemak Bay, the Distant Time exists through stories of the Sugpiaq Alutiit and Den'aina Athabascans who still live in three villages on the south shore of Kachemak Bay. In the Distant Time, animals and people could communicate with each other directly using human language. Animals could transform themselves into human-looking beings by taking off their animal skins. Humans could put on animal skins and become animals. Elders say the animals have not lost their ability to understand humans, but unfortunately, humans can no longer understand the messages from the animals.

As I began to peruse the data, to muse over what Daniel Pauly and other scientists consider anecdotes of explorers and Russian Orthodox priests, and to plumb the Native stories that have survived a turbulent and cruel history, I began to despair. What was normal and natural was *always* shifting, depending on your point of view. Stability seemed to be only a matter of perception and desire in relation to what was really dynamic and interactive. In Kachemak Bay, as elsewhere, the ocean is far from pacific. It's a restless soup that has been rising and falling over millennia as glaciers and ice sheets made their glistening advances and gritty retreats. Hour by hour the winds and waves change, and the edge of land and sea shifts constantly with the tide. Earthquakes, tidal waves, and volcanic eruptions happen at regular intervals. If nothing has ever really been stable, why should it matter if change was happening faster? Or that some humans—not me—were at the helm of the careening environment? Couldn't I just seek out the beauty and wildness remaining, at least to the end of my life, which is now much closer than its beginning?

Sitting by the waterfall above Bishop's Beach, feeling both still and in movement with change, is another one of my baselines. My self and the world flowed together like a gentle river. My own aliveness and that of the natural world were all and more than enough. When I returned to ordinary mind, I felt not only a sense of kinship but also one of obligation, to the aliveness and beauty that permeates the world.

This place that existed before me has a history. Its past is a labyrinth of time and tides and the leavings of the people who conjured up the Distant Time and its lessons in story and song and dance. If I search the past for clues, I may be able to conjure up the ghosts of former ecosystems and earlier humans enmeshed in their webs of life. I might hear the messages from the animals.

The places I love best on this planet are changeable. Glaciers melt. Windstorms scythe down forests. Rivers change course. Sea cliffs melt away. Volcanoes make their way to the sea, burning everything in their path. But looking backward—reconstructing an ecological and cultural history of one place, Kachemak Bay—may be a chance to dispel a small portion of the amnesia, to sustain the past as the means to move forward into the future, discovering its former abundance and entreating it to return.

THE BIDARKI STORY

On my low tide rambles in China Poot Bay, I often spied a small patch of black on the dark gray rocks. Looking closer, window-panes of white in a distinct line signaled the presence of a flat, armored mollusk called a chiton. By moving quickly, I could snatch it off the rock faster than it could clamp down. It fit neatly in my hand but immediately began curling up, like an armadillo, flexing its rubbery black back and hard shells around to its pink, fleshy underside.

In its strangeness, this chiton was a single-footed candidate for a bestiary of Kachemak Bay. Like other chitons, after it died, it would leave behind eight white butterfly-shaped shells. They were a real find on the beach, especially when all eight remained in an overlapping stack. I thought they added a touch of class to my windowsill displays among the duller but more common mussel and clamshells. I've worn earrings made from polished versions of them along with a particularly large one on a blue satin cord as a necklace.

In Kachemak Bay, this chiton goes by many names. The common name, katy chiton, is a nickname for its Latin genus, *Katharina*, bestowed by science after the lady biologist who sent the first specimens to a London museum. She really was a Lady—Lady Katherine Douglas—displaced from England to Canada. While her husband was some form of colonial governor, she kept up a spirited correspondence with museums about her collections. I always wondered if she would have approved of this nickname business. *Tunicata* is the species name, derived from the animal's fleshy covering of skin that was thought to resemble a tunic, just as the word *chiton* refers to a long garment worn by men and women in ancient Greece that never achieved the long-lasting fame of the toga. The common name has morphed into something more contemporary, in the way that common names are allowed to flourish in their local corners of freedom. In Alaska's coastal towns, I've heard it called the katy chiton or black chiton, but most often, the black-leather chiton, which I like to think is an homage to Marlon Brando's *Wild Bunch* era. Two other common names are used most often in the Native villages on the south shore of the bay: *urriitaq* and *bidarki*. Urriitaq is the name of the animal in Sugt'stun, the language of the Sugpiaq Alutiiq people. Bidarki, is after *baidarka*, the Russian word for "boat," or "little kayak," from the time that Kachemak Bay was an involuntary part of Russian America. I can see how the flattened, chunky, oval animal resembles a seaworthy kayak turned upside down to dry. The centers of its overlapping shells poke up in a straight line like a keel above the black leatherish covering that's as waterproof and tough as gut skin. The variety of names reflects the long history of the Sugpiat and their relationship to chitons, which they harvest and eat.

I found a recipe for the preparation of bidarkis on the Internet that begins with cautions: "Safe to eat if picked at the right time of year and cooked. Always beware of red tide." This was followed by helpful advice: "Pick the black bidarki but do not pick the hairy bidarki as they are not good." Presuming these conditions are satisfied, the process begins: "Gather the bidarki from the beach. Boil a kettle of water and slowly pour over the bidarki. Do not cook them." The next step is my favorite: "Push the bidarki (with a stick) back into the hot water until the black skins come off." It reminds me of my experiences trying to keep bidarkis in live tanks from which they often tried to escape. At the field station they would crawl down the legs of the wooden frames that supported our box-like tanks and begin moving across our deck. They moved slowly but steadily and seemed to have a notion of which way they needed to go to reach the sea.

The rest of the recipe describes eating their red eggs and making gravy that begins with sautéing onions in Wesson oil to pour over the meat. I never actually followed it, heeding a stern warning that it was not advisable to eat bidarkis "unless they were prepared by the Native people of Alaska."

Alaska Native Distant Time stories explain the origins of many things, including the animals, but none are told about *urriitaq* by the Sugpiat, even though the lineages of both have been intertwined for thousands of years.

The evolutionary story of the chiton does place their divergence from other mollusks in a distant time—500 million years ago. Like other animals now well-established on Kachemak Bay beaches, how and when they first arrived would be difficult, if not impossible, to reconstruct. The only possibly relevant baseline I could find for the coastline of Kachemak Bay was around five thousand years ago. Some scientists generalize that at that time wild swings in sea level after the last Ice Age and a subsequent long melt slowed and stabilized the sea level over much of the North Pacific Ocean.

The first chitons on Kachemak shores would have needed stable rocky beaches, where waves kept sand and glacial silt from accumulating. They would have needed to stay in the lower intertidal zone because they feed only when submerged. Big waves and high surf wouldn't have daunted them. Chitons keep a low profile, an adaptation that works well to blunt the force that would sweep them away. What they really do best is cling to rocks. Like many mollusks, they clamp down their muscular foot, which takes up most of their underside. With a unique chiton move that smacks of intertidal yoga, they hunker down to dissuade a potential predator—say, a Sugpiaq woman intent on a meal. They clamp down the outer part of their foot while lifting up the inner part, a process that creates a vacuum seal, an invention for which they've never been given proper credit. If they do get pried off, their drop-and-roll response works to protect their fleshy parts and land them in the water where they can make their escape.

To persist in the same area over several generations, chitons would also have needed relatively stable patches of seaweeds, especially the large kelps they prefer to eat. They move around like a bulldozer, scraping away other small barnacles and limpets that attempt to settle in their territories. The destinations of their descendants depend on tides and currents that bring together eggs and sperm broadcast into the ocean.

The Sugpiat who live in the villages of Nanwalek, Port Graham, and Seldovia trace their own lineages to people who historically wintered to the east of Kachemak Bay on the steep and rugged outer coast of the Kenai Peninsula and ranged into the bay for fishing and marine mammal hunting. Natives were camped near the current location of Nanwalek when Russian fur traders arrived in 1781, and a village with several houses stood near present-day Port Graham when British explorers arrived five years later.

But when did these people first come to Kachemak Bay? This is another question of origins that is impossible to answer precisely. When the Russians first began keeping written records in the late 1700s, they referred to the Natives in Prince William Sound as "Chugaches," who in turn referred to the people of the Outer Coast as *Unegkurmiut*, "the people out that way," implying a separate and unrelated group. In the 1800s, the traditional hunting and fishing territory of the *Unegkurmiut* extended to the head of Kachemak Bay and across Cook Inlet to the bays on the Alaska Peninsula. The Sugpiat, which in their Sugt'stun language means the "real" or "true" or "genuine" people, remember grandparents and great-grandparents who moved from the villages of Nuka, Yalik, and Aialik in what is now Kenai Fjords

National Park. They came westward by kayak to hunt and fish from seasonal camps before they settled permanently in the villages in the far outer part of Kachemak Bay, the Russian fur trading post at Fort Alexandrovsk and then to a place where the Russians established a coal mine. After that, fish processing and cannery jobs drew more people to the villages that were named Nanwalek and Port Graham. The winter villages on the outer coast were abandoned in late 1880s at the urging of Russian Orthodox priests who wanted to consolidate their flock in Kachemak Bay. Still everyone remained nomadic, moving around to seasonal camps until the 1960s.

We don't usually think of scientists as having lineages in the same way we think of species as having evolutionary lineages or more exotic cultures as having lineages of ancestry over centuries. I didn't, until I attended a conference of the American Geophysical Union in 2010, several decades after the end of my career as a state wildlife and habitat biologist. I was in the midst of twenty thousand scientists gathered to talk about everything geophysical, from the biological oceanography that satisfies my nerdy interests to volcanic eruptions to global patterns of climate change to the physics of asteroids. In my latest professional incarnation as science outreach specialist, I felt like an anthropologist dropped into a different culture whose social structure was a puzzle.

I hadn't thought about what a crowd it would be, something rare in Alaska and nonexistent in Homer. Yet everyone seemed to know someone, and many traveled in small groups consisting of several young people who were sure to be graduate students and a gray-haired one, more often a man than a woman, who was sure to be their major professor. I was struck by how each mini hierarchy functioned like those of other primates, even to the extent of sharing food and drinks. Instead of chest-poundings, they flashed PowerPoint with data-heavy slides. Challenges to authority took the form of hard questions. When I eavesdropped on conversations, I realized that scientific lineages went back several generations. People introduced themselves as the student of Dr. X who was the student of Dr. Y and often received a similar response, placing themselves not only in an extended kin group of scientific specialties but also within certain approaches and ideas within each field. I felt a bit left out. Having completed my master's degree work in wildlife management thirty-five years prior, I was literally a stranger to this community of interlocking families of thought and practice, no less than I am when I visit Nanwalek or Port Graham.

I didn't know anything about Anne Salomon's scientific lineage when she arrived in Homer, nor did I foresee that her passion would be to braid the three lineages—bidarkis, Sugpiat, and scientists—together. I can't remember how we first met, but in a town like Homer, it was as likely to have been over the avocados in Safeway as at one of the many fund-raising events of the town's plethora of nonprofits, which made for an easy, if expensive, social life. She told me almost immediately that she was Canadian, distancing herself, as most Canadians did, from the abysmal reputation of America during the Bush years. She was a lithe woman with hazel eyes framed by long spun-gold hair.

As soon as I learned she was an intertidal ecologist, I felt kinship. Here was another person who lived by the tides. Someone I could gossip with about interesting sightings and relationships, not among the residents of Homer, but on the beaches. She cared when someone spotted an unusual species, like a fish-eating sea star or a flat-bottomed star, in China Poot or Peterson Bay. She was a graduate student from the University of Washington who had come to Homer to become a research fellow at the Kachemak Bay National Estuarine Research Reserve, which locals called simply "the reserve."

It was about a year after Anne came to Kachemak Bay that we adopted each other. Toward the end of that first year, she decided that it wasn't working out so well for her at the reserve. She confided that she had resigned her fellowship after unhappy experiences with the science director. One day he had gotten so angry at her that she feared he was about to throw her out of a skiff in the middle of the bay. That left her stuck in Homer with a PhD project idea and only a small Canadian scholarship. She needed a place to stay in Homer until she found the funding she would need to accomplish her research. It just so happened that the Center for Alaskan Coastal Studies had an apartment upstairs from its office. She needed volunteers to help her collect data, and we had a staff of naturalists who would be eager to help.

I surprised myself by offering her the apartment because it meant overturning my ironclad rule about employees only, my means of screening out visiting boyfriends and girlfriends and the strangers who sometimes turned up after employees' nights out at the bars. I surprised myself further by telling the center naturalists they could go work on the project as part of their job. Anne made the center her home base.

The alliance between Anne and the center solved a long-standing problem with the name of our organization, because while we did a lot of education, we didn't really do research. I was tired of having no answer to the question I was frequently asked: "So what do you study?" For the small price of in-kind lodging and labor, we became an official sponsor of a research project. When Anne was in town, she often came down to talk to me as I toiled away in the office over the logistics of boats, people, food, toilet paper, and esoteric plumbing fittings. I began to feel like a member of her scientific pit crew, engaged in her research project vicariously, but blow by blow.

Anne's PhD project idea had come to her one day when walking on Nanwalek Reef, one of the last Kachemak Bay beaches she was surveying as part of her fellowship work at the reserve. She had been cataloging all of the seaweeds and marine invertebrate species in the intertidal zone at each site. Based on her own baseline of studying intertidal communities in Washington and British Columbia, she expected to see katy chitons occupying more intertidal real estate than any other marine invertebrate. Instead, they were sparse and small. She traced her scientific lineage to the University of Washington's Robert Paine, considered the father of the ecological concept of keystone species. Anne also thought in these terms. Not only should katy chitons be abundant, but there should be a certain mix of other species as a result of their role as a predator. When she saw a pattern different than what she expected, Anne knew that something was up. The germ of an idea for a project began to grow in her mind, research she was uniquely suited to pursue.

A different scientist—even one looking for a PhD project like Anne, even one wedded to the concept of keystone species in intertidal communities—might have stopped there in terms of the scope of their research. But when Anne saw some local people on the beach, what she did next was something that many other scientists would have avoided. She went over to talk to them. It was instinctive, she told me later.

"I was in their front yard," she said. "Talking to them was just the right thing to do." She knew they were Alaska Natives. As she had grown up in British Columbia where the traditional ecological knowledge of First Nations people was respected, this respectful attitude was also part of her scientific lineage. Jennifer Ruesink, the scientist at the head of her PhD program at the University of Washington, favored involving community members, especially indigenous people, in research. The conversation Anne had with members of Nanwalek's Sugpiaq community that day was as important to the formation of her research project as her observation of the pattern of the community living on the reef.

"It was clear," she said, "they knew a hell of lot more than I did, and they could teach me."

During that first conversation, the mystery of few and small bidarkis on the beach seemed to have a simple solution.

They ate them. This could be the new ecological twist for Anne, one that wasn't part of the ecological picture on Washington coasts. Overharvesting could have simply depleted the reef of chitons and taken the largest ones first. But then the people she was talking to presented her with a mystery of their own. They told her that while they and their Elders had been harvesting in the same way and eating them their entire lives, bidarkis had begun to decline in number and size in the last ten years and some thought as long as fifteen years. Since they hadn't increased their harvests during that time, the changing densities pointed to some change in the environment.

A more complex study began to unfold in Anne's mind. Ecological questions bubbled up: Were katy chitons a keystone species on the rocky beaches around Nanwalek and Port Graham as they were on Washington and British Columbia beaches? If not, what *did* control the intertidal ecology? The people on the beach had their own questions: How fast did bidarkis grow? How many could be harvested before it was too many? How could they keep harvesting bidarkis, which were important to them as a traditional subsistence food? In the katy chiton, Anne had found an animal that she predicted played a major role in the entire structure of the rocky intertidal community. In addition, the animal the Sugpiat had named bidarki played a major role in their culture, a relationship they wanted to sustain. You need to learn science, I often tell children, and myself, because it can solve real-world problems. The bidarki project as it was conceived seemed to present a perfect opportunity to do so.

Over the time I was involved in Anne's research, mostly as a cheerleader, much about it reminded me of my own days studying moose as a graduate student in wildlife management. My scientific lineage through the human biology program at Stanford included Jane Goodall, the field biologist who made watching animal behavior famous, and Paul Ehrlich, purveyor of a general sense of impending human-wrought environmental doom. Evolutionary theory was the explanation of choice then. Ecology was a relatively new science and organizing principle of biological theory. In the aftermath of the first Earth Day in 1970, however, *ecology*—derived from the Greek word *oikos*, which referred to house, household, and family—became, literally, a household word as well as a political one. When I thought about ecology, my gaze was firmly terrestrial during my moose-watching days—on energy flows through a food web with willows, moose, and wolves—so I took little note of what might be happening in the intertidal zone or the ocean. If I had, I might have read Bob Paine's classic study, published in 1969 in the *American Naturalist*.

It was years later after I moved to Homer that I sought explanations for the patterns I saw on the beaches in China Poot and Peterson Bays and answers to hard why questions that fifth graders asked. I learned that Paine's experiments in the intertidal zone had made him one of the rock stars, not just in the field of intertidal ecology, but in the entire field of ecology. In his own tide pool excursions, he could see that the bottom of mussel beds on his beach had an abrupt horizontal edge that could only correlate with a certain level of the tide. The mystery was why the pattern existed. Putting together what he knew about the mechanics of sea stars, he came up with the hypothesis that the line in the sand, or rocks, represented how high the most common sea star on the beaches he was studying, the ochre star, could venture up the beach at low tide, powered by the hydraulics of its multiple tube feet, before perishing in the desert above the tide line before the water returned. He reasoned that if they were dry too long, particularly as they digested a mussel above the tide line over the course of several hours, they would cease to function and die. Mussels that settled and anchored themselves below the tide line would be at the mercy of the predacious sea stars, but those above the line would escape being dinner. The sea stars, in other words, were controlling the distribution of the mussels.

To test his hypothesis, he simply removed the sea stars from small study plots and watched what happened. The mussels did indeed begin settling and growing farther down on the beach. What surprised him was that they were such successful competitors for available space that as many as fifteen other species were eliminated from the biological community while barnacles increased along with the mussels. Paine concluded that the ochre star, whose Latin genus is *Pisaster*, not only controlled mussel distribution but was also critical to a particular structure of the food web.

Paine coined the term *keystone species* as a metaphor. His removal of *Pisaster*, he said, had been like pulling out the keystone of an arch, the single brick at the top of the arch that is critical to its structural integrity. Pull out the keystone, and you end up with a jumble of bricks; remove the keystone species in a biological community, and you get a different architecture of interacting species—with either more or less diversity. When Paine pulled out *Pisaster*, a top-level predator, he ended up with less because the mussels that had been its primary prey flourished and expanded the extent of their beds seaward. If you're a snail or chiton, an expanding mussel bed is the equivalent of a mountain range in the landscape of the intertidal zone, the equivalent to Alaskans of the Alaska Range expanding by hundreds of miles, covering the gentle slopes and flatlands of habitat where we like to build our houses and tend our gardens. Pull out katy chitons, a grazer, however, which Paine also did in his experiments, and he ended up with more diversity because the chitons were no longer cropping back the kelp or bulldozing away other settlers. Both the predatory sea star and the predatory grazing chiton were keystones as Paine defined them because they held the system in check by being efficient and voracious consumers. When they were removed, the numbers of the prey animals they usually consumed exploded. In the case of the removal of the sea star as predator on mussels, mussels took over the community—both in numbers and in the relative amount of area they occupied. In the case of the chitons, it was the kelp that became a lush forest for other animals that settled and thrived at their base.

The concept of keystone species has reverberated through the ecological literature ever since. Scientists, and then people seeking reasons for the conservation of various species, may have overreacted a bit—soon many mammal species were being called keystones, including prairie dogs, wolves, sea otters, and even moose, whose selective appetites can change the composition and structure of forest communities. Paine refined his definition in response to some debates in the scientific literature to focus on the "strength of interactions" between various species that could be determined mathematically. By the numbers, the bulldozing chitons would be "strong interactors" if they influenced what else was in the biological community out of proportion to their actual numbers. The real test of influence remained, however, in demonstrating what happened when the species was absent.

Anne was careful to talk of the strength of interactions between *Katharina* and other species when engaged in "science speak" with other scientists. Locally, however, she talked about "keystone-ness" quite often in terms of bidarkis being the real movers and shakers in the community that lived between the tides. Some of the players in a food web, she would say by way of explanation, can give bigger tugs on the connections they have with other players. Keystone species were the ones with the really strong tugs. If you remove them, Anne would say, "the system can change quite dramatically."

Over a glass of wine one evening, Anne told me that after a bit more reconnaissance of the area around the villages, she realized she had stumbled on to a natural experiment. She found beaches where bidarkis were small and few and beaches where they were large and abundant just a short skiff ride away, so she could quantify their interaction strength and test the bidarki's keystone-ness. Then she would need to do the removal experiments pioneered by Paine. I could see how her research questions tugged on her science mind. But I could also feel how the long-standing connection of the two Native communities to the bidarki was also tugging on her heart. She summed up the difference in the types of answers desired quite neatly: "They're interested in the causes of the declines. As a scientist, I'm interested in the ecological consequences."

Anne began her research by setting up sampling sites at varying distances from Port Graham and Nanwalek, where she counted and measured bidarkis. Her data established that at sites closer to the villages, bidarkis were smaller and at lower density. But if what she'd been told was true—that the rate of harvest hadn't changed—harvesting alone didn't account for her results.

She began sampling other variables, including water temperature and the force of waves hitting the beaches, but she couldn't find any pattern. To get at the question of how fast bidarkis grew and how many were in the population, she tried a classic mark/recapture study by organizing a bidarki rodeo. Compared to the ups and downs of moose populations, which people react to like a state sport in Alaska, no one really cared about the size of bidarki populations except the people in the two villages. No one had ever marked bidarkis, or apparently ever wanted to. Anne had to devise a technique with small numbered tags, epoxy, and an etching tool to scrape a code onto one of their plates. She set up her removal experiments by creating small plots in the intertidal zone that she encircled with sticky putty covered with anti-fouling paint and then picked out, one by one, any bidarkis within the circles and convinced herself they wouldn't cross the poisonous barrier. Just in case, she set up controls—other plots, encircled with sticky putty alone.

As she collected data, she seemed almost magnetic in how she drew resources and people, me included, to her project. She rallied the center's naturalists and volunteers to help her tag bidarkis. Over the course of the first summer, they tagged more than nine hundred. Paul McCollum, a non-Native fisheries scientist working for the tribes, provided her with boat rides to her study sites and a place to stay in the hatchery when she worked in Port Graham. Before very long, she had a crew of volunteers in the villages that ranged from the older women who were the main collectors of bidarkis to teenagers with rainbow-hued mohawks. On days she wasn't out sampling, she visited the schools and helped students create intertidal food webs out of construction paper and yarn featuring, of course, bidarkis making large tugs on their ecosystem. She said she was also learning from the community members.

"Mmm, smells like bidarkis," one older woman declared when she stepped out of the skiff onto a beach where the bidarkis were thick. Anne, too, began to recognize that smell.

At the end of that first summer, Anne invited me to a potluck dinner in Nanwalek where she was planning to give a short talk to the community about her research. By then I'd gone to hundreds of Alaskan potlucks. In Fairbanks they had been the best meals during my time as a poor graduate student. In Juneau and in Homer they had brought together various "families" of unrelated people who had been gathering together for years or people who had in common music or a cause such as saving clean water, children, or everyone's sanity during the long winter. This potluck, however, was the first one I'd been invited to in a Native village. Everyone in the village, related in knots and skeins of lineage that went back hundreds of years, was invited. They came bearing enormous amounts of food and set it up on long tables in the school gym.

As people gathered, Anne introduced me to community members she had enlisted in her study. The women tutoring her in how to smell bidarkis were short and stolid, with manes of silver and gray hair. They teased her and called her "the bidarki lady." Although I was a white stranger, I felt entirely welcomed as a guest of Anne. She made a special point of introducing me to Nick Tanape Sr., an Elder. I knew he took the revival of his culture seriously because he had already shared his skills in kayak building and other traditional ways with the younger generation. He was a compact, soft-spoken man, with still-black hair and a mustache just beginning to show threads of silver and gray. He carried a dignity I remembered in my immigrant grandmother, who had straddled two worlds most of her long life.

Like all potlucks I had ever been to, we milled around, eyeing the food, pretending we didn't want to be the first in line. An announcement was made that invited the Elders to go first, one that I learned later was made in every village when food is shared, so that they can enjoy traditional Native foods they may no longer gather and prepare.

When I reached the food, I could see that it, like many things in the village, was a hybrid of traditional and modern. Rich grease floated on the top of soup made from harbor seal meat set beside a bowl of chicken salad. Dark green, chewy beach greens accompanied salads made with lettuce grown in local gardens. Deviled eggs dulled beside glistening magenta fish eggs. Bones emerged from an enormous salmon baked whole, head and all, as each chunk by generous rosy chunk of flesh was carved away. Slices of bidarkis appeared in their natural habitat among the other traditional Native foods with some modern twists. In one bowl, bidarki slices had been pickled in a spicy marinade that someone declared to be ceviche.

I thought about my first taste of bidarki, served to me raw on the beach near Seldovia when a Native woman levered one off a rock with her knife and cut the foot into slivers that she handed to her sons and to me. It was salty and gamey and chewy, as mollusky as it could be, absent butter and garlic. I looked forward to tasting the ceviche.

The other end of the table was all cakes, pies, and sweet confections, laden with sugar and other store-bought ingredients. People went back for seconds and thirds, intent on the year's last sharing of fresh fish and garden harvests. Like my Jewish grandmothers, the Sugpiaq grandmothers urged me, and everyone else, to eat more.

"Bidarkis are the lawn mower of the intertidal," Anne began her talk after the meal, as I had heard her start other talks in Homer. Everyone listened as she told her scientific project as a story.

I couldn't help but think back to my lonely graduate student meals at Mom's Restaurant and my sleepless nights in the Fish and Game boat shed in Soldotna. Like Anne, I had been immersed in a different culture, but mine had been the culture of "real" Alaska men in the woods, and I had been shown again and again I would never belong. The only moose stories told at Fish and Game potlucks were those of men against beasts, of epic hunts that had transformed a moose into a pile of meat.

I also knew that what Anne was doing was exceptional. A lot of research had been conducted in Alaska Native villages, and I had been told bitter stories about scientists who had come and asked the people in the village many questions, even poking and prodding them to collect data about the contaminant load in their bodies and other health problems. These scientists were all given traditional hospitality—boat rides, places to stay, meals, and endless cups of tea. Most collected their data and left. Worse yet, they never told the people the results of the study, or if they did, they mailed reports so technical and laden with science-speak that they were impossible to decipher. In contrast, from the day Anne first stepped foot on the beaches in front of the villages, she made it clear to the people in Nanwalek and Port Graham that she respected them and their knowledge.

In her second year of research, Anne was able to call on her scientific lineage and get substantial grant funding for her project from the *Exxon Valdez* Oil Spill (EVOS) Trustee Council, which was still doling out the money from Exxon's fines to support the recovery of subsistence resources from damage caused by the spill. Anthropologist Henry Huntington joined in on the grant, lending his experience in bringing together knowledge gained by Alaska Natives in their traditional ways with that gained by the methods of science. With grant funding, Anne was able to pay some of the locals as field assistants. She went out with them and community members who continued to volunteer each morning in a brand-new skiff purchased with EVOS research funds. The bidarki team wore matching orange survival suits that gave each of them a stiff, Gumby-like shape.

Henry interviewed the Elders about their experiences of harvests on the reef in the past and what had changed in the villages in their lifetimes. As the Elders spun out their older baselines, Anne collected data for three years to understand the baseline of a short scientific now. It was at that point that the bidarki project became its own type of potluck event. The gatherers and eaters of bidarkis brought their traditional tastes and their questions to the table, Anne and Henry brought their scientific questions and methods, and the Elders brought their memories and the stories transmitted over generations of the Sugpiat through oral tradition.

The challenge of oral tradition, as I learned trying to get the attention of an excited and unruly group of kids on the beach, is that younger generations need to be willing to listen to their elders. The Sugpiaq Elders in Port Graham and Nanwalek had stopped telling their stories of what was required to survive as Sugpiat because the younger generation had stopped listening and then stopped asking to hear any stories at all. Without the stories of the past to anchor them, the younger generations became part of the shifting baseline in which everything they depended upon had become fewer and smaller almost imperceptibly. Scientists rarely asked the Elders anything, relying only on data. But what

Anne and Henry understood was that to extend their baselines backward beyond short-term datasets, they needed to ask and to listen for how the Sugpiat had survived during a long period when the environment and the culture had surely been changing. It began with Henry listening to the Elders, and the Elders listening to Henry's questions, and all of them pondering together over the patterns hidden in the answers.

Two kinds of stories emerged. The science story arose from the experiment of removing the bidarkis. The results were nothing short of spectacular. In plots where there had been no bidarkis for a year, ribbon kelp grew profusely in long, green blades. But in plots with a high density of bidarkis, there was almost no kelp. The bidarkis had reduced the density of kelp by a whopping 94 percent and the total amount, or biomass, by a factor of seven times—statistics any scientist would envy. Bidarkis chowing down on the fast-growing, productive ribbon kelp left behind only a short, slow-growing community dominated by seaweed called sea cabbage. When no bidarki bulldozers were around, the number of species in plots rose by nearly 40 percent. You couldn't ask for better scientific evidence of the consequence of the bidarki's strong tug on the community than what happened in its absence.

The second story had never been written down or even told before from beginning to end. It was what Native people call a "real story" about causes—how the current situation of the bidarki and the Sugpiat came to be. This story emerged like a string of beads. The Elders could remember back to the 1940s and 1950s as the good times, when many different subsistence foods had been available on the reefs close to the villages. Then beads in the string began to fall off: green sea urchins became scarce, then sea cucumbers, and then gumboot chitons, the much-larger relative of bidarkis that they called the lady slipper. Some animals remained on the reefs and waters near the villages, but by the late 1970s to early 1980s, more beads were missing. The large commercial fisheries that had developed in Cook Inlet for shrimp and crab crashed. The number of crabs available for subsistence use continued downward until the bay was eventually closed to the harvest of king, then Dungeness, then Tanner crab, never to reopen. Clams were next to decline in abundance, followed by cockles. Looked at in this historical way, the pattern of a sequence of declines was obvious, but no single person that Anne and Henry talked to had seen the pattern as a whole. The decline of the bidarkis was, for the Sugpiat, not just any decline—it was the last subsistence food that could be collected on the beach.

Other things had changed as well. The Elders remembered the 1989 oil spill as a time when animals they harvested for subsistence had been killed or contaminated by the oil. It was a sad time. As Walter Meganak Sr., an Elder and then chief of Port Graham, described it: "We walk our beaches. But instead of gathering life, we gather death. Dead birds. Dead otters. Dead seaweed."

The oil companies had immediately offered cleanup jobs to people in the villages, which not everybody had welcomed at the time. As the chief described it: "Before we have a chance to hold each other and share our tears, our sorrow, our loss, we suffer yet another devastation. We are invaded by the oil company. Offering jobs, high pay. Lots of money. We are in shock. We need to clean the oil, get it out of our water, bring death back to life."

There was another change the Elders remembered. In the early 1960s, they all agreed, they began seeing sea otters in the bay for the first time in their lives, and they had been slowly increasing in numbers ever since. Sea otters preyed on chitons, Anne knew, and on sea urchins, sea cucumbers, and clams.

One evening as she was returning to Nanwalek in her skiff with Nick Tanape Sr., something clicked into place suddenly for both of them. They realized that when the otters had returned to the bay after their long absence, a new baseline had begun. After the years following the fur trade when there were no sea otters in the bay, the abundance and diversity of marine invertebrates that were their usual prey had built up. Based on another classic series of ecological studies in the Aleutian Islands, what had returned was a second keystone predator.

After their aha moment, she and Nick developed what she later called an "alternative hypothesis" as the basis on their continuing study. The hypothesis depended on the story provided by the Elders as context for interpreting the scientific data. Perhaps the series of declines had been caused by the combined impact of two keystone predators—humans and sea otters—which began competing for the same prey. They could have worked in tandem to deplete one prey species after the other at an accelerated rate, racing each other down the food web. This fit the pattern of people who, when they first began living permanently in villages, concentrated their harvest effort in the places that were closest, in contrast to their historical pattern of moving to salmon streams or clamming beaches every season. Later, with the addition of outboard motors, they had ranged farther from the villages. When electricity and freezers became more widely available, they had harvested more and stored more. They put boxes of frozen bidarkis on airplanes to send to relatives in Anchorage. Every change made the Sugpiat into more efficient and wide-ranging predators. Meanwhile, the sea otters munched away, consuming a quarter of their body weight they needed each day to survive. Both sea otters and Sugpiat were down to their last move in the intertidal game in a food web that had been constantly changing.

The new hypothesis required that Anne and her crew look up from their plots in the intertidal zone and out to the nearby waters. Sure enough, they counted more otters rafted offshore of the places where bidarkis were smaller and fewer. The counting and measuring and the traditional knowledge converged into a history that explained the causes of the decline. It also fit ecological theory.

Anne found additional data about when bidarkis became important as a subsistence resource. When the Alaska Department of Fish and Game had conducted subsistence surveys in 1987 and in 2003, people in both Port Graham and Nanwalek had reported that bidarkis made up more than half of their harvest of marine invertebrates each year, followed by butter clams and octopus.

But this had not always been the case. An archaeological site with a midden, or garbage pile, near Port Graham provided the means to go back even farther, to find out whether bidarkis had been important in the diet of people who'd lived in the village sites in even earlier times. In comparison to the number of bones from fish and marine mammals and other shells, the number of bidarki shells was small. Bidarkis were thus only a very small part of the traditional diet from around 1300 to 1500, and even later during the early 1900s. This made their importance as a subsistence food a recent phenomenon, Anne concluded, related to the disappearance of the other food animals they preferred more. Like other people who depend on their local environment, the Sugpiat had adapted not only in terms of what they used to fill their dinner table but in what they could claim as the heart of their culture and identity. As the people in the villages participated in the telling of the bidarki story, the bidarki evolved into a cultural keystone.

The bidarki story was told as a science story at science conferences. The scientific results were well-grounded in ecological theory and supported by statistics of more than acceptable significance. Anne, Nick, and Henry published an article titled "Serial Depletion of Marine Invertebrates Leads to the Decline of a Strongly-Interacting Grazer" in that holy grail of science, a peer-reviewed journal. But the full story was first told during conversations on the beach and while pounding over waves in a skiff. Later, the three wrote a book together—*Imam Cimiucia* in Sugt'stun, *Our Changing Sea*, in English. The story in *Imam*

Cimiucia, they said, was "told through the eyes of tribal Elders, subsistence hunters, village residents, an artist, a social scientist, a photojournalist, and a marine ecologist, each one of us bringing our observations, skills, and knowledge to tell, with many voices, a single story about our changing sea." Lisa Williams, the photojournalist, captured the spirit of the people in sepia tones. It was the ultimate potluck story.

"We, the Sugpiat, are sea people," *Imam Cimiucia* begins. "Our lives are sustained by the sea. The sea is part of our spirit, our stories, our history, and our future." The book underscores the profound value of the knowledge of the Elders as necessary in preventing what is recognized as a case of shifting baselines syndrome for young subsistence gatherers and scientists alike.

Anne was never able to answer the questions about bidarki population dynamics—how fast they grew or reproduced to replenish the numbers that had been harvested by people or sea otters. The summer after she and her crew had marked nine hundred bidarkis, they searched and searched. Anne offered a reward for any that people collected and turned in. Only one was ever retrieved. Still, in *Imam Cimiucia*, the possibility of overharvest is acknowledged. The book includes the seeds of a management plan for the bidarki harvest that might include size limits, seasonal closures during the spawning season (which the Elders say was a traditional conservation practice), protection of nursery areas, or closing of some beaches entirely to promote the recovery of bidarki populations.

The bidarki story told in *Imam Cimiucia* contains no conclusion about what, if anything, should be done about the otters. Anne, Henry, and Nick, speaking on behalf of the Sugpiat, affirm that "amid all that has changed in our ocean home, some things have stayed the same. Sharing remains important, valued, and practiced." But in regard to sea otters, they say, "Sharing, however, has limits. . . . We have a strong connection to the land and the sea and we recognize all creatures have a place and need to eat.

Yet . . . we perceive sea otters as one of our main competitors, an uninvited guest feasting at our table."

After Anne completed her project and her PhD, she moved back to Vancouver. I met her for dinner in Seattle a few years ago. She was busy with the hectic life of a junior professor at Simon Fraser University—shepherding her own group of graduate students, teaching, and heading up an ambitious research program centered on the role of sea otters in the marine ecosystem on the wild coast of central British Columbia and the home of the Haida G'waii.

We talked about how we had first met. I was surprised to see tears in her eyes as she told me how much my offer of a place to stay had meant to her. It had happened at one of the lowest points in her life, she told me. She had been nearly broke after giving up her prestigious fellowship in a town where she knew almost no one. She had been preparing to return to Seattle in academic disgrace. When she'd found a home among everyone associated with the Center for Alaskan Coastal Studies, she said, it had meant to her that someone believed in her and her work at a time when she was about to give up.

I hadn't thought very hard at all when I made the offer of the apartment, which was something in my power to give. But I had received so much in return from my time with Anne, not the least of which was a new understanding about bidarkis, which few people outside Kachemak Bay and a small group of scientific specialists paid any attention to at all. Anne's study showed me how bidarkis were enmeshed in a web of connections, both natural and cultural, that stretched backward into the Distant Time and forward into the future. She had invited me to the potluck where I had eaten bidarkis with the Sugpiat who prized them, but it was really an invitation to a larger and richer potluck of ways of knowing and being in Kachemak Bay, where the cold dish of science lay side by side with bidarkis that had been eaten by the ancestors.

Part II
ARTIFACTS

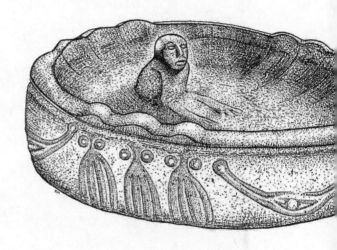

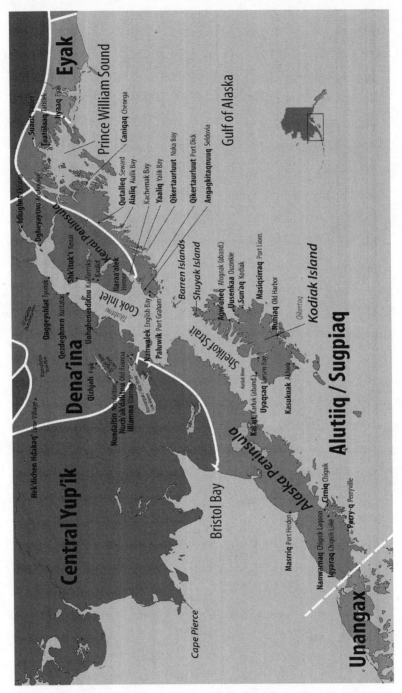

Area traditionally occupied by Alutiiq/Sugpiaq, Dena'ina, and neighboring indigenous language groups with place names in English and the Alutiiq/Sugpiaq language (Sugt'stun in the Sugpiaq language).

Adapted by the UA Press from the Alaska Native Language Center's Map of the Indigenous Peoples and Languages of Alaska (www.uaf.edu/anla/collections/map/).

Sniffing Down the Scent of the Past

To reach the remnants of the long-abandoned house site near Peterson Bay Field Station, you climb up from the beach on China Poot Bay and into the forest. The path begins at a short stairway at the edge of the cove we call Shipwreck. Salvaged driftwood planks covered with fraying netting provide traction against the slickness. These boards washed up from somewhere else in the North Pacific onto the steep, churned-up beaches in Peterson Bay. They're now part of this sturdy structure, resuming their pitted, knotty journey toward total decay. Even brand-new boards take on a graybeard appearance after the first winter. Dead wood has a short life on this edge of the rainy coastal forest.

On the trail that follows the coastline, the salmonberry shrubs are taller than I am. Their greenish-white berries are a signal that they still contain gritty kernels but are on the verge of softening into their ripe tang and turning as golden-pink as their namesake fish. I pick carefully, popping the juiciest-looking ones into my mouth, but keep an eye out for the stinging nettles that twine their duller leaves through the shrubs. Just a few hundred feet along the trail from Shipwreck Cove, another path branches off and winds its way upward to a point high above the beach. On a short, steep section, monkshood, that solitary nodding purple cowl of a flower, offers a private audience for buzzing bees.

The trail levels out into a bench with a grassy meadow above the cliff edge. Down below, the rocky beach vanishes beneath the incoming tide. It's a perfect place to beach or launch a kayak as it has been for thousands of years. High above the bay, people looked outward for whoever might be paddling this way from the north side of the bay or from the west, where the bay opens out into Cook Inlet. Five miles away, Homer is a long grayish smudge of coastline below a ridge that undulates in mirage.

Another short hike up an even steeper section of trail leads to an arbor of drooping alder branches that frame the entrance to another flat spot of bare ground. A short section of flimsy railing stands next to a depression. A wooden kiosk, obviously as home-made as the stairs, sits on the far side of the clearing, alerting everyone coming to this place that there is something of interest here. The weathered wooden box of the exhibit has a bottom shelf heaped with shells, bones, and stones. Signs and illustrations provided by Janet Klein, the resident archaeologist at the wilderness lodge, convey what we know about the people who may have lived here. But what's being interpreted appears to be only an empty hole in the ground.

In the mysterious way that things appear here, someone from the wilderness lodge built a rope fence around the perimeter of the hole years ago. Barely visible in the tall grass, the rectangular form of the rope provides the entry point to the significance of the hole. It's the square corners that give it away as an archaeological site—a house pit dug by people, because only people make straight lines. People from more than one prehistoric culture made their home on this bluff, and the last of them were Dena'ina Athabascan. The bones and tools in the display weren't left by the Dena'ina but by an earlier people who discarded things in deep piles covered over now by soil. During the period from around AD 1000 until 1800 and the arrival of European trade goods, however, the Dena'ina left nothing behind—no tantalizing shards of pottery, no discarded tools, not even the remains of a meal. They left only empty house pits like this one, with at most a hearth in the center where their log houses once stood. On its surface, this archaeological site is a baseline of blankness. Digging down into the house pit would add little to the body of knowledge that requires cold, hard artifacts.

Whenever I stand at the edge of the pit, I feel the absence of the Dena'ina in that space once filled with smoke and breath that has long since drifted away. There's loneliness there, an abandonment that even the magenta spikes of summer fireweed in full bloom fail to dispel. I strain to detect echoes of songs and drumbeats and conversation, but I hear only the soprano trill of an eagle or the chatter of a red squirrel.

In the past, I heard my enthusiastic naturalist voice unrolling facts to people who mostly wanted to know when and where we'd be eating lunch. This is a deep place, I really wanted to say to them, its meanings layered in rock and shell and seeming emptiness. There is so much we need to learn from its ghosts about how to live in this place *now* as the world shape-shifts around us. The people who lived here weren't my ancestors, I wanted to say, but this is the place where my roots are firmly in the soil, still clawing themselves downward, nurtured by the past.

A dead spruce with a broken top grows up out of the pit, another clue to the time that has elapsed since the lower logs of the house were laid below the surface of the earth. Ed Berg, a curious local ecologist, cored this tree in 1994 and counted 170 rings, alternating between the dense clusters laid down during the rainy years and the wide bands of the dry. The house must have collapsed years before the seedling got its start in 1824, about forty-five years after Captain Cook anchored his ships at the mouth of the bay and the Russian fur traders established their first settlement on the mainland of North America at Alexandrovsk. It's unlikely they ever encountered the last inhabitants of this house.

Ed cored more trees in the coastal forest around Peterson Bay. Back at the field station, a tree cookie wedge displays the history of a tree from the last generation in a road race of tiny flag pins. That tree was a young sapling of 16 when America made its Declaration of Independence, 18 when Captain Cook arrived in Cook Inlet, and well into its maturity at 117 when the United States was purchased Alaska from Russia. During its elderhood at 209, Alaska became a state. At its death at 250, the tree succumbed to beetles.

Archaeology is a spooky science, with its tales of the long dead and the most imperishable of human possessions. The bones in the display are slowly dissolving away. I've always been drawn more to what is living or recently dead in the forest and on the beach. I caught the excitement of archaeology, however, from the man I lived with one long, dark Fairbanks winter.

We led very different lives during the summer. We both spent them in the field, but while I swept the horizon for moose and caribou and seabirds, he was doing archaeology, tramping through Arctic valleys and climbing ridges, his eyes on the ground scanning for out-of-place flakes chipped from rock cores. It was as close as he could come to being an Arctic explorer after he read about the journeys of Peary and Rasmussen and Nansen.

He prepared himself in childhood, he told me, by flinging open his bedroom windows to stand bare chested during New England blizzards. If he and I were to look together at the same bare expanse of Arctic landscape, I would look for what was alive and moving while he would think about where he would camp and look out for game as he rolled back the landscape through the changes it might have undergone over millions of years. He knew in a deep-time way that rivers shifted their courses, riverbanks eroded, and the permafrost melted and thawed in cycles that moved and shaped the land. Field archeology, he would say, was "all about who can tell the best stories" because no one could actually know what really happened.

It was the late 1970s when the era of pipeline archaeology fell into the laps of University of Alaska Fairbanks archaeologists. They interpreted the area of the oil pipeline corridor that needed to be surveyed for archaeological sites to be a broad geographic area of archaeological interest in northern Alaska. As a result, they spent summers in remote camps, miles away from the Haul Road but well supplied with steaks and the occasional lobster flown in from a crowded pipeline camp. Nights around the campfire were whisky-fueled, mostly male affairs under the midnight sun and nothing like life in biological field camps where we huddled in our wall tents over freeze-dried food heated on Coleman stoves. We transcribed our data about plants and animals that no one could argue might not have existed and built our fragments of data into habitats and ecosystems that we imagined to be more real than vanished cultures reconstructed from rock chips.

I regarded the pipeline archaeologists around those campfires as field camp buddies who would never make anything of themselves. Little did I know they were imagining their way toward finding the prize of the oldest archaeological sites on the eastern side of Beringia, from a time when a land bridge connected Asia to North America. Michael Kunz was one of those archaeologists, and he went on to discover the 14,000-year-old Mesa site in the foothills of the Brooks Range. Jim Dixon was there, and he later helped excavate On Your Knees Cave in southeastern Alaska, which entombed the then oldest-known human remains of a man who died 9,700 years ago. Jim also excavated a flint station, dated originally at 10,500 years old and one of the oldest sites on Alaska's North Slope, which the man I spent the winter with discovered. I was privy to the inside joke that he spotted the first twinkle of flint while relieving himself.

Archaeology in Kachemak Bay began as a somewhat tamer affair. Johan Adrian Jacobsen, a Norwegian, was not the first to dig in the ruins of abandoned Native villages in Kachemak Bay, but he was the first to send his collection off to a museum in 1881. He made his excavations because he had time on his hands while waiting for the next schooner to arrive at Alexandrovsk, renamed Fort Alexander (now the village of Nanwalek), so he could travel to Kodiak. According to his questionable account, the product of a ghostwriter much given to exaggeration, he was guided from a Native village near the present community of Seldovia to what was left of Soonroodna, at "the foot of the third glacier on the south side of Kachemak Bay," a location that remains an official archaeological mystery. Jacobsen had none of the tools of modern archaeology. His duty was the sheer act of collection to salvage the artifacts of vanishing cultures for German museums. He collected more than sixty-seven hundred of them during a two-year odyssey that took him the length and breadth of Alaska. Kachemak Bay was just one of his time-killing stops. In the book about his travels, Jacobsen comes off as possessing a strange sense of humor that led him to play what he described as a practical joke on the Natives by dressing up like a shaman and proclaiming to them that Jacobsen had died.

Jacobsen and his Native guide dug for several days at the old village site. According to local oral history, it had been a sizable settlement when the Russians arrived and then carried off all the women as unwilling wives to Fort Kenai sometime between 1792 and 1796. The men had then abandoned the village and gone to Kodiak. Without attention to the careful spade work that preserves the context of each item, Jacobsen still made passable notes about the layers in which he found the artifacts he salvaged, or looted, depending on your point of view. The result, however, was an archaeological jumble—arrow and harpoon points of bone, a stone spear point, an iron knife and blade, a glass bead, pieces of pottery, and three massive wooden slabs of masks.

This assortment of artifacts tells us only that people from several cultures lived there over a long period of time, as late as the 1800s when trade goods made their appearance. Bits of ancient pottery, whose nearest makers lived on the Bristol Bay side of the Alaska Peninsula, have only been found in Kachemak Bay on Yukon Island, five miles to the west of China Poot Bay. Despite the large number of wooden masks collected from sites on Kodiak Island 150 miles to the southwest, no other masks were ever found around Kachemak Bay.

Jacobsen shipped everything he dug up at Soonroodna to a museum in Berlin. Janet Klein, a naturalist for the wilderness lodge in China Poot Bay and an archaeologist, traveled to Germany in pursuit of Jacobsen's artifacts, which she learned had miraculously survived two world wars. When she finally got a look at them, the 120-year-old labels were deteriorating and fading. Some had fallen off, making the connection to a specific artifact tenuous, and others contained the uncertainty of question marks, including, unfortunately, the one on the mask that read "Kachemak Bay? Prince William Sound?"

Janet cut her archaeological teeth in Kachemak Bay. As curator of collections at the Pratt Museum, she organized the museum's first dig. Since receiving more training as a professional archaeologist, she's always on the lookout for more sites in the bay. She's been involved in the excavation of several, often with another archaeologist, Peter Zollars. They don't always agree. Janet is nearly certain that Soonroodna was located somewhere in China Poot Bay, most likely near its entrance to the north of the house pit on the bluff. Peter places it in a different bay than China Poot, reconstructing a different map of the "third glacier" up the bay from Seldovia. Peter Kalifornsky thought it might have been in the bay now named Halibut Cove east of China Poot.

With its uncertainties, Soonroodna's not any kind of an ancient baseline. Yet I want its location to have been in China Poot Bay. Someday I'll stumble across it and see stone points spilling out of a cutbank or shards of pottery beneath my feet. I like to imagine I might discover a well-preserved cache of slab-like wooden masks that will be the missing link to a time of dancing and the presence of animal spirits.

In 1931 Cornelius Osgood was the first modern anthropologist to live among the people he called Tanaina. (The spelling "Dena'ina" has been reclaimed as a more appropriate translation from the Native language.) The Dena'ina are now thought to have arrived on the Kenai Peninsula from the north, reaching Kachemak Bay around a thousand years ago. This migration coincided with the Medieval Warm Period, one of the warmest periods ever recorded until present time.

Osgood was a freshly minted PhD student of Edward Sapir, who studied with Franz Boas, who in turn pioneered the study of how language and culture interact and influence each other. Sapir particularly favored the various languages of the Dené Indian cultures, which include all of the Athabascan languages. He wrote in a private letter to the anthropologist Alfred Kroeber that Dené was "the son-of-a-bitchiest language in America to actually *know* ... most fascinating of all languages ever invented."

By making recordings and compiling word lists in all of the dialects being spoken, Osgood thought, as did Jacobsen and Boas, that he was salvaging a culture destined to vanish. In Osgood's case, he was salvaging it for the Yale Peabody Museum whose Department of Anthropology he would soon direct. He lamented that the Tanaina culture was "almost completely gone." Nevertheless, he managed to write a painstakingly detailed two-hundred-page book, *The Ethnography of the Tanaina*. Osgood based his tome on the accounts of a small number of elderly informants at a time when most of the Tanaina lived near Kenai and the abundant salmon runs of the Kenai River. By the time he arrived, only two Tanaina men still lived in Kachemak Bay who remembered enough about traditional life there to be his informants. Fitka Balishoff was sixty-five and Wassila, "half Kodiak Eskimo and one-quarter Russian," around sixty years old. Fitka remembered hiding in a corner of a house when Russian sailors first arrived because he was too small to run off with everyone else in his village. By the 1930s he was the last speaker of the Seldovia dialect, the only Dena'ina dialect ever spoken in Kachemak Bay.

People of Dena'ina ancestry still live in Seldovia, on the south shore of the bay. To the west, the majority of Alaska Natives in the outer bay villages of Nanwalek and Port Graham are Sugpiat. The Dena'ina are, more generically, Indians, in the terms of anthropologists, and the Sugpiat are descendants of people the anthropologists once generically described as southern Eskimos. But *Eskimo* and *Indian*, *Dena'ina/Tanaina* and *Sugpiat/ Alutiit* are names that encompass groups of people with two mutually unintelligible languages who fought each other at times but also traded and intermarried. The terms also homogenize what were once vibrant and diverse villages and family groups until fragmented and displaced by war, economic slavery, and disease.

To Osgood we owe our ability to visualize the semisubterranean house, or *nichił* in the Dena'ina language, that stood on the bluff above China Poot Bay. The Russians later called this type of house a *barabara*, the name given similar types of huts in Siberia. One thing is certain—it was built of spruce, the only trees that surround it and that make up nearly the entire evergreen portion of the forest around Kachemak Bay. Only a few western hemlocks at the northern edge of their range are scattered about.

Since I am particularly carpentry-challenged, I used to bring along a copy of a section of Osgood's book on my tours and pass around his illustrations to help me explain how the house would have appeared, inside and out.

The outside would have had a covering of spruce poles over the unpeeled logs, and the corners would have been square, not notched, and tied together with spruce roots. Osgood explained that crosshatched rows of peeled spruce bark would have covered the sloping side-by-side poles of the roof. The walls and the roof would have also been completely thatched underneath with long strands of beach rye grasses. The inside would have had the rich, dark look of any wooden box bigger than a coffin. In the diagram, it looks cozy, with benches lining two walls for lounging upon during the day and sleeping under at night on top of sea otter skins. The central log-cribbed fireplace filled with sand would have warmed the space. Dirt piled high around the walls and moss chinking between the logs would have kept the cold out.

Two smaller, barely visible depressions adjoin the largest indentation. These would have been side rooms that could have had only a few possible purposes. While one might have been a sleeping room, the most important use would have been a sweat bath area. The smaller room, about six feet square, could have been the place that women whiled away the days during their menstrual periods. The Dena'ina built *nichiłs* as winter houses in groups for four or five families to spend late fall, winter, and early spring together. Janet Klein assures me that this was a winter house. I have trouble imagining how many people could have spent the dark and cold months together there. The main room is only twenty-one square feet.

The Dena'ina people's origins within Alaska are inland, like other Northern Athabascan groups. Oral history and archaeological evidence differ, however, about whether their ancestors came north to Alaska from the south, where the Navajo and Apache are speakers of related Dené languages, or eastward to Alaska from Siberia as speakers of an ancient Ket language that originated there. Stories about when they first arrived also differ. Some archaeologists place the Dena'ina in upper Cook Inlet before Eskimo-type people arrived from the west thirty-five hundred years ago. Others place their arrival along the Kenai and Kasilof Rivers and Kachemak Bay around a thousand years ago and not as a return to lands from which they were earlier displaced. Dena'ina Elders, like those of the Alutiit, say they have been on their lands and the sea from time immemorial. In the oral tradition of the Dena'ina, the sky clan came to Cook Inlet on a cloud.

The Dena'ina were unique among Northern Athabascan groups in their migration into territories bordering the ocean. In Kachemak Bay, they adapted to hunting marine mammals, waterbirds, and shellfish rather quickly in archaeological or cultural time, which remains a bit of a puzzle since archaeological sites contain no record of overlap between the Dena'ina and the distinctly maritime people who came before them. The answer may lie in the pattern of their migrations from an ancestral Northern Athabascan homeland in the interior of British Columbia. Again according to the linguists, the speakers of the Dena'ina language dialect used in upper Cook Inlet arrived from the west by migrating down the Copper River, while those who spoke the Outer Inlet dialect used on the Kenai Peninsula came from the east. As salmon people they followed rivers, first the Yukon River to the upper Kuskokwim River drainage. Then they moved southward to Lake Iliamna on the Alaska Peninsula before crossing the inlet. Lake Iliamna still has a population of harbor seals adapted to fresh water, and Dena'ina people still live there. Perhaps the two groups overlapped around what is now the coastal village of Tyonek in the northwest part of the inlet and began hunting seals in the ocean there.

Their adoption of maritime ways might also have begun through trade. The Dena'ina were prolific traders, as were all the people living around Cook Inlet and south to Kodiak. Oral histories describe caribou skins from the mainland exchanged for seal skin covers and kayaks. The skills could also have been spread by intermarriage and the taking of hostages and slaves from the losing side of battles.

However it happened, the Dena'ina in Kachemak Bay adapted their harvest patterns to benefit from the combination of forest and sea, an edgy world of woodlands, streams, beaches, and ocean. According to Osgood's records, they traditionally hunted sea otters and porpoise from kayaks using tools made from the bones of black bears and caribou. Their diet was varied, extending much more widely to animals they hunted inland, including porcupines and beavers in addition to the larger mammals that provided the bulk of their meat. Likely one of the biggest attractions to the bluff on China Poot Bay was a spring-fed stream in a low-lying and undulating landscape of tiny watersheds. Coho salmon run in the streams across China Poot Bay in late summer and into the fall. When the tide recedes from the flooded delta, you can pick them up still gasping where they're stranded in the grass just inches away from the channel.

It's an easy kayak paddle across China Poot; I've done it myself to a stream where I could dip net for salmon. The weighty harvest that I collected in a matter of hours was enough to fill my freezer and elevate the entire plane of my winter nutrition. A group of harbor seals hauls out regularly on the sandbars of the bay at low tide. The Dena'ina would have done well to come in late summer for the salmon, the seals, and the clams on the beach below, with berries to top it off.

Despite this long-lived culture in Cook Inlet, it wasn't until 2013 that the Anchorage Museum examined and celebrated Dena'ina traditions in a major exhibit, *Dena'ina Huch'ulyeshi*, which translates as "the Dena'ina way of living." The culture had become nearly invisible in its own homeland as the small number of descendants had become swamped by more recent immigrants to Alaska's most populous region. Artifacts that existed anywhere in the world, including those in the museum collections made by people like John Adrian Jacobsen, numbered less than a thousand.

Osgood's careful records of the Dena'ina language helped stave off its demise, and in the 1970s it underwent a revival. The language lives on as an endangered species with a small number of fluent speakers. For many years, it had its own website, quenaga .org, and Dena'ina writings and recordings are now preserved in the Alaska Native Language Archive at the University of Alaska Fairbanks. Linguist James Kari compiled a Dena'ina dictionary, but it contains no place names in the extinct Seldovia dialect, the only one used in Kachemak Bay. In the Outer Inlet dialect,

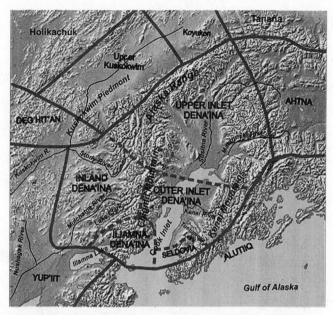

Map of Dena'ina language area and dialect areas by Alan Boraas.

Dena'ina Language Map: *Dena'ina Qenaga*. (http://web.kpc.alaska.edu
/denaina/pages/territory_pages/map_pages/denaina_language_map.html)

Soonroodna was *Ts'enghutnu*, which meant "bone fur stream."
Yukon Island, later named after a government schooner, was
called *Nika'a*, "the big island." A tantalizing place name also
survives for a village in China Poot Bay—*Tsayehq'at*, "place below
rock,"—which would put it in the outer part of the bay on the
east side, along the stretch of cliffs north and south of Shipwreck
Cove, where chert stone for tools and spruce trees abound. The
word for the Kenai Peninsula is *Yaghenen*, translated as "good
land." The Dena'ina name for Cook Inlet, *Tikahtnu*, meaning "big
river water," could have alerted Captain Cook as he sailed up the
narrow arm of the ocean that bears his name that it wasn't the
Northwest Passage he sought.

Despite a flurry of archaeology in Kachemak Bay beginning in the 1970s, the emptiness of ancient Dena'ina house pits shatters our western logic of using bones and stones fashioned into tools, weapons, and clothing to assign cultural identity. The memories closest to their prehistory were transferred to paper nearly 140 years after the first European contact, when Cornelius Osgood wrote his mountains of notes.

"Prehistory," we often say, as if it weren't history at all, as if it were almost but not quite unimaginable. As if it were a ghostlike existence until it was inevitably transformed into what it was meant to become by the people who took its scanty clues and material fragments and wrote it into being. Oral history preserves the deeper structure of a culture, the massive part of the iceberg below the waterline that again and again tips over the boats of the smugly rational. Linguists went swimming in the depths of the Dena'ina language and stories. Forty years after Osgood, in the 1970s, Kari took on the task of preserving the language. His wife at the time, Priscilla Russell, who became the first naturalist at the Wynn Nature Center, learned and recorded the plant lore. Their work began when they met a man named Peter Kalifornsky, his name alone a story from the Dena'ina past.

Peter was born in 1911 and raised in the traditional Dena'ina way until his village was decimated by an influenza epidemic and abandoned in 1929. In school, he was punished like all of the other children for speaking their native language. It's no wonder that so many of his generation lost their ability to speak it at all. As an adult, he got by in a variety of ways—running a trapline, building boats, working in canneries and on fishing boats, and working as a laborer on military construction projects. He suffered from tuberculosis and arthritis. He was sixty years old and one of only four speakers of the Outer Inlet dialect when he began to collaborate with James Kari to become the first Dena'ina writer.

Peter wrote down Dena'ina place names, then he wrote down word lists, and finally he began to tell stories. He was the great-grandson of Qadanalchen, who was taken by the Russians with other Dena'ina and Alutiiq men to hunt sea otters in Fort Ross, California, and forced to remain there for ten years. Peter was the first to write down Qadanalchen's song of homesickness:

> Another night has come over me.
> We may never be able to return home.
> But do your best in life.
> That is what I do.

"This is my great-great-grandfather's story," Peter wrote, "and the reason why there are no more potlatches." When Qadanalchen returned to his village, the chief told him he would be the next chief, but he refused. He took his relatives to found a new village he named Kalifornsky after his time in California, that faraway place where he had been taken. (The area around the village site still goes by this name, even as the spelling of nearby places has become "Kalifonsky.")

Peter's collected writings, *Dena'ina Legacy: K'tl'egh'I Sudku*, were published when he was eighty years old. James Kari and another anthropologist, Alan Boraas, were his editors and translators. His picture has the look of a Chugach Alutiiq mask in which the face is barely wrested from a tree, as if he was growing into the spruce tree the Dena'ina think of as their companion. Peter died two years later, after filling the emptied basins of Dena'ina memory with a flood of words and stories.

Through the stories and the language, and even the convoluted carpentry of the Dena'ina verb, Boraas began to plumb Dena'ina culture in the tradition of Edward Sapir. He and Dena'ina language teacher Donita Peters suggested that one Dena'ina word explains the absence of their leavings on the land as well as their entire worldview. The word is *beggesh*, translated as "a scent" or "a trace," to describe a type of negative energy that clings to objects and places. We humans are born into the world, the Dena'ina believed, in a state of *beggesha*, a state of purity without taint, without pollution, but then the possibility of influencing things of the world negatively or positively began. Our thoughts of ill will, our evil actions, and even our bad dreams bring *beggesh* into the world, where it becomes entangled with anything we use and any place we go. For this reason, the killing of animals—who by their nature were *beggesha*—for food, required rituals to eliminate *beggesh* from their remains. The bones of animals were placed in water or burned in fires to send them back to the reincarnation place presided over by K'unkda Jelen, "the Mother of Everything Over and Over." If they had been treated respectfully by humans, they arrived in good shape and would return to life as animals again by "putting their clothes on," meaning they turned back into animals as they appear to people.

Boraas and Peters understood *beggesh* to be a form of negative energy that could communicate across different dimensions of the Dena'ina cosmos that included humans, ancestors, animals, animal spirits, spirits, and *Naq'eltani*, literally, "the spirit that passes through us" or "awareness of the spirit that passes through us." Objects could "speak"; the *beggesh* entangled with things was information that could be relayed much like light across dimensions. Animals could detect *beggesh*. They withdrew from the places where they sensed it, so the attachment of *beggesh* to people, places, and things had implications for survival.

At the end of each human life, the possibility that a person's *beggesh* could harm someone else was so great that the body was cremated. The possessions of the deceased might communicate their *beggesh* to the ancestors and other spirits who might haunt the village, so they were also burned. It was a form of housekeeping and recycling within the ecosystem that we moderns could never begin to approach. We would need to consider the garbage of our lives and our negative thoughts to have such a titanic and ambiguous power that it must be washed clean or transformed into smoke after our death.

The Dena'ina feared that their actions would speak into the future, that they could offend the ancestors or harm someone, even those of us a thousand years removed, who gaze at their empty house pits, seeking older baselines of human need and desire. What speaks to me is their treatment of this place and its bounty as a spiritual baseline, an ethic that took into account the potential for human actions to have negative effects on other living beings. But this acute awareness of potential harm by thought and action brought the ancient Dena'ina no dispensation from a future of human cruelty and epidemics. As we move away from this baseline into that of the modern, industrialized world, the spiritual books do not balance. Neither do the ecological ones—it is the smoke we make now that imperils the entire web of life.

When I first learned the meaning of the word *beggesh*, I strained to detect tracings and scents from the past and to find places and things in which I could sense a purity—to try, once again, to live differently. True to my culture, I wanted something I could use. But it's hard to put myself in the mind of a group of people who so willingly and completely returned their outward possessions back to where they came from or to ash, down to the table scraps. My modern mind worries over their belief system like a dog with a musty bone, from within a culture that exhorts me to construct my identity out of my possessions and to accumulate them as a measure of my success. Eating locally and living garbage-less isn't particularly practical. A summer garden with a compost pile is as close as I can come to local recycling of nutrients. Other than the salmon in my freezer, frozen only hours after they were swimming in China Poot Bay, all the other healthy foods in my cupboards selected for the word *natural* on the label have been flown here from thousands of miles away, accruing *beggesh* like frequent flyer miles. I feel virtuous when I remember to bring a cloth bag when I shop and accumulate guilt over my leavings. My identity is embedded into my stuff like glue in a way that would terrify the ancient Dena'ina. They might describe me as someone slightly insane, a person who "hears the barking dog" that no one else hears and wanders off into the woods seeking what she's lost.

Perhaps the *beggesh* of a place could be what was once there but is now absent, in memories still attached to the holes in the ecosystem that are left behind after people or nonhuman beings leave a place, or die. My science brain connects me to places in their particulars: the names of plants and animals and the weather, the cycles of tides and seasons and how they are all structured and how they function. But science provides no basis by which the history of things or places is palpable. It doesn't describe how the intention with which an animal is killed attaches to its bones, to the spear that was used, to the place where it happened, or to the flesh and spirit of the person who killed it. There's no acceptable evidence that demonstrates that the trace and scent of an event can be seen or smelled long after it occurred.

I sense nothing at the house site—no violence but no great joy either, only my own aloneness in a place where people once shared food and songs and told stories.

Maybe something like *beggesh* is the source of my uneasiness in the built world in general, my sense of displacement when walking on paved trails with bicycles zooming by as I pretend to share the path with good cheer. When I first came to Alaska, I wintered in a log cabin in an aspen forest and lived for seasons in field camps smaller and more remote than that Dena'ina house. I inhabited those seasons among moose, seabirds, and salmon in what felt like a pure way of living after the recurring thoughts that circled through my mind during a long Fairbanks winter were washed away by the long light of summer. In those years, I craved wilderness and spent enormous amounts of time and much of my meager income on hiking trips to places where I wouldn't see any sign of human presence. A single piece of litter was devastating; a sign with the nerve to tell me to stay on the trail made me furious.

I'm not sure where that fury went. When faced with inevitable change to the environment or to a culture, maybe it's a notion of scale I've acquired about what is worth holding onto and what I need to release.

Another possibility is that my constant modern reliance on what is tangible has dulled my capacity for direct perception of the imprint of other lives. My wedding took place in a park in Sitka, Alaska, in a meadow I later learned had been a battlefield, the place of the last stand of the Tlingit against the Russians. I only connected the location of the battle, which remains a sad and bitter memory among the defeated Tlingit, to the place of my marriage vows (and their eventual defeat) years later, when I read the plaque placed as a memorial. But there are places, always wild places, where I have stopped and lingered and stayed for a while and left reluctantly. I've felt a quality without name or form, without smell or taste or sound. I've crossed the paths of wild animals in those places—bear and deer and raven and hawk—and they crossed mine, in a convergence that seemed to have been arranged a long time ago. Everything in nature changes and moves, slow like trees, swift like hawks. But in those moments, we met in places where nothing, and everything, changed.

Alan Boraas came to regard the culture of the Dena'ina who lived in Kachemak Bay during the period of late prehistory as "one of the most sustainable and egalitarian in terms of equitable access to resources the world has ever known." Archaeologists have only located a few Dena'ina camps and villages from the period after the Dena'ina began trading with the Russians. The uppermost layers are laden with metal buttons, gun parts, nails, and fragments of Spode china cups and saucers likely used to drink Chinese tea. In the collision between Dena'ina and European culture, the practice of accumulating possessions and garbage won out, at least for trade goods.

Were the Dena'ina convinced by the constant demonstrations by the Russians and later by the Americans that *beggesh* could be ignored without consequence? The forces that shamans appealed to seemed indifferent to the rule of Europeans who forced the Natives to turn animals into furs and commodities and to discard their bodies without ritual. They were offered objects never seen before, so perhaps untainted, in trade for pelts of sea otter, fox, beaver, and black bear. At the same time, the ecological consequences of killing began rippling through the food web in the forest and even outward through the food web invisible below the surface of the ocean. The trade goods the Dena'ina received may have been perceived differently, the stuff of a new and different kind of reality that they were no longer responsible for dreaming and thinking into being and returning to a state of purity.

As the killing continued without traditional rituals, the Elders still told the cautionary story of a man who did not believe in performing the rites, who cast out animal bones where people could walk on them. Mice came to him, and he clubbed them or poured hot water on them and threw them away. In a dream, he traveled to a mythical place where a beautiful woman, the mother of the animals, showed him the creatures he had mistreated. They were horribly disfigured. Unless he changed his ways, the animals would never return to that other realm where they were hunted and transformed again and again. Perhaps no one heard the story or its lesson, so the monsters that were the animals returned only in dreams. If they reappeared at all during waking hours, they barked like dogs. The failure of the shamans to neither foresee nor heal the smallpox epidemic that came in the 1830s may have been one of the last blows to the survival of their power. We will never know the stories of that time in the Seldovia dialect that is now extinct.

The nothingness that the Dena'ina left behind is a strange kind of gift from the past. When I hiked with the man who introduced me to archaeology, he would argue, half seriously, that we should leave our candy wrappers and pop cans behind for future archaeologists. But in the tracings of the *nichił* that vanished into the soil and air, the Dena'ina left the scent of a possibility that humans can become so much a part of the natural world that they can disappear into it for nearly a thousand years. Only their words linger to point the way to what cannot be seen. The scent that lingers at the house site is that of bones and flesh transforming, from life into smoke and ghosts.

IN THE SPIRIT OF THE LAMP

Past the weathered display at the edge of the Dena'ina house pit overlooking China Poot Bay, the hill drops away steeply. Drop to your knees after the snow has melted and before the grass and fireweed have spread their interlaced mat, and you'll find the white of shell and bone poking out of the matrix of soil. Other people lived here before the Dena'ina, and they left much more behind, in the manner of those who feast on clams and mussels and seals. Among the plant roots and below is a garbage pile fifteen feet deep. Archaeologists call it a *midden*, just as biologists do the massive caches of cones amassed by red squirrels nearby in the forest, and the remains of clams and crabs tossed outside the entrance to an octopus den on the beach below. Dig down carefully through layers of time and garbage and you'll find what people harvested from the sea and the land, and what they chose to discard.

I found my first evidence of these earlier people in my backyard in Homer, right on the surface and miles inland from any beach. My house had belonged to Sam and Vega Pratt, founders of the local museum now named for them. They obviously favored native plants, a positive spin on what many gardeners would call weeds. When I moved in, the enormous yard surrounding the house was mostly a spruce stand with a couple of lone birches, one wild cherry tree, and two bunches of lilies. In a few spots, circular metal fences driven into the ground corralled perennials but only half-heartedly excluded the natives. Each spring for me went by in a whirl of school field trips across the bay that left no time for planting. Spruce and birch trees soon obscured my view of the water; elderberry shrubs curtained the windows; the trails on the lot narrowed under a massive tangle of goatsbeard, cow parsnip, wild geranium, giant ferns, and forget-me-nots. During my infrequent forays into weeding and control, I kept coming across odd rocks—pumice and lava and rounded river rocks with striations and bands. Then I found arrowheads that looked suspiciously like the ones my father had collected as a boy on the Great Plains of Montana. One day I found a heavy, flat stone with a depression on one side, which I recognized as half of a stone lamp that would have been used to hold oil from a marine mammal, most likely a seal. The lamp had been sheared apart, almost neatly.

No, I wasn't living on an ancient house site. I soon learned that Sam had been a collector all his life, and he had incorporated his finds into the landscaping. Perhaps he and Vega had founded the museum because he needed a bigger repository when his treasures threatened to engulf his life. The more I looked, the more of Sam's eclectic artifacts I found scattered around the property. Excited about what might be valuable archaeological specimens, I filled a bucket with the arrowheads and the stone lamp fragment and took them to the current curator of the museum.

She was amused. The piece of lamp was the only thing that she was reasonably sure might have been collected locally. She explained to me what it meant for an artifact to be without provenience, to be displaced without information about where it had first been found. It had lost its precise placement on the cultural map of the past that archaeologists patiently construct. Sam, it seemed, had committed an archaeological sin that he couldn't atone for—he was long dead and settled into his last place below the ground himself. Vega, who might have known something about the objects' origins, was still alive then but stranded in dementia. To the museum, the displaced lamp was stranded in time as well, as good as dead to the past, present, and future.

I could understand the hard science of it—the digging slowly into the earth and mapping human things to their latitude and longitude and exact deepness that could fix them in place and time. But rather than being impressed that the presence of the lamp on the surface of my property meant nothing, it suddenly seemed odd to me that out of such fragments any story at all about human culture could be told, especially one told backward past language and memory. I had a vision of archaeologists around the campfire in the Arctic conjuring up ghosts of people who may have become ancestors or who may have left only their broken remains as they passed through. Real people had moved over the land, going and staying, staying and going, doing all the things that people must do to survive day by day over thousands of years. What had they been thinking when they chose their campsite or the place where they ended up remaining for generations? What made them decide to move on?

Here in Kachemak Bay, there certainly must be a real history about how people survived, or didn't, as the world shifted and changed around them, and they shifted in response and then changed their world. If we could read the signs, what knowledge of survival in the face of an unstable environment have they bequeathed us?

We need that baseline now as we weather changes so rapid that the concept of a modern baseline becomes harder and harder to fathom. Perhaps the people changed first, before being forced by desperation, inventing different ways of shaping stones, of traveling over water and snow, of sewing, of carving patterns into rock and bone and ivory, and of adorning themselves. The stone lamp was one of many inventions that made life in a cold, somewhat rainy environment possible. The world was different then, of course, but it's the many worlds conjured up by humans, living in groups, that we try to capture by the word *culture*. It feels

like casting a net to catch other nets of invisible connections—
between birth and death, humans and other animals, people and
the restlessness of the winds and the sea and the rumbling land.
This is the story I'm after, a story of cultural baselines

It seems best to start at the beginning, at the origin, which is the
original meaning of provenience, from the French word *provenir*,
"to come from." But my own history gets in the way of feeling I
have the right to claim human origins in Kachemak Bay as my
own. These are not my ancestral lands.

As a child I was taught the origin stories of my ancestors,
the Jewish people who began in the desert. We're the people of
the original Diaspora, forced to leave Jerusalem when the Holy
Temple was overrun by infidels. We wandered in the desert for
forty years led by Moses in our return from slavery in Egypt. The
Holy Temple has its own sacred lamp, likely also made from
stone in the beginning, which we're commanded by God to light
and keep lit forever—in Jerusalem and in every synagogue in
the world. Some say it's the light of eternity, the eternal light
of God's presence and the Torah. We are people of the Book and
of the Laws handed down by God in that desert. We carry them
with us wherever we go. "Next year in Jerusalem!" is our ritual
chant during the Passover seder held by Jews all over the world
that has little to do for many, like me, with any actual travel plan.

As far back as our origin stories go, we were never hunters;
we were never gatherers, except of God's manna. Yet I feel a pull
toward the life and death in the tide pool, toward the invisible
webs beneath the surface of the sea, toward the people who first
came here, who were mariners, arriving before the coming of
the strange comfort of trees. Perhaps, in the ecology that weaves
together all living beings in a matrix of great forces, I can begin
to trace the human strands backward into the landscape and seascape. Perhaps I can better navigate our shared future, changing
at a global scale, now encompassing all life.

I'm a descendent of people who spread out over the entire earth. My inheritance is a culture of displacement. My great-great-grandparents on my father's side emigrated in the late 1800s from what is now Lithuania to Ireland, which seems to me an unlikely bastion of religious tolerance. My grandfather left Ireland to homestead and become the keeper of a general store in Montana. My grandfather on my mother's side left the Island of Rhodes, off what is now Turkey, for Alabama. As a Sephardic Jew, his ancestors had been cast out of Spain in 1492. After his first wife died, he sent for a suitable picture-book bride from the old country. My grandmother Ida, in Smyrna (now Izmir), Turkey, responded.

I study other diasporas of people who hunted and gathered and who settled down in places and often abruptly disappeared. In the provenience of the people who lived here long before me—in their beginnings and their endings—perhaps there are lessons about staying put.

Still, the price of staying echoes through my family stories. I owe my existence to my ancestors who moved on.

The story told by the archaeologists began in Kachemak Bay with an artifact of dubious provenience—another stone lamp seemingly stranded far away from where they were usually found. An Alaska prospector unearthed it in 1919 as he plowed land he'd settled along Fish Creek, in upper Cook Inlet. He gave it to the University of Pennsylvania Museum. The lamp was elaborately carved, which impressed the prospector so much that he invented his own theory—that it had been looted from a temple in India by pirates who were later shipwrecked in Alaska. J. Alden Mason, the chief of the museum's American section, thought it was an Eskimo-type lamp that would have burned seal or whale oil, although one unlike any in museum collections. It was a flattish, dark gray affair, about a foot long with a narrow edge to hold moss or cotton grass that would have been its wick.

But the narrow edge was beveled and the sides were circled with what looked like garlands or eyes peering out of long, sweeping lashes. More surprising, the head and shoulders of a man with a broad, flat Asiatic face and almond-shaped eyes rose from the seat of the bowl in full relief. When the bowl was filled with the burning seal oil, he would have slowly emerged in the flickering light, as if from the ocean in which the seal once swam.

The southerly location of the lamp in Alaska created an interesting anthropological conundrum. Stone lamps had just begun turning up in archaeological digs along the coast of northern and northwestern Alaska and were considered an artifact of Eskimo culture. Anthropologists at that time used the word *Eskimo* to refer to indigenous people who occupied the northern rim of the world. It was later that it carried layered meanings of insult and disregard of the diversity of peoples the word tried to encompass.

Beginning in the late 1920s and early 1930s, archaeologists traveled to Greenland, northern Canada, and Alaska with a quest to learn where Eskimo culture had originated and how people had survived for thousands of years in the harsh Arctic environment. Stone lamps that burned oil from seals and whales came to be viewed as an ingenious invention. They provided the only source of heat in shelters, were used to melt snow and ice for drinking water, and provided light during the months-long Arctic night. An Eskimo lamp in Cook Inlet far south of even seasonal sea ice was definitely out of place. Moreover, for several centuries, Cook Inlet had been known as the territory of Dena'ina Athabascan Indians. Most archaeologists wouldn't even consider looking for the origins of Eskimo culture in southern Alaska at the edge of the boreal forest.

A stone lamp with ornately carved decorations was also unique. The hard rock and soapstone lamps found on Arctic archaeological digs lay alongside ivory figurines and tools whose entire surfaces were inscribed with intricate patterns, but the lamps were plain. Carved animal hunting charms or amulets had also been unearthed from house pits and graves in the Aleutian Islands and in western and northern Alaska, but sculptures of human figures were rare. A carved figure inside the bowl of a stone lamp was doubly intriguing.

The lamp that arrived at the Pennsylvania museum immediately piqued the interest of Frederica de Laguna, a young anthropologist. Although her full name was Frederica Annis Lopez de Leo de Laguna, all her life she answered to Freddy. The lamp was all she needed to convince the museum to send her off to Alaska in search of evidence of an Eskimo culture far south of any that been discovered so far.

Freddy's interest in Eskimo culture was shaped by her fieldwork in Greenland and her membership in the anthropological lineage of Franz Boas. Boas had been deeply involved in determining the origins of Eskimo culture his entire life. He had, however, assigned Freddy a PhD project involving the painstaking job of comparing Eskimo symbols and images carved into ivory and bone with those in Pleistocene-era cave paintings, which he hoped would help refute a connection between early Eskimo and European cultures. For Freddy, an opportunity to follow a mysterious and artistic lamp to Alaska was an opportunity for a grand adventure. Archaeological studies were just beginning in Alaska and few of them were done by women.

In the summer of 1930, Freddy landed first in Cordova and set off bravely to explore Prince William Sound in a rented skiff whose owner she described later as "a jailed bootlegger." The Danish archeologist Kaj Birket-Smith had planned to join her there, but he fell ill, so Freddy and her brother, Wallace, went on to Anchorage and rented a dory. After an unsuccessful visit to Fish Creek that was characterized by mud, rain, and no-see-ums that bit with a vengeance, her brother departed for school. Undaunted, Freddy chartered the thirty-six-foot-long *Dime*, captained by Jack Fields, who claimed he knew about sites on

Kachemak Bay where artifacts were spilling onto the beach. One of the first places Jack took her was Cottonwood Creek on the north shore of Kachemak Bay.

Jack's words proved true; Freddy found a midden almost immediately, and she and Jack started digging. Nine feet down, Jack pulled out a piece of stone lamp. The decorations on the outside and the rim were similar to those on the lamp in the museum and, to Freddy's delight, decidedly Eskimo.

That first summer, she surveyed the bay, locating sites that weren't excavated until several decades later. She returned the next two summers to dig in the site on Cottonwood Creek as well as at two sites on Yukon Island, near the middle. She dubbed one Yukon Island site the Great Midden, and she named the second the Fox Farm, in reference to its use in the 1920s. At the end of the season in 1933, she found a complete lamp at the Fox Farm site; it was the first unearthed in place.

This lamp was plain on the outside, without bevels or garlands, but it had the same upper half of a stocky man carved into the bowl. He looked like he was hunching his shoulders, face upward instead of outward, "in an attitude of prayer," as she described it. The arms were again outstretched, the hands flattened and almost paw-like. She had found her precious provenience for an Eskimo culture in Cook Inlet.

In addition to the lamp and lamp fragments, Freddy found more tools and weapons characteristic of a lifeway focused on hunting marine mammals. She named the culture Kachemak, following the convention of archaeologists to name new cultures for the first place where they are found and described. As she troweled through the top layer of the midden, she found that the lamps were not the only things the early people had decorated. They had evidently adorned themselves with beads, pendants, and nose pins. They made rings from ivory, jet, amber, and red-baked shale and regarded themselves in mirrors of polished slate. The pierced lips and cheeks of both men and women would have sported labrets, circular plugs of jade or jet—a custom of indigenous peoples along the coast of Alaska and in the Pacific Northwest that persisted into the nineteenth century. They'd also crafted combs, buckles, human and animal figurines, dolls, and toys, like miniature harpoons. They'd incised some of their well-crafted tools with spirals and hatch-marked lines and circle-and-dot symbols that matched ones she had seen on artifacts dug from archaeological sites of northern Eskimo cultures.

She also found human bones and bodies buried in the middens, some of the latter folded up in neat packages with knees and arms to chests. She found two skeletons, an adult male and a child, in one grave. Not only were they fully articulated like current-day medical mounts, but beside them were two more adult skulls. Diamond-shaped eyes carved from bone stared back at her from all three adult skulls, and they were covered with what appeared to be white clay masks. A long marble labret had been inserted near the center of the child's jaw and one made of gypsum was embedded in the clay on one side of the man's. Other skeletons were dismembered and the bones themselves broken, cut, or drilled and thrown into the midden. In yet another grave, Freddy found the skeleton of a woman with long strands of bone and shell beads.

Freddy had uncovered the first people who settled in the bay, a people who had ritually buried their dead and had created what we now describe as jewelry and art perhaps as a demonstration of an awareness of identity and status.

As she dug down to the bottom of the Great Midden, she saw a cultural sequence that had changed over time but in phases that were remarkably stable for hundreds of years. The workmanship on the lances and arrows noticeably improved. Earlier layers had grooved stones to weigh down fishing lines and notched stones that could have functioned as sinkers or weights on nets, but the size of the stones was substantially larger in the earlier part of the sequence than in later years when the nets might have been flung at waterfowl and seabirds. She found stone and bone harpoon parts and lances suitable for being launched from the deck of a skin boat. Even in the lowest layer of the midden, the harpoon heads were of the type that toggled, or swiveled, once they pierced the hides of marine mammals and caught them fast—another ingenious innovation thought to have originated in the North.

The overall picture was one of people who had occupied settlements long enough to accumulate deep middens, living a way of life fully adapted to maritime subsistence. Over time, a society had developed and become more elaborate, while the types of tools they made changed less, in only a few ways that made them more efficient hunters and fishermen.

Freddy returned to Bryn Mawr College in Pennsylvania to write up her findings. In 1934 she published *The Archaeology of Cook Inlet, Alaska*, the first book of its kind about Alaska. Forty-five years passed before archaeological excavations began again in Kachemak Bay, many of them headed by Bill Workman and his wife, Karen. They surveyed and excavated Kachemak sites with budding archaeologists Janet Klein, Alan Boraas, and Peter Zollars, groups of college students, and eager local volunteers. Excavations at Yukon Island and at other sites in the upper bay reinforced Freddy's early picture of Kachemak culture. After the invention of carbon dating in the late 1940s, archaeologists were able to assign dates that bracketed the Kachemak period to three thousand to fifteen hundred years ago in Kachemak Bay. Whether their occupation ended abruptly around AD 500, give or take a century or so, or they lingered until around AD 1000 is still debated, but the last dates of four major settlements—one at the mouth of Cottonwood Creek, two on Yukon Island, and one on Chugachik Island near the head of the bay—converged around AD 500 to 600.

Other archaeologists found evidence of Kachemak people on Kodiak and nearby islands, including some along the Pacific shoreline of the Alaska Peninsula. They also found the remains of an earlier culture that they named Ocean Bay in several locations in the same large region from which Kachemak culture appeared to have evolved. The timeline for Ocean Bay occupation in this region eventually stretched back to a site forty-five hundred years old in Kachemak Bay and to several sites farther south seven thousand to seventy-five hundred years old. Later, during the summers of 2000 and 2001, Janet Klein and Peter Zollars excavated an eroding site near the head of Kachemak Bay. The carbon dating on charred wood from a campfire came back with a range of seventy-five to eighty-two hundred years old. Stone flakes and points, Janet Klein told me, lay on top of less than an inch of soil deposited in the glacier's wake.

The scientific origin story for Ocean Bay people is still a confusing one. Their earliest camps were on islands they could have reached only by boat, and the diet revealed by their middens was almost exclusively marine. But where did they come from? Archaeological stepping-stones from slightly earlier marine cultures in the eastern Aleutian Islands and the Alaska Peninsula are still missing. At the end of the last Ice Age, the warming climate may have forced people who hunted caribou, elk, and bison on the northern side of the Alaska Peninsula or in upper Cook Inlet coastward and southward as the great Pleistocene herds dwindled. Evidence of this type of transition from living off the land to living off the sea is also missing. Ocean Bay people appeared on the scene, archaeologically speaking, with all the adaptations necessary to thrive as a marine mammal hunting culture.

The debate about the origins of Ocean Bay culture closely parallels one about the means by which the first people reached Alaska. Did they first come on foot over the Bering Land Bridge, reaching Interior Alaska around fourteen thousand years ago, where a number of archaeological sites demonstrate their presence? Or did they sail and paddle from Asia and reach the coast of South America around the same time or even a thousand years earlier?

I must admit the hypothesis of people arriving first by boats has always intrigued me. It's predicated on the extent of lush kelp forests that thrive in shallow seas from Japan around the Pacific Rim to Baja California and has been dubbed the "kelp highway hypothesis." People in skin boats paddled eastward and southward as the world warmed and the ice sheets receded, flooding the Bering Land Bridge seventeen thousand years ago. I imagine a flotilla of skin boats bearing whole families paddling amid the swaying fronds, stopping to camp on beaches with shellfish for the picking, and fishing and hunting seals and whales as they moved past a continent still walled with ice. A recent date of fourteen thousand years ago for a settlement on the coast of British Columbia has recently breathed new life into the hypothesis. But here too, a solid scientific trail backward is also missing; the skins and wooden parts of boats have all melted away with time. Evidence of more camps or settlements has been drowned by rising seas. If the ancestors of Ocean Bay people were part of this early migration by water from Asia or even of a later wave, the evidence is submerged on the shallow Continental Shelf that now girdles the seaward edge of southern Alaska.

The indigenous people the Russians encountered on Kodiak in the late 1700s had their own origin stories duly written down by explorers and Russian Orthodox priests. One is a migration story that began on the banks of the river that is now named Yukon. Two others begin on the Alaska Peninsula, which the Koniag called Aliaska. Those involved dogs who swam for love. In one story a dog swam from the mainland across to Kad'yak to find a mate. The story was possible, the storyteller told the Russian captain Yuri Lisianksii, because the crossing from the mainland to Kodiak was a river in those times, not a treacherous strait. It was a large otter who decided one day to create a wider channel. In another version, a male dog swam to be with his human wife. They produced five half-human, half-dog children after the woman's unhappy father banished them to an island north of the Alaska Peninsula. Like many Native tales that involve women marrying dogs or bears, this story didn't end well. The dog drowned and his dog-children killed their grandfather. In both dog stories, the dog-children become the first ancestors on Kodiak.

If the origins of the earliest people and the ones the Russians encountered on Kodiak are both mythically and scientifically murky, the end of the Kachemak people in Kachemak Bay is even more mysterious. When I gave naturalist talks next to the house pit in China Poot Bay, I would say that the Dena'ina still live along the Kenai River and in Seldovia. But when it came to what happened to the Kachemak, I could offer no explanation. Neither could Bill Workman. In a scientific article he published in 1980, he asked why such a "rich and stable cultural tradition in an apparently rich and stable environmental setting" should have been vulnerable to disruption in its ancient homeland. He and his fellow archaeologist and wife, Karen, sought an answer for several decades.

At first I was mildly curious, but as I began my search for ancient baselines, their disappearance began to seem more ominous to me. If the environment during the end-time of Kachemak culture looked rich and stable to anthropologists, what could buffer any culture from calamity? When my own ancestors left eastern Europe and Rhodes with only the richness of their laws and the eternal lamp of God's covenant to guide them, how could they have hoped to survive their wanderings? How can I survive in a land going strange?

Bill and Karen Workman considered the possible environmental catastrophes that may have precipitated the Kachemak peoples' departure: earthquakes, volcanic eruptions, and tsunamis. All three are a good bet on the southern rim of Alaska, a region where tectonic plates lock up and release regularly. It's so wildly seismic that geologists have dubbed this part of the North Pacific

Ring of Fire the Megathrust Zone. In 1980, however, no evidence existed that an environmental catastrophe of this nature had swept the Kachemak people away or forced them to leave. They considered possible social catastrophes, such as a raid by another group, famine, and even famine accompanied by cannibalism. But if the Kachemak were less than peaceful, their violence left no traces of bashed-in skulls or spear points lodged in skeletons. Their ending was not abrupt; it stretched over several centuries.

The first solid clues to the riddle came from the work of John Lobdell and David Yesner in the 1980s. Both were zooarchaeologists, with a background in archaeology and biology. They applied their skills to the middens, approaching them as garbage piles that could reveal the relative quantities of different animals the Kachemak harvested over time, like a series of collective dinner plates writ large and arranged in layers. Lobdell took on the midden on Chugachik Island near the head of the bay, and Yesner did the same for two ancient settlements on Yukon Island.

Their initial surveys turned up a pattern that appeared to have been stable for fifteen hundred years. No animal disappeared from their diverse hunting and gathering repertoire of mammals, fish, shellfish, and birds. With the exception of short-tailed albatross and beluga whales, all of the species in those middens still frequent the bay today. By the numbers, Kachemak hunters had been most successful in harvesting harbor seals and harbor porpoise, the latter of which spend so little time at the surface you can miss them in the blink of an eye. Bones of beluga and other small whales were also scattered through layers along with smaller numbers of sea lion and sea otter bones. Like the people the Russians later called Aleut in the Aleutians and Koniag on Kodiak Island, the Kachemak likely dined on meat and fat from marine mammals and used their intestines to make gut-skin clothing. They would have rendered seal fat into lamp oil and used it as a dip for other foods and a preservative for meat and berries, just as it is traditionally used today. In the circular nature of hunting, they needed seal skins and sinew from the tendons of porpoise and belugas to make the skin boats they then used to hunt them.

More surprisingly for a people who depended primarily on the sea, the Kachemak harvested an inordinate number of marmots, a distinctly terrestrial animal that would have yielded only a small amount of meat. But no doubt their lustrous silver coats provided warm fur clothing. They hunted other animals on land, including caribou and bears. They captured seabirds and waterfowl from their kayaks or with nets. They fished for cod, halibut, and starry flounder but brought home a surprisingly small number of salmon (or perhaps only a small number of salmon bones were preserved). Bones found in the middens were surrounded by chalky shells, primarily fragments of mussels that crumbled into powder along with the intact and thus countable shells of clams, cockles, and whelks.

When the zooarchaeologists compared the relative volume and number of individuals of different species in each midden, they saw a difference in the layer laid down at the end of the Kachemak period. The sheer volume of bones and shells had increased, although this might have been partially due to the much longer period of time the ones in the lower levels had had to decay. More significantly, the proportions changed, signaling a change in harvest patterns. The question shifted to *why*.

At the head of the bay, the harvests of seals, porpoise, marmot, and shellfish had all increased sharply until AD 250, but then they declined just as sharply over the next 250 years before the settlement was abandoned. Lobdell calculated that, at the peak, the annual harvest of harbor seals had doubled from eight to sixteen. Because most of the seals were juveniles, he assumed they had come from the rookery near the village. At this rate, he reasoned, the harvest would have become unsustainable from a population that he estimated to have been no larger than fifty seals. To him this was evidence of an inevitable food crisis and likely the cause of a crash of the Chugachik seal population. Switching to shellfish seemed to be a desperate and ultimately unsuccessful effort to compensate after the harbor seal population declined.

Similar to the pattern on Chugachik Island, Yesner found increases in the harvests of seals and porpoise compared to all other species on Yukon Island. In addition, a new ceremonial status seemed to have developed around the elusive harbor porpoise. He found several porpoise skulls and articulated skeletons that had been carefully laid out and surrounded by rocks.

Fishing and gathering also became more specialized. The harvest of marine fish became concentrated on halibut. Shellfish harvests narrowed from more than twenty species, to just four —two types of whelks, butter clams, and Pacific littleneck clams. In the uppermost layer of the midden, their shellfish diet had apparently narrowed even further—three-quarters of all shells were those of butter clams.

Like Lobdell, Yesner speculated the changing patterns to be in response to an increasing number of mouths to feed, resulting in depletion of some species that forced them to switch to others. This was something new in the way anthropologists had been pondering the endings and transitions of cultures along the Pacific coast. They had been focused on social behaviors like the invention and spread of new tools, trade, and intermarriage, meanwhile treating the environment as a stable backdrop to what was essentially a human drama. The coastline from the Aleutians to California was also assumed to be uniformly rich, especially in marine mammals and salmon, which eventually supported large, wealthy societies.

Yesner published a paper in 1992 that chided his colleagues for this type of thinking, which he referred to by the rather grandiloquent name, the North Pacific Maritime Stability Model. He challenged the assumption of environmental stability with examples of Alaska Peninsula settlements wiped out by volcanic eruptions and tsunamis. He was also starting down the track of the possible effects of climate change during periods of cooling after the last Ice Age. His Kachemak case study was a direct challenge to the notion of uniform richness of the environment. He marshalled evidence from the patterns in the middens to narrow down potential causes for the changes in harvest patterns to two—either overharvest or environmental change, much as Anne Salomon had done in the bidarki study. Since he lacked direct evidence that the environment or climate in the bay *had* changed before the Kachemak people disappeared, his best answer to the riddle of their eventual disappearance was that it was a classic case of people growing out of balance with their resources. In other words, humans have a propensity to settle down, overpopulate, and overharvest.

Scientists are still arguing about the human role in the demise of thirty-three species of Pleistocene land mammals that vanished around the time people arrived in North America, whether it's early proof of the tragedy of the commons enacted by humans again or extinction by global warming. According to Yesner, the Kachemak culture's claim to anthropological fame was as an illustration that the tragedy of the commons could also happen along the coast, in a region believed to have a nearly limitless abundance of salmon, seals, and whales. In the following decades, he and many other scientists—from anthropologists to ecologists—would reexamine their assumptions about the long-term stability of the North Pacific Ocean.

The same year that Yesner published his article in the archaeological literature, glaciologists Greg Wiles and Parker Calkins published evidence of a climate pattern in southern Alaska after the last Ice Age that oscillated between cooling and warming every few centuries. One period had been so cold that the icefields and complexes that drape the southern Kenai Mountains had moved forward, sending glacial tongues to engulf the forest above the southern shore of Kachemak Bay. When Wiles and Calkins counted rings to date trees that had been buried by glaciers and measured the growth rates of lichens on rocks that had been scraped bare, they bracketed the period of ice advance to AD 100–600. This meant that during the last centuries of Kachemak occupation of the bay, the climate and environment had been anything but stable. The changes in the harvest patterns might also be explained by changes in the marine food web related to colder ocean conditions or, as we are learning now during a period of rapid warming, unpredictable swings between extremes.

In 2010 Bill and Karen Workman published their last words on the disappearing Kachemak in the *Alaska Journal of Anthropology*. They seemed to wish to lay the question to rest with their unequivocal title "The End of the Kachemak Bay Tradition in Kachemak Bay, Alaska." They reiterated all of the possible reasons the Kachemak may have left, including some of the potential impacts of a colder climate that might have covered the head of the bay with ice during winter. They still weren't aware of any evidence, however, that a major earthquake, volcanic eruption, or tsunami had occurred during Late Kachemak times. Unable to say anything at all with scientific certainty, they characterized Kachemak Bay as a "marginal place," particularly because of its relatively small salmon runs, a place where no more than two to four hundred Kachemak people had likely ever lived at one time. They reiterated their points with a hint of asperity: "Displacing such a small marginal population," they said, "is not equivalent to bringing about the fall of the Roman Empire."

The Workmans left out another clue that had been published two years earlier in the *Journal of Volcanology and Geothermal Research* by a team of volcanologists headed by James Begét. They'd surveyed Augustine Volcano on an island forty miles due west of Kachemak Bay for evidence of eruptions that had sent enough lava, ash, and mud into the ocean to have triggered tsunamis.

They calculated that a tsunami aimed straight at Kachemak Bay would reach it in fifty minutes. They found one debris flow dated to AD 400 that matched a layer of sand twenty feet above the high tide line on beaches near Nanwalek and Seldovia in the outer bay. The timing, they claimed, could well have contributed to the collapse of the Kachemak culture in the bay.

This conclusion has been disputed, not because they were volcanologists dabbling in archaeology, but because two years later, a team of seismologists dug down through four thousand years of muck in Beluga Slough, on the other shore of Kachemak Bay, and found no evidence of a tsunami or a major earthquake. They found this lack of any evidence of an earthquake to be curious, because by then they had dated an earthquake at least as large as the infamous 1964 quake to around AD 400 or 500, which had caused massive subsidence in Prince William Sound and along the eastern shore of Cook Inlet north of Kachemak Bay. How Kachemak Bay escaped the effects of that megathrust Earth movement remains a mystery. The lack of tsunami evidence was even more confounding in light of the ash layer found by the volcanologists. Nonetheless, at a meeting I attended in Homer, scientific modelers assured me I was safe from a fast-moving, high-tide tsunami coming straight across Cook Inlet from Saint Augustine because it would dissipate as it moved through the bay. I could stand on top of the Homer Spit, they said, and watch it roll in and never so much as get my feet wet.

I've never experienced a tsunami that raised the tide more than a few inches. But I have experienced eruptions of the string of volcanoes across Cook Inlet from Homer. Viewed from the spit on a clear day, I remember them as AIR, from south to north: Augustine, Iliamna, Redoubt.

Augustine erupted again and again the winter of 1975 when I was following moose around in the Moose Research Center north of Homer. On some days, dark puffs of smoke arose from it, a sight both alarming and thrilling. Isolated in a field camp without radio reception, I was blissfully ignorant of any immediate danger, which was just as well because snowshoes were my only means to escape an approaching ash cloud. In the winter of 2005, Augustine erupted again, hundreds of years sooner than expected, but by then I was settled in Homer with a connection to a Volcano Watch website that I could tune into 24-7. Following oft-repeated instructions, I was prepared with panty hose stretched over my car's air filter, a box of survival gear, bottled water, goggles, dust masks, and blankets to fling over my computer. Despite a series of eruptions whose trajectories I could watch online, all Kachemak Bay got was a single dusting of ash that turned the snow a drab brown.

Redoubt erupted again and again during the winter of 2009. One day I knew a cloud was coming over Homer when the U.S. Geological Survey webcam broadcasting a picture of the smoking peak suddenly went black in the middle of a clear day. My phone, smart by then about volcanic eruptions, told me to stay put and to seal my windows with duct tape against ash so fine it could sift through the edges of the glass. Against these urgings, I had a duty to warn the naturalists at the Center for Alaskan Coastal Studies office a short drive away from my house. As I walked to my car, I looked toward the bay's mouth. The air thickened, choking me with every gritty in-breath. A roiling blackness filled half the sky. It moved at an incalculable speed. The lightning! Wispy bursts of pure light I never imagined radiated outward from the darkest center of the ash cloud, which looked like it would speak at any moment, would boom and roar, telling me something deeper than words.

Suddenly, I knew the way the world could end.

Following scientific bread crumbs, the most solid suspects at the end of the Kachemak people's trail are a volcanic eruption that would have been seen from Kachemak Bay, an earthquake that would have shaken the ground for long minutes, and global cooling. The year attached to each clue is not precise. In the way of science, they all have a plus or minus that could move the events as much as one hundred years in one direction or another. There is other evidence, however, that the sixth century AD was a time of cold and drought throughout the world, leaving behind a record of crop failures and famines. The Kachemak people could still have overharvested their resources, but they were also coping with an environment and a food web that was changing in unpredictable, incomprehensible ways.

In my habitat biologist mind, I've been thinking for so long about the potential impacts of a rapidly warming world that it's hard to wrap my mind around a cooling Kachemak Bay. In the warming world, glaciers on the south side of the bay are quickly retreating, dumping sediment that clouds the vision of animals searching for food in the ocean. Warmer waters leave salmon gasping for vanishing amounts of oxygen in streams. They're stopped far short of their spawning grounds when streams run dry after a sparse snowpack melts. Bark beetles double their reproductive rate and attack spruce trees weakened by drought.

I imagine a cooling world where ice crept ever downward, cutting short the trails used by hunters to travel inland in pursuit of caribou and moose. I imagine salmon turned back from spawning grounds by ice, not drought, and seals having pups on ice floes instead of rocky haul-outs. In this colder world, a food web topped by harbor seals might actually thrive as it does now in bays in Alaska where tidewater glaciers and harbor seals still coexist.

Mostly I think about life on the beach. What's left out of the accounting of bones and shells is timing. For someone foraging for food, Kachemak Bay is a series of patches in space and in time. Anyone who survived here with a kayak, harpoon, and a throwing stick would know when seals and seabirds returned to their rookeries, when salmon ran in each stream, when ducks and geese moved through. After the summer stores of dried fish and meat were exhausted, marmots and bears would still be sleeping the winter away, and the return of birds, seals, and whales in spring would still be far off, but there would be food on the beach. In this place where timing is everything, where winter storms can pin hunters on land for weeks, there are beach foods—available to everyone, including women, children, and men too old to hunt. Eating from the beach would yield a steady diet of protein but not much else in the way of carbohydrates, fat, and vitamins. People can starve even when they can fill their stomach with protein.

Clam and mussel beds themselves are far from stable; they're subject to spectacular die-offs. When the 1964 earthquake dropped the land six feet in Kachemak Bay, hundreds of acres of clams and mussels were suddenly drowned. In 2005 little-necked clams that had been so abundant the harvest limit was set at a thousand clams per day disappeared from China Poot Bay in a single season for reasons no one could explain. In 2010 farther up Cook Inlet, thousands of deeper-burrowing razor clams were churned up by a single powerful winter storm that deposited their dead bodies in a berm of sand at the top of the beach, ending the harvest five years later. Scientists sampling butter clams and little-necked clams in Kachemak Bay began finding only older ones.

Clams and mussels can also die of cold. I learned this lesson during my first field trip to a Kachemak Bay beach. Daisy Lee Bitter, a legendary teacher and naturalist, led the tour that day on Bishop's Beach. She may have been one of the only people who could have found something to be enthusiastic about on that frigid day in early March, luring me unwittingly into my future as a naturalist. I fixated on the solid black mass of mussels gaping open and empty next to my numb feet.

Kachemak Bay is on the cold edge of the Pacific Ocean and is prone to occasional winter bouts of below zero temperatures that I had thought happened only in Alaska's Interior. That year temperatures plunged as low as -24 degrees Fahrenheit for nineteen days in a row in January, long enough to freeze everything on the beach exposed all the way down to the extreme low tide line. Nearly every barnacle and mussel was dead and, along with the mussels, an intertidal forest providing shelter and food for snails, chitons, crabs, and small fish. The butter clams, that last favorite beach food of the Kachemak on Yukon Island, burrow deep inside the beach and were possibly the only clams best able to survive cold winters. The event whose aftermath I witnessed had been an extreme one. The temperatures were the coldest recorded in seventy years and more than a hundred years after the glaciers had begun melting after their last surge during the Little Ice Age.

Although I don't remember the date in early March when I walked on the beach, I certainly remember the year—1989—the year of the *Exxon Valdez* oil spill, which occurred only weeks later. The black tide of spilled oil never reached Kachemak Bay, although tar balls and oily brown mousse washed up. The dead, frozen mussels in Kachemak Bay became the control group for experiments by scientists to see how fast they could recover from a natural disaster compared to the un-natural one of being drowned in oil in Prince William Sound. By 1992 mussels had only begun to take back the beaches in Kachemak Bay.

Shellfish beds recover when their zooplankton larvae settle and young animals grow large enough to escape hungry predators or bulldozing chitons. A single storm can uproot baby clams and break the slender golden threads that bind young mussels to rocks. Recovery always takes several years. The Kachemak people, beset by a volcano and walls of descending ice, wouldn't have had a few years to wait.

I like to think that the decision to leave a place that is home is one of mind and heart. But it can surely be a matter of survival, of stomachs empty too many years in a row and winters that seemed never-ending.

Perhaps there was another factor. The Kachemak people, in their last centuries in the bay, kept raising children and making beautiful lamps. On Yukon Island, they buried not only the skulls of harbor porpoise but also the bodies of certain people with ritual. Sometime during that period, they buried the body of a woman with three strands of beads made from cockle shells that reached to her waist. In the midden on Cottonwood Creek, they laid out the body of a second woman with two very large labrets made of jade and jet, and nearly thirty-three hundred bone and shell beads still attached to the shreds of a dance cape. Both burials tell a story of a culture in which women could become wealthy and live much longer than men. The bones of the woman at Cottonwood Creek told still another story. When John Lobdell peered into them by X-ray, he saw the telltale marks of annual bouts of starvation. Perhaps the deaths of the women had been a great blow. They were buried with rituals that might have been accorded to shamans at a time when the environment was becoming unpredictable and harsh. With these deaths, perhaps the people lost their belief in a means to predict the future and what they may have believed was their means to intercede with the great powers on their behalf.

That the Kachemak, with tools of stone and bone, survived fifteen hundred years in this changeable place remains a singular, surprising fact. It's easier for me to understand why the Kachemak might have left than how they managed to stay.

Of course, this version of the past is one I've constructed, a story of bone piles and long-dead people in a place beset by implacably marching glaciers, fiery sky paintings of volcanoes, and rumblings of the fissured earth. Kachemak storytellers would have told it differently as reflected in the titles to Alaska Native stories that have survived. They might have told the story "How the Glacier Ate the Forest." Or the one about "When the Sleeping Monster Beneath the Ground Awoke."

I often reach for the fragment of the stone lamp I found in my yard and hold it. I imagine the work that must have gone into creating a rough, functional depression in one rock, using only another rock. The lamp became, for the archaeologists, a talisman of Eskimo, and maritime, culture. But among the scores of cultures unearthed along the coast of Alaska, the figures inside the lamp and the raised patterns on its sides remain unique to the Kachemak tradition.

Bill Workman was the only archaeologist to speculate in any depth about the possible meaning of Kachemak art. At first he was wary of what he called "obsessively high levels" and "almost compulsive levels" of craftsmanship found even on simple everyday tools. He called their treatment of the dead "bizarre burial ceremonialism" involving "mutilated corpses." But in trying to make sense of the decorated lamps, he later noted how many had been found associated with burials. He tied this to traditional Eskimo beliefs that lamps were necessary for ghosts to find their way between the worlds of the living and the dead. Lamps were also lighted when shamans traveled to the spirit world. Masks and covering one's eyes were means to enhance spiritual vision. Perhaps, he speculated, the Kachemak ritual dismemberments of their dead were based on one of the most ancient ideas of all—the inherent power in the human body that must be taken apart after death in order to regenerate into a new, live whole.

When I look at my lamp, I feel what was really lost from the bay with the disappearance of the Kachemak people. I feel what would be lost if the people in Nanwalek and Port Graham no longer harvested bidarkis from their beaches. I see what's lost in any diaspora when one is separated from the place where one's ancestors still remain.

All that time I obsessed over the Kachemak lamps, I never saw or touched one. Those collected by archaeologists are sequestered in museums; others have disappeared into private hands. So I was surprised to see one on display at the Anchorage Museum as part of the exhibit about the Dena'ina people. The provenience of this lamp was limited to the notation on the label: "Stone Lamp, found 1913, Fish Creek, near Knik (Kachemak Culture?)." Knik is in upper Cook Inlet, which is now Dena'ina territory, the place where Frederica de Laguna searched fruitlessly to find a lamp after her first skiff ride in 1930.

The squat upper body of the human figure emerges from the bowl of the lamp. The arms stretch forward and the hands are flat and end in large, distinctive fingers that merge into the bowl's surface. The figure was now familiar to me from pictures of lamps in other museums. Under the soft light in the display case, before me in its three-dimensional form, however, the lamp had a presence that no photo could convey. All of the surfaces on the hard rock had been polished to an almost impossible shining smoothness. The face had distinct features, the nose broad and flat and the head flattened on top.

Protected from me in its glass case, the lamp was another stranded thing, its provenience and significance uncertain. It was meant to be filled with a miniature ocean of seal oil. The figure in its center was meant to be surrounded by a circle of burning moss and by an outer circle of people, feeling the warmth of the flame and seeing the figure and each other in its glow. The face looked outward in the direction of outstretched arms, speaking a language of entreaty to something invisible.

I had trouble moving away from the lamp, held there by the lone half figure and meaning I could never hope to plumb. I accorded a reverence to its echoes of the eternal light burning in every Jewish temple. Its design united stone and moss—things of the land—with seal oil—a thing of the sea. Its spirit of a home under the care of a woman united with the spirit of a man who went out to hunt seals and whales. If the lamp had been needed to light the way to the world of the dead, it might have also been necessary to light the way back.

The Kachemak impulse to add images to the items they gathered around their homes comforts me. As long as it was burning, there were enough seals to feed the lamp, the people, and the imagination. When there were not, a woman could live into middle age, accumulate thousands of beads, and still starve, again and again, in her failure to intercede with the powers that brought abundance.

In the winter of my own life, with the animals disappearing, this strikes close to home. In the midst of great forces and uncertainty, the stone lamp still speaks to me of Kachemak rituals of death, of being part of a circle, a great circle of life into death and life again.

Part III

FUGITIVE RESOURCES

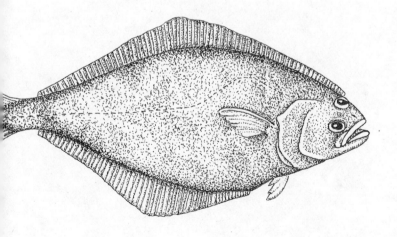

Chasing Abundance

Consider once more the universal cannibalism of the sea, all those creatures that prey on one another, carrying on eternal war since the world began.

—Herman Melville, "The Savage Sea," *Moby Dick*, 1851

"Homer, Alaska: Halibut Fishing Capital of the World," the chamber of commerce sign proclaims as you top the hill from the north and get your first glimpse of Kachemak Bay.

You notice the sign only after the panoramic sweep west to Cook Inlet stops you cold. To the east, the major jutting-out piece of geology that is Homer Spit bisects most of the bay. Across are the mountains. Watery washes of blue-gray clouds wreath them above the slopes draped in blue-green forest. The jagged white southern rim contrasts with the constant motion of the textured bay below.

This landscape draws artists just as surely as the bay attracts scientists and fishermen. Fish and science and, of course, money and politics have been entangled here since the first case of salmon was shipped from a cannery in Port Graham in 1911.

I tasted Kachemak Bay almost as soon as I recognized it as more than a name on the map of Alaska. In the late 1970s, it was all about crab. A poster on a kiosk at the university in Fairbanks lured me to a dinner where spidery legs and chunky crab bodies were pulled from massive boiling pots and piled high on plates by burly, bearded men. Compared to my usual graduate student diet of rice and vegetables and the occasional gift of moose meat, this was manna. By my third helping, crab juice dripped down my arms and was smeared into my hair. After dinner, fishermen made speeches about a pristine bay the state had leased to oil companies. They told the story I've heard many times since about the *George Ferris*, the oil rig that had gotten stuck in the mud that winter and then leaked oil into Kachemak Bay. The dinner was our bait to become hooked into the political battle against oil development. As the fishermen told it, the equation seemed pretty simple: we could have Kachemak Bay crab forever or Alaska could have oil development. But not both.

The abundance of Kachemak Bay that existed then is mythic. A 1975 report depicts a watery Eden in a single map. According to scientists whose job it was to come up with numbers, the bay was stuffed with a plentitude of all forms of marine life. "1.5 billion shrimps" the map declares, paddled about in its center. At the mouth of Halibut Cove, east of China Poot Bay, up to 160 million herring eggs were laid during the spawning season. The inner bay's north shore was home to 30,000 marine birds. Harbor seals hauled out and pupped in the exact area that would have offered convenient settlement places for the Kachemak people— at the head of the bay and the north shore of Yukon Island. And that wasn't all: 25,000 waterfowl congregated in the flats at the bay's head and 300,000 salmon spawned in the lower reaches of streams on its south side. There were halibut, rock sole, yellowfin sole, and scallops in the bay's depths. A crab "sanctuary" had been established along the north shore of the bay to protect the nursery area for half a million Dungeness crab, a million king crab, and somewhere between 3 to 5 million Tanners.

The numbers seem utterly fantastic, but a second map in the same report shows the results of dragging a trawl net along the bottom to sample shrimp. A dense cluster of numbers appears in the middle of the bay, each of which represents the results of a single haul. The numbers are in terms of shrimp in the thousands per mile, the highest of which is more than 4,000. "To convert to average number of shrimp per mile," the map legend says, "multiply pounds by 102," which converts to nearly a half million. But, the scientists caution, "it must be underscored at this time that such figures are only a *partial* estimate of the amount of marine life utilizing or living in the bay." The report and its treasure maps became the basis of the claims that Kachemak Bay was "the richest bay in the world," a mantra invoked again and again to stave off oil development. It even showed up in the speeches of a fisherman named Jay Hammond running for governor of Alaska. His embrace of the issue may have flipped the balance toward his victory.

By the time I moved to Homer two decades later, I was told again and again that I had missed out. During the good old days, the bay had been filled with crab pots. I was shown pictures of boats awash with pink masses of shrimp. In China Poot Bay, you could walk along the beach and flip a king crab onto the beach with your kayak paddle. The owner of the Kachemak Bay Wilderness Lodge told the story of collecting enough mussels and clams in just minutes from the reef in front of the lodge to feed appetizers and chowder to fifty people. I heard stories from the now-respectable citizens of Homer who began their lives here as part of the ragtag army of beach-partying Homer "Spit Rats" who spent their summers in a haze of fish slime from their cannery jobs.

At the beginning of my first summer there in 1998, a tent camp embellished by driftwood, blue tarps, and Visqueen was still a feature of the summer landscape. When the fishing boats returned to Homer Harbor, there was work for anyone who wanted it. But before the summer was over, Homer's only fish processing plant blew up and burned. The Spit Rat tradition disappeared with it. Deliveries of commercial catches were sent to floating tenders or other ports. When fish were offloaded at Homer, they were shoveled into refrigerated trucks and sent on their way to

Seward, four hours away. Motor homes laden with retirees and families soon filled the vacant camping spots on the spit.

The fishermen with their seining nets and tall trolling poles continued to overwinter their boats in the harbor or the nearby boatyard, but their captains began nosing them out through the breakwater for salmon openings as far away as Bristol Bay. Fishing boats with names like *Predator* and *Mercenary* set forth for the Gulf of Alaska and the Bering Sea for crab and cod. The captains of the crabber *Time Bandit* became stars of the reality TV show *The Deadliest Catch*. In actual reality, they probably made more money from ship tours and souvenir sales online than from crab seasons fraught with monster storms, vessel repairs in near-freezing weather, and the occasional man overboard. Some years, salmon fishermen still set their purse seines on the point across from Peterson Bay Field Station and occasionally threw me a large salmon as a reward for watching as they pulled in their bulging net.

Commercial fishing boats tie up now amid fully equipped dreamboat cruisers captained by vacationers, retirees, and second-home owners from Anchorage. These boats have leisurely names like *Spare Time* and *Change of Pace*. Unnamed skiffs owned by locals have their own float. From Memorial Day to Labor Day, a flotilla of charter boats and their well-paying clients now sets off for Cook Inlet in search of halibut and salmon, but they rarely stop to try their luck in the halibut hidey holes in the bay that used to be a sure thing.

Like the Sugpiaq Elders and the fishermen, I've accumulated my own litany of how it used to be, even though my baseline goes back only to 1998. The crab pots we set (with educational permits) on oceanography field trips for kids used to come up with bronzy red Dungeness crabs among the duller Tanners. A solid band of sea stars lined the beach in China Poot Bay at every low tide. One stretch of that beach was so covered with sea urchins and squishy sea cucumbers that there was nowhere to step without committing a massacre. A Kodiak king crab, three-feet across, was mounted on the wall of Peterson Bay Field Station.

It's no wonder that fishing stories told in Homer tend to harken back to baselines of a golden age, like that of the Sugpiaq Elders when herring, shrimp, crabs, clams, and mussels were all abundant and the fish were much bigger. These stories create nostalgia in me for times I never even experienced. The treasures mapped in the 1970s faded away soon after the map was published. Herring populations were already a shadow of their former selves from the heyday of the 1920s, when salteries lined the shorelines of Halibut Cove and Seldovia. In the 1980s the shrimp fishery ended, followed by near-complete population crashes of king and Dungeness crabs. In the 1990s halibut began getting smaller. When I moved to Kachemak Bay in 1998, you could still set crab pots for Tanners on a sport fishing license, but that fishery also ended in 2003.

Now Kachemak Bay fishing stories always seem to lead to the question of who's to blame for the crashes and shrinkages. Fishermen blame greedy fishermen (the other guys, never themselves), the Alaska Board of Fisheries, the Alaska Department of Fish and Game, the feds, bad science, poor management, other predators. Sometimes stories check the box "all of the above." The Sugpiat blame commercial fishermen for the crashes of crab and shrimp. Scientists and managers defend themselves by blaming the economics and politics of the fishing industry. Since the earliest days of Alaska as a U.S. territory, fishermen have been chasing fish and shellfish, and scientists have been chasing fishermen, trying to head off crashes.

When Alaska became a U.S. territory in 1912, a strange brew of capitalism and democracy had already taken hold. Beginning in the 1700s, the colonial nation-states had a tacit agreement in the doctrine of *mare liberum*, "freedom of the seas." No nation could claim to own any part of the ocean, and every nation had the right to exploit fish and whales wherever they could find them. The colonial powers claimed land, of course, in the name of their king, queen, empress, or president, regardless of whether or not the land was already occupied. Since Russia claimed Alaska, the United States was obliged to buy it. Immediately upon signing the check, all of Alaska became public lands owned by the federal government.

Fish were legally unowned things, a notion that had its roots in English common law. Ownership could only be established by their capture. Along with wildlife, fish were wild, *feris naturae*, and legally "fugitive resources." Their "fugitive" nature seems whimsical in retrospect—fugitive from whose justice, exactly? But the original meaning of the term was more of the nature of being unconstrained, like air, or, later, like outer space and the Internet. The "resources" designation was more ominous, spelling the transformation of fish from food and the stuff of regional trade in Alaska to something to be extracted and sold anywhere in the world where there were buyers.

The right to catch fish has its own legal history. The Magna Carta, signed by King John of England in the thirteenth century, included a stern rebuke to rights of monarchs. "The king's fish" became fish that no one owned but everyone had the right to attempt to capture. In the wake of the Indian wars in the western United States, this equality wasn't extended to the Sugpiat, the Dena'ina, or any other Alaska Natives. Natives were essentially transferred from one occupying power who granted them full citizenship rights as Russians to another, the United States, who granted them no citizenship rights at all. They couldn't own title to property or legally operate commercial boats. In the Sugpiaq and Dena'ina territories, centuries-old fishing rights held by clans were thus conveniently ignored. The rights of other Americans and people from other nations who flocked to Alaska for gold and then stayed were also overrun by those with the capital to invest in the fishing industry. As absentee owners of canneries and salteries competed fiercely to control the lion's share of harvesting, processing, marketing, and profit, the territory's residents were left far behind.

Alaskan fish had been a selling point for the purchase of Alaska. "All authorities unite on this point," Ivan Petroff reported to Congress in 1881, that Alaska fisheries resources "are regulated by demand . . . the supply is simply inexhaustible." His report echoed that of Tarleton Bean, the first federal fisheries scientist to travel to Alaska in 1880. Bean also bemoaned the use of fish by Alaska Natives as waste: "The proportion of Alaskan fish brought into the markets of the civilized world, when compared with consumption of the same articles [by Natives], are so very small that it barely deserves the name of an industry," he complained. "Any development in the fishing industry," he went on, "must necessarily be an improvement causing a saving in supply."

The industry ramped up quickly. The development of the science and its use in fisheries management fell well behind the rising curves of fisheries responding to demand created in distant markets. The history of the fisheries in Kachemak Bay was just one step behind the history of the entire North Pacific Ocean as American and Canadian fishing fleets expanded northward and seaward along the West Coast. Russian, Japanese, and Korean fleets expanded eastward.

Sarah Gaichas, a computer modeler of Alaska's fishy ecosystems, took on the task of compiling the harvest statistics for all species fished commercially in the North Pacific as part of her PhD dissertation for the University of Washington. In an ocean with hundreds of fish species, her statistics demonstrated that fishing fleets consistently chased after only a handful for the better part of the twentieth century but with all the technology they could muster. Gaichas compressed the data into a single graph of cumulative tons of each species removed by fishing. The graph was a surfer's nightmare; waves of harvest rose in succession, each one more steeply than the one before, and then crashed precipitously.

The job of heading off the crash of fish populations has always been underlain by conflicting motives. On one hand, it's straight-up math for biologists: numbers into the population through births and numbers out through deaths, with the management goal of keeping those numbers even, or at least the biomass of fish relatively constant over time. But from the fishing industry's point of view, fish are commodities to be harvested at a maximum level and profit.

In line with mare liberum, it's perhaps no surprise that "maximum sustained yield" became standard policy for federal and international management of fisheries around the middle of the twentieth century. In practice, the maximum could only be determined after the harvest pushed past the magic number and biologists marshaled evidence of declining, or depleted, stocks after the fact. This didn't seem to trouble the fisheries managers after the theory that fishing controlled fish populations became the cornerstone of fisheries politics. Once the harvest level was reduced, so the theory went, the next generation of young fish would be less crowded, eat heartily, and grow faster, with fewer large fish of their species to compete against. The population required only a brief respite, like a field left fallow, to replenish itself and go back to yielding itself to the fishing industry.

I thought there was something a bit shortsighted about this viewpoint when I first encountered it in wildlife management even without the same economic implications. Like wildlife, fish populations are referred to as *stocks*, the language of livestock. The notion of *yield* has a similar ring, like that of crops. It also implies a certain willingness, or maybe subjugation, of the ecosystem to lend energy and matter to our species that could otherwise have been used and recycled within the system. Lawyers still refer to fish as fugitive resources to which our species are the rightful owners, only temporarily at large until we catch and kill and use them. As to which among us are the rightful owners, democracy and capitalism continue to disagree. Since the 1920s in Kachemak Bay, anticipated rapid rebounds of fish and shellfish populations have been rare. Fisheries close and never reopen.

The battle against oil development in the bay was won in favor of the crab and the fishermen and ecological sense, an unlikely outcome in a state that has run on oil ever since. Signing the buy-back legislation passed by the legislature in 1978, Governor Hammond called it a victory of the people over a government that did not listen to their wishes.

"It was a time," he said, "when Alaskans rose up to say in this state there are some places we consider so valuable that we will not risk their destruction, even if we produce a little less oil and make a little less money in the process." It felt like the greenies had won. He was the first, and possibly the last, Alaska governor to declare a decision to forego development as a victory for the people and the conscience of Alaska.

Each crab we caught on our oceanography field trips stirred my memory of the long-ago crab feed. Within a few years of my arrival in the bay, though, the crabs the students dutifully measured and dropped gently back into the ocean were always Tanner crabs, never Dungeness. The monster-size king crab on the wall of the field station began to crumble into dust. Eventually, the legs fell off, and I reluctantly took it down. The only signs of Dungeness crabs in the bay were fragments of small shells in the midden pile of wily octopus.

We didn't have crab forever.

The Scotch Cure

Everything in Peterson and China Poot Bays is "rustic," even the
upscale wilderness lodge with its trail sculptures made from
washed-up floats and driftwood. All sizes of rubber boots are
lined up neatly in its mudroom where the floor is tiled with beach
rocks. On the other side of the peninsula, the field station melts
slowly back into the landscape. The signs along the trail grow
grayer and less readable every season. *Wabi-sabi*, the Japanese say,
to describe this inevitable melting and graying of the things made
by people as natural processes proceed. Nothing lasts. Nothing
is permanent. Nothing is perfect.

Halibut Cove lies just a few miles up the bay, tucked behind
Ismailof Island along the south shore. The area was occupied not
only in Dena'ina times but before that in Kachemak times. Even
earlier, a group of hunters left behind a collection of finely worked
tools made of jasper, quartz, and obsidian. Their workmanship
has been traced to people who carried stones exotic to Kachemak
Bay eastward from Bristol Bay on the Bering Sea side of the Alaska
Peninsula. The obsidian had made its way, likely through trade,
from its source in a quarry far north on the Koyukuk River in
Interior Alaska.

The modern era began in Halibut Cove with herring, not the fish
that gave the cove its name. In 1911 a Scandinavian fisherman
"discovered" a herring run in the cove. A new rush was on, not
for gold, but for the silvery fish that arrived fat with oil in late
summer or fall. Thousands of people came to the cove each year
to pack the harvest.

By the time Frederica de Laguna arrived in 1930, Halibut Cove was a ghost town again. In the last few decades, however, it's been repurposed into a combination of an upscale vacation home community, summer tourist destination, and artists' colony. Its collection of cabins and two- and three-story trophy homes are the equivalent of a gated community for Alaska, where private land is scarce away from communities and private docks even scarcer. A handful of people winter over. Glaciers still flank the cove.

Halibut Cove gets much of its current character from a clan headed by Clem Tillion. I still think of him as the Codfather, his nickname when I lived in Juneau during his long reign at the center of state and federal fish politics. He created his own empire in Halibut Cove, buying up homesteads and building boardwalks and docks and a large salt box house in the New England style of his birthplace. When he tells the story of why he came to Alaska, he cites the dilemma of being a younger son in a family with a limited inheritance of land. "Ye can't make more land," he says his father explained to him as he left home, "but ye can always make more sons."

Clem's wife, Diana Tillion, now passed away, was a gentle woman and artist who spent many evenings in her studio talking with visitors. Their artist daughter, Marion Beck, paints oil landscapes and owns the Saltry—in my opinion the best restaurant in Alaska. Its name is a reminder of the vanished salteries of the industrial-scale herring fishery that filled the cove in the late 1920s.

When I dine at the Saltry, I arrive like everyone else on a venerable wooden boat, the *Danny J*, which lumbers across the bay from Homer on a nightly run for those of us fortunate enough to have a reservation for one of the restaurant's two seatings. Unlike those who might have arrived by skin boats in the distant past, we visitors come in peace and are allowed to stay for a short time in the cove to trade money for seafood and art.

Like all summer visitors to Halibut Cove, I stroll on a board-walk perched high above the water to a series of art galleries. In the first one, classical music wafts from a baby grand piano. Sea otters and cormorants wrought of gold, abalone, and pearl twinkle from velvet trays. Marion Beck's landscapes emerge from bright patches of oil paint. The next gallery still displays Diana Tillion's paintings. Silhouettes of birds as spare as glyphs fly across the page in calm sepia tones. It's hard to believe they were painted with ink that she extracted from an octopus with a hypodermic needle. Visiting the last gallery requires crossing a narrow gravel isthmus slightly wider than a trail to a pottery studio where large-breasted, molten mermaids guard the walls. Plates, cups, and bowls fill racks in sheds. The doors are always wide open, no artist anywhere to be seen, with a sign proclaiming that payment is on the honor system.

When I amble through these galleries, I feel the pull of art that seems to have been made in this place from the earliest times, such as the small ivory sea otter amulet found in one of the oldest layers excavated by archaeologists nearby. I'm grateful for the ways artists have always chosen to create beauty, not just usefulness, in the materials they craft. Their notice of patterns, colors, and textures gifts me with the sense they make of the world.

On a perfect summer evening on the deck of the Saltry, my fork is poised above a hand-thrown plate graced with a slab of perfectly cooked and seasoned salmon that was swimming in the bay just hours ago. I reach for my wine glass and sip a burst of bloom with a lingering aftertaste of light tannin and some spicy fruit at the edge of my ability to recognize and name.

The Saltry's menu boasts salmon, halibut, cod, shrimp, clams, and oysters along with more exotic buffalo, labeled heart-healthy, and a divine cheesecake. The salmon and halibut are always local and wild. Oysters, also local, are raised nearby on watery farms, grown up from tiny spat imported from

Washington State. As sure as the unique *terroir* of a wine is composed of the chemistry of soil and climate of a place, these oysters have a particular Kachemak Bay *merroir* from the chemistry of the tides and currents that flow through them.

As I gaze out over the calm mirror of the bay to snowcapped peaks, the midnight sun warms my face. The environmentalist tirades I'm prone to deliver vanish into mental smoke as I bring my fork to my mouth for a taste of *my* salmon without a thought about the sustainability of any other member of the ecosystem but myself.

While waiting to order dinner at the Saltry, I've read and reread the history of Halibut Cove's short-lived herring fishery, written by Diana Tillion and printed on the menu. She wrote that after the 1911 discovery of the large run of herring so enormous in size they were called "bloaters," the "herring salteries immediately filled Halibut Cove."

The herring fishery stayed small until 1916. In 1917 a perfect storm gave Halibut Cove bloaters their moment of marketing fame and profitability. World War I closed shipping between Europe and the United States, so no Norwegian herring could reach the East Coast. Fortunately, the transcontinental railroad was in place to bring Alaska seafood from Seattle to New York City. The transformative moment, however, was the arrival of U.S. Fish and Wildlife Service agents in Portland and Seattle to provide training in the Scotch cure method of processing pickled herring. The Scotch had kept their secret until it was leaked to the British and then to the Americans. The superior product was the key to dominance of the world herring market.

The Norwegian method was to gut and lightly salt the herring at sea, but the Scotch took them directly to port where the removal of heads, guts, and gills was accomplished more neatly with sharp knives. The fish were then stacked in wooden barrels between layers of salt. This method resulted in firmer-fleshed fish, much preferred by finicky East Coast consumers who had disdained earlier shipments from Alaska.

The Scotch cure changed the method of harvest as well. Instead of large ships that ranged far offshore, salting the herring as they went, the fleet shifted to smaller boats that stayed close to shore and brought the fish into the salteries daily. A seasonal work force was needed to process and pack the catch.

Floating salteries appeared in Halibut Cove and other coves in the bay. More were hastily built along the shoreline. During territorial times, the U.S. Bureau of Fisheries reported annually on Alaska fisheries and fur seal harvests. In 1918 they reported that fifteen of the thirty-six herring plants along the Alaska coastline were in Kachemak Bay. The herring harvest was valued at $1.8 million. The numbers of plants dipped between 1919 and 1923, but in 1924 there were again fifteen salteries operating in the bay. Ten of those were "recorded as being in Halibut Cove although according to local accounts, some of those were in Halibut Cove Lagoon, a narrow pursed area at the head of the cove. Surrounding forests were stripped from the hillsides for building materials. When the number of salteries in the bay peaked in 1926 at thirty-two, seventeen of those were in Halibut Cove or in Halibut Cove Lagoon. Others had been built on Homer Spit and in Seldovia and a few were on the water.

According to Diana Tillion's history, a thousand people were employed in Halibut Cove on a steady basis at the peak of the harvest, with up to three thousand taking part for short periods of time when the herring returned. In Seldovia, whose Russian name Zaliv Seldevoy translates to "Herring Bay," there were another twelve hundred people supporting the herring fishery.

Tillion described a hectic scene in Halibut Cove in the mid-1920s: "There were ocean docks built for the steamers that came to pick up the kegs of salted fish. There was a pool hall and, as prohibition was in full swing, there were bootleggers as well. The population consisted of Scandinavian fishermen and girls from Scotland to 'Gib' the herring (clean them) and pack them in large kegs called tierces."

But the heyday of herring was short-lived. In 1925 more than eighteen million pounds of herring were harvested from Cook Inlet. In 1926 the harvest dropped to fourteen million and, in 1928, to only four. Although four more salteries were added in Seldovia that year, only small numbers of herring returned to Kachemak Bay. In 1929 the number of salteries operating was zero.

Diana Tillion blamed the demise of herring primarily on pollution, something barely considered a problem in the 1920s. The notion that Alaska's fish resources were inexhaustible translated into a belief that fish habitat was similarly vast. According to Tillion, the historian Morgan Sherwood found a letter in the archives in Washington, D.C., with a curt reply from a federal government official to someone making a plea that the salteries should be stopped from dumping their waste in the lagoon for fear that pollution would harm the spawning grounds: "On a huge coastline like this? You have to be kidding!" With the guts of thousands of herring unceremoniously dumped each year on the beaches below the salteries, so Tillion's reasoning went, the eelgrass where the herring spawned had been smothered.

The use of purse seines by the herring fleet may have added to the pollution problem. At first herring were caught using gill nets with meshes large enough to let smaller fish slip through. After 1923, however, fishermen switched to smaller-meshed purse seines to encircle entire schools of herring and "purse up" the bottom to capture herring of all sizes and ages. With no use for those too small even for the smallest grade of marketable matjes—ranging in length from 9½ to 10½ inches long—the processors dumped these fish on the eelgrass beds too, according to Tillion.

The tidy cause-and-effect story resonates more with our latter-day awareness that organic wastes from fish processing plants pile up in shallow areas if the tides don't sweep them away or the crabs don't work them over. As the waste decomposes, stretches of the bottom become places where only organisms that need little or no oxygen can survive. It's easy to imagine the waste that would accompany gutting the herring and the use of purse seines in such a small bay and in a shallow lagoon with limited circulation.

But is this really the whole story? Aside from the numbers of barrels of herring packed and the shifts in the placement of salteries, the only scientific data collection during that era was conducted by George Rounsefell, one of the very few federal fisheries scientists who worked in Alaska during territorial times. With limited support from the federal government, scientists struggled to gather evidence to prove whether or not overfishing was occurring, or, to use the more genteel term, that a fish population was being "depleted" and in danger of a precipitous crash. Rounsefell described the purpose of his study of the herring fishery accordingly: "The rational use of this fishery depends on two things. We must know how the species is withstanding the strain of the fishery; we must know what natural changes in abundance are occurring, so we will not be confused about the effects of the fishing, that they will be understood, and if possible, foretold."

The number of barrels packed in Alaska, and in Cook Inlet in particular, increased every year except two from 1918 to 1924. Rounsefell had to figure out if there had really been an increase in the abundance of herring or if the rising harvest reflected only more boats and more gear.

Rounsefell was the first scientist to describe the biology and population dynamics of Pacific herring in Alaska. To do so, he made tedious measurements of herring heads and vertebrae and counted the fin rays of each fish he sampled from the catch from Southeast Alaska to the Aleutian Islands. His goal was to distinguish several different stocks, or populations, of Alaska herring based on physical characteristics. In the era before genetic methods, he used the measurements to infer relationships among groups of herring in different areas. The goal was to manage the harvests of each stock separately, ensuring enough adults returned to spawn every year.

Based on his laborious methods, he grouped the Kachemak Bay herring into a stock with herring that showed up in Shuyak Strait at the north end of the Kodiak Islands. He singled out what he declared to be a well-defined winter migration to Halibut Cove: "Six weeks after the appearance of schools in Shuyak Strait, schools of herring appear on the south shore of Kachemak Bay. . . . They gradually work farther up the bay until September or October when they appear off Halibut Cove. Herring now enter Halibut Cove and lagoon where they are found until the following spring."

Rounsefell spent the spring and summer of 1926 and 1927 in Kachemak Bay making observations of spawning herring. His first sightings in late April of 1926 were of schools of herring surfacing in Halibut Cove Lagoon. When he dropped nets down fifty fathoms, he found more schools in the deeper water where they had apparently spent the winter. Whatever cued their return to the surface also attracted a pageant of their predators. As the herring rippled the surface in schools, Rounsefell wrote, "About 50 belugas were raising havoc, and thousands of sea gulls were scattered everywhere. Cormorants, murres, and scoters, and divers, were there in tens of thousands, and scores of bald eagles were circling about."

These feeding frenzies, so-called by the most staid of biologists, happen relatively rarely in the bay now, but when they do, a ball of small fish is at its center. Within a few days, Rounsefell watched a steady stream of herring come out through the narrow entrance to the lagoon on an ebbing tide. The procession lasted for longer than half an hour. In 1926 and in 1927, herring spawned in several places around Kachemak Bay after they left Halibut Cove Lagoon, not only in the harbor of Halibut Cove behind Ismailof Island, but westward to Peterson Bay, farther out the bay on the south shore, and even along Homer Spit on the north shore. They weren't particularly choosy when it came time to spawn, coating rocks or eelgrass beds. On Homer Spit, they spawned at the extreme high tide line in the grass, which Rounsefell observed to be spectacularly unsuccessful, not only because the eggs dried out before the next high tide, but also because of the feasting by gulls that gathered in the thousands and trampled the grass flat. The timing and location of spawning varied somewhat each year but occurred both years in late April and early May. These observations make it harder to place the blame for the demise of the herring population solely on pollution of the spawning grounds near the Halibut Cove salteries.

According to the 1928 report by the federal government's Division of Scientific Inquiry, the purse seiners gathered in July in Shuyak Strait but caught nothing, and in August the run of large herring failed to appear in Kachemak Bay. Later in the fall some small catches were made, but the report noted the fish were unusually small for the area. Two years later, Rounsefell published a fishery bulletin summarizing the results of his studies. With respect to the intent of his investigations, his 1930 bulletin can only be read as a study in hindsight, and cautious hindsight at that. He had the rueful opportunity, although there is little evidence of rue in his measured scientific prose, to use the failure of the fishery as the basis for his conclusion that there had been a decline in abundance.

So why did the herring population crash? Rounsefell reasoned that what might look like an increase in abundance when harvests increased in 1923 and 1924 could be explained by the geographic expansion of the fleet into Shuyak Strait, Kachemak Bay, and Cook Inlet. He looked at changes in the amount of fishing effort, arguing that what mattered wasn't the number of barrels of herring shipped but the relationship between the biomass of fish extracted, the number of boats, and how hard everyone fished. After purse seines became the method of choice after 1923, changes in the fathoms of purse seine nets deployed and the number of pounds of fish caught provided a telling comparison. The length of net fished over the course of the season increased dramatically by a third (from four thousand fathoms to six thousand) between the 1925 and 1926 seasons, but only half as many pounds of fish were caught the second year. He reported that fishermen stuck to gill nets inside Halibut Cove (whether he meant only the cove or the lagoon or both is unclear), but the numbers of seiners fishing for herring in Kachemak Bay and Cook Inlet outside the cove increased in 1927 and again in 1928. With more boats, more feet of net in the water, and a more efficient method, the catch per unit of effort, or CPUE, should have gone up. But it went down. Rounsefell concluded that the abundance had to be declining dramatically each year.

Rounsefell described the fishery in Shuyak Strait that was incredibly efficient during its few years of operation. Fishermen created a fish trap by stringing a wall of nets across the entrance to a small, sheltered cove and trapped the fish in an area about one by one and a half miles. One graph in his report shows that in 1926, the year after the estimated harvest was nearly ten tons, three times as many boats were fishing in the small impoundment area with gill nets and purse seines. The packing facilities, Rounsefell said, "were taxed to the maximum possible pack, since owing to the ease of impounding, surplus fish could be held for many days and the plants kept constantly busy."

Rounsefell never connected any dots between this method of fishing in Shuyak Strait and the fact that no large herring returned to either Kachemak Bay or Shuyak Straits in 1928. In the end, he didn't sound entirely convinced that overfishing was the sole cause of the precipitous decline: "The decrease in abundance has been so rapid and so great as to cause one to question whether it can be due to depletion, but the concentration of large quantities of gear in the very restricted area makes it appear quite probable that such has been the cause."

If the bloaters bound for Kachemak Bay and Halibut Cove passed through Shuyak Strait, most, if not all, could have been dispatched during the 1927 season—the larger, marketable fish to the Shuyak Strait saltery and the smaller ones caught but then discarded and left to rot there.

After the fisheries crashed in 1928, the fleet and the floating processors moved on, as they always do, westward to the Aleutian Islands, where the herring were even larger on average than the never-to-be-seen-again Halibut Cove bloaters.

Throughout both of his reports, Rounsefell maintained the neutral voice of the scientist. "Depletion is thought to have occurred," he concludes. His final recommendation? "It is deemed necessary," he wrote in the report published in 1930, "that additional protection be applied to herring in Cook Inlet."

And there the story seemed to rest, with a letter in government files about polluted spawning grounds and the mildly conclusive evidence of extinction of the bloaters by fishing. I checked in with Ted Otis, the local Homer herring biologist who's responsible for managing herring in the fishing district that stretches from the mouth of Kachemak Bay across Cook Inlet. After several decades surveying spawning herring by airplane and crunching numbers through computer models, he didn't think much of Rounsefell's measurements or his mere two years of spawning observations. Still, despite sophisticated genetic techniques now available, he said there was no way yet to reliably connect or separate herring stocks that spawn, or are harvested, in different places. So Rounsefell's painstaking measurements don't support a scientific conclusion that the herring in Shuyak Strait and Kachemak Bay were really the same stock.

Ted provided me with more information from recent research that might shed light on the past ways of herring and fishermen. Herring, it seems, abandon their spawning grounds and entire bays on an unpredictable basis. Many eventually return. In keeping with this erratic pattern, herring come back in small numbers to Kachemak Bay to spawn some years along the south shore. They winter in two of the deep fjords close to the mouth of the bay, but never in Halibut Cove or in the lagoon. The run of Halibut Bay bloaters has completely disappeared.

This baseline narrative of brief, intense fishing and a lone and beleaguered government fish biologist isn't necessarily a cautionary tale for latter-day fisheries managers with an aim of managing for maximum sustainable yield. The statistics provide a modicum of support for the theory that fishing can control fish populations and that unregulated fishing can drive herring populations to at least economic, if not total, extinction. But there are at least two other explanations for what happened. For one, herring have leaders and followers. Ted told me about the repeat spawners, the large, older herring that show up earliest in the places where they first spawned. When fishermen efficiently targeted the largest herring with purse seines and gill nets; the younger fish could have ended up somewhere else for *their* first spawning. The second possibility is disease. Older fish are also more vulnerable to certain diseases such as the one that is the likely cause of a recent sudden decline in the spawning run in Kamishak Bay on the west side of Cook Inlet. But herring also fail to show up in the places they're traditionally found for reasons known only to herring.

The business of managing herring fisheries remains tricky. Biologists still strive to define populations and track their trajectories upward and downward. Staving off crashes is a matter of avoiding fishing on the down-curve of a population graph beginning its plunge. A warming ocean also seems to complicate the equation for herring and fishermen in ways that scientists have yet to fathom.

Well into the 1920s, Sugpiaq hunters from the villages at the mouth of Kachemak Bay rowed wooden dories to Halibut Cove on the incoming tide to hunt seals, sea lions, and beluga whales that chased schools of spawning herring into the bay. The hunters spent days on the beach around sultry fires that rendered the rich fat into oil.

Lush coastal forest now covers the ruins of the salteries. When I walk along Halibut Cove's boardwalks, I imagine the voices that must have echoed through the woods. I can almost hear the lilt of the Scottish girls who were said to have been the best packers as they sliced and gutted the herring and stacked them carefully in salty rows.

One night I walked Halibut Cove's only public trail, which winds through a meadow to a point overlooking the bay. I didn't see any belugas, but then none have been seen in at least a decade anywhere in the bay. I spotted a pair of mergansers and a lone murre close to shore where seabirds and sea ducks now hang out in groups of fewer than ten rather than in the tens of thousands that George Rounsefell saw. A few pairs of eagles nest along the southern shore.

My eyes landed on the rising backs of two harbor porpoise just as they broke the water's surface and swam under a rock arch. They dropped out of sight a moment later, ghosts of an ecosystem that used to teem with herring every spring and where their ancestors were often served for dinner.

People have ebbed and flowed through Halibut Cove more slowly than the tides but faster than the glaciers. Each of the cultures left scant artifacts of their passions and their intelligence, their celebrations and sorrows, in a place that can change in an instant, shake the ground beneath your feet, or overturn your kayak in a rushing wave.

We moderns have removed so much more than we are trying to sustain.

In their analysis of the middens, the anthropologists applied Optimal Foraging Theory, as did Anne Salomon, the ecologist, comparing humans and sea otters as predators. The theory assumes that predators are rational, that they seek the "sweet spot" where the expenditure of effort and energy to find prey is balanced by sufficient calories and energy captured. Any more than that is just plain gravy.

For me, dinner at the Saltry and a tour of its art galleries is an experience in optimal foraging. My wine glass drained, my meal consumed, my patronage of the arts completed, my walk to the overlook having netted no incoming warriors or shy harbor porpoise tonight, I would know it was time to return to Homer. Not only in the sense that it was time to move away from my contemplation of the ten-thousand-year-old human history of this place to the present, but more immediately, my time in Halibut Cove—the only community I know in Alaska with restricted visiting hours—would be up. I'm not nearly wealthy enough to have a second home here or skilled enough to be one of its resident artists, so I must leave. My long but seasonal tenure in Peterson and China Poot Bays just to the west earns me no neighborly status. I must board the *Danny J* with the other visitors on its last run back to Homer tonight, the one that someone will politely make sure I don't miss.

We All Live in Homer for the Halibut

The race for halibut is a daily sport during Homer's short summers. I always miss the 6:00 a.m. start when charter boats leave
the harbor. On days I led tours across the bay, I ambled down
the ramp for a 9:00 a.m. boat departure, and we passed rows of
empty slips on our way out of the harbor. When I returned at 6:00
p.m., I often paused in my walk back up the ramp, steepened by
low tide, to get out of the way of young men trundling buckets
of flopping halibut. On warmer days, they stripped down to
their rain pants, the eye candy effect slightly marred by ragged,
grubby suspenders across their muscled chests.

It's hard to avoid halibut in Homer. They're the subject of
our art and the smell that permeates our clothes. I rest my back
on a halibut-shaped pillow on my couch, serve halibut and even
salmon on a halibut-shaped platter, wear a T-shirt with a grinning
halibut, and even wear earrings in the shape of dangling halibut
skeletons. But while halibut fit Homer's mystique as a fishing
town, they're still hard to feature as aesthetic objects. Their chief
anatomical exuberance is their extraordinary flatness and the
bulging eyeballs clustered together like a pair of grapes on their
topside.

Like all flounders, halibut begin life as upright, fat-bodied
larval fish, peering out in two directions. Within weeks of their
birth, however, they, and their existence, flatten. One eye migrates
toward the other in a single vision of ocean above. Members of
the right-eyed flounder group, they lie next to left-eyed starry
flounders. As a parable for Homer—a community shot through

with science, art, and fishy ideas that lead to conflicting ideas about which way is up or down—it's not half bad.

Homer rightfully claims its status as halibut fishing capital of the world in terms of being the #1 port for pounds of commercial landings of Pacific halibut in the United States almost every year. The fish brought back on charter boats aren't even counted in this competition; their captains stoutly maintain they aren't commercial fishermen at all, just taxi drivers and guides for their clients. Catching a halibut remains a task of hooking it on or near the seafloor and pulling it upward to the light through too much oxygen too fast. Successful fishermen duly gaff them with a long, wicked hook on a pole and shoot the big ones in the head.

Every summer day, a small crowd gathers around the naughtily named Buttwhacker's gibbet-like contraption from which the day's catch of halibut hang tail-down in order of size before being expertly filleted and handed back to the fishermen in tidy packages. Their successful slayers pose, often wearing the crooked grin of people recently recovered from sea sickness. The halibut themselves, however, began to resemble the "after" pictures used to illustrate the concept of shifting baselines in fisheries. Since I first began taking in the scene, the halibut seem to shrink more and more each year (even as the tourists themselves expand in girth, according to my frustrated kayak guide friends).

It's not just my eyes or my faulty memory—the halibut are getting smaller, a trend that began decades before I moved to Homer. A mount of the world-record halibut greets visitors at the Anchorage airport. Caught in 1996, it was thirty-one years old, nine and half feet long, and weighed in at 459 pounds. The locals who run the annual Homer Halibut Derby lamented recently that an eighteen-year-old female halibut caught in 1997 in the central Gulf of Alaska fishing zone that includes Homer was likely to weigh 80 pounds, on average, and in 2015, one of the same age was likely to weigh half that.

Jane Sullivan, a University of Alaska Fairbanks graduate student I heard speak at a marine science conference in 2016, took up the question of *why* as her research project. The data she amassed from the fish tickets required from every commercial fisherman extended the timing and magnitude of the shrinkage back another decade, to the beginning of the 1990s. There's a good reason to pay attention to the size of older female halibut. They can live for more than fifty years, but they don't reproduce until they're twelve. Like the punchline to the joke the Woody Allen character tells in *Annie Hall* about letting his crazy family member believe he's a chicken, "We need the eggs." A 50-pound female halibut produces five hundred thousand eggs while a 250-pound female produces four million.

This shrinkage would seem to provide evidence of a classic case of a shifting baseline, or of overfishing, or both. William F. Thompson, the first halibut fisheries scientist, began his illustrious career in 1913 measuring halibut and trying, like George Rounsefell, to detect depletion of stocks by a rapidly expanding fishery. In a picture of Thompson as a boyish graduate student from that era, dressed in a dirty slicker and cuffed rubber gloves, he intently reads the measurements of a white-bellied halibut on the back deck of the schooner *Flamingo* while the sea roils behind him.

"The decks were always so slippery and slimy it was necessary to lash the fish down 'fore and aft,'" Thompson wrote later, "to guard against the rolling movements of the vessels as they lay in the trough of the seas." Several other halibut are draped nearby, so small they look like chickens, the name for those weighing less than ten pounds.

Perhaps I admire Thompson because of his seeming immunity to halibut slime. One of the few and last times I went halibut fishing, it was in an open skiff that a friend navigated cheerfully out into what seemed to be the middle of the Pacific Ocean. I saw no trace of land in any direction. My friend hooked into a halibut and pulled against its weight, and for some reason that I can't remember, he tasked me with doing something requiring that I place my head, and thus my nose, close to the bottom of the skiff from which wafted the scent of previously caught halibut.

The smell reminded me of the biologists I'd roomed with after the *Exxon Valdez* oil spill who spent their days examining dead and decaying whales. When they returned at the end of the day, we insisted they march straight into the shower, rain gear and all. The stink that lingered in the room after they passed by was a distant second to that of the leavings of halibut.

My stomach revolted. After landing and cleaning his halibut with a heaving companion, my friend quickly ended our fishing trip. Word must have gotten around the small town of Homer because I haven't been invited to go halibut fishing since. I've become an armchair historian of halibut fishing, content to buy my halibut already packaged into meal-size chunks.

William Thompson was a pioneer in the development of fishery statistics, particularly the catch per unit effort, or CPUE, calculations that Rounsefell used later to detect depletions of herring stocks. CPUE isn't an accurate measure of the abundance of fish in a population since it's a statistic that portrays only the success rate of the catch from the population, but it provides insight about that success in relation to the amount and type of gear deployed in specific areas. Thompson was thus able to get ahead of the curve of rising harvests by calculating and comparing the total number of pounds of halibut caught on all the hooks on long lines set over a specific period of time. Then he analyzed his CPUE data shrewdly in the context of observations of the movement patterns of the fleet to new grounds.

In 1915 Thompson declared halibut seriously depleted along the British Columbia coast. As he wrote later in a paper co-authored with F. Heward Bell, the early statistics of increasing harvests had masked depletions.

"Were this [harvest] to have come from a single stock of fish its consistency might have been regarded as legitimate evidence of a healthy fishery," he wrote. "But we know that in 1911 the fishery spread out of sheltered waters onto deeper banks." After 1911 the fishery that began in Puget Sound, British Columbia, and Southeast Alaska captured more than half the harvest from Alaska districts. In addition to overfishing the halibut off British Columbia, the fleet had, in fact, first overfished the more southerly stocks in Puget Sound and along the Washington and Oregon coasts before heading to British Columbia and Southeast Alaska. Thompson described the "exceedingly heavy" winter fishery that began in the Gulf of Alaska in 1913. It later expanded even farther west to the rich new banks along the Aleutian Islands.

The history of depleting and moving on stretched back in time even farther. The high demand for Pacific halibut came after halibut banks off the coasts of New England and Norway had been exploited and began yielding smaller harvests of Atlantic halibut.

Armed with Thompson's evidence, a winter closure was imposed on the fishery in 1916. By the early 1920s his studies spurred the development of a treaty signed by the United States and Canada that marked the first international regulation of a deep-sea fishery. The treaty was to be implemented by an International Fisheries Commission (IFC). Thompson became its first director.

Pacific halibut harvests grew at a phenomenal rate between 1888 and 1910 and then leveled off. After 1922 longer trips became possible as the fleet switched from sail-powered dories to boats powered by diesel engines. The availability of ice from glaciers in Southeast Alaska and from cold storage plants allowed more time to fish and improved the product delivered to processors. In the 1920s, however, harvests started to plummet. The stocks appeared to be on the verge of crashing.

By the late 1920s, halibut in the harvest were noticeably smaller. The IFC began imposing catch limits. In 1934 they claimed credit for saving the fishery from the fate of Halibut Cove and Cook Inlet herring stocks. The IFC published the much-cited *Scientific Report Number 8* that year. Authors Thompson and Bell concluded that the imposition of the caps had reduced fishing effort to a third of its former intensity while the harvest had increased by 25 percent. This success story for fisheries management, with international cooperation no less, was widely hailed. A few years later, Thompson laid out his theory of the effect of fishing on the stock of halibut in the IFC's twelfth scientific report. He began with the analogy of the ocean to a fish farm and expanded into another analogy of the ocean as a bank that accumulated a stock of fish as capital. Since there was evidence that the intensity of fishing could reduce the yield, or profit from the bank, he concluded that reducing the amount of gear fishing was the only way to increase the yield.

Not everyone agreed, however, that management of the harvest was responsible for the apparent recovery of the population. In 1947 marine biologist Martin Burkenroad published an opposing view, considered radical at the time. He challenged the assumptions made to derive the statistics and suggested that halibut and other fish populations had natural ups and downs, related to cyclic changes in the marine environment.

So began the Thompson-Burkenroad debate, famous in the narrow niche of fisheries science. This was one more variation on the long-running debate about the relative impacts of environmental conditions from the "bottom up" and fishing pressure on fish populations from the "top down." What's at stake in the debate is becoming increasingly urgent as a rapidly changing climate affects the conditions of survival in unpredictable ways. Fisheries managers are challenged to keep up with shifts in numbers, size, and distribution of fish in every stock.

Burkenroad was a scientific maverick. He was first an expert on crabs, but he also published in astrophysics and anthropology and was an accomplished poet. He was reportedly "encouraged to leave" Tulane University, where he'd published his first scientific papers. Many years later, he returned to continue his studies at Yale but worked so long on his graduate thesis that the time limit for submitting it was finally waived. He never turned in a thesis. Thompson, on the other hand, was a director of the School of Fisheries at the University of Washington at the same time he was director of IFC.

The IFC was deeply troubled by Burkenroad's challenge. They took it as an attack on their scientific integrity and their professional role in what one reviewer called "biological book-keeping." In the 1940s and early 1950s, other scientists weighed in. Although Thompson never directly responded to Burkenroad's criticisms of his methods, the debate hardened into an either-or proposition: if natural cycles of environmental conditions con-trolled population dynamics of fish, then depletions weren't scientific evidence that overfishing had occurred. As the ages of long-lived fish like halibut varied in the annual harvest, it became possible to detect "strong" age classes—cohorts born in a "good year" that were large and robust and pulsed through the population and fishery. This made the position that fishing alone controlled halibut population dynamics difficult to de-fend. Increased survival rate of an age class pointed to favorable conditions in the earliest, and riskiest, year in the life of a young halibut. Ocean conditions must thus have been more favorable in some years than others.

In 1975 the commission, now renamed the International Pacific Halibut Commission (IPHC), published its fifty-sixth scientific report. It was written by Bernard Skud and contained a thorough review of Thompson's methods and results. Skud found flaws in some of Thompson's methods, like calculating CPUE without taking into account changes in the number and spacing of hooks on longlines when the fleet switched dories to steamers. Skud's corrections and recalculations led him to the conclusion that fishing had indeed depleted the fishery from Puget Sound to Alaska, but the magnitude was smaller than declared by Thompson. The contribution of skillful harvest management by the halibut commission to population recovery was also smaller than claimed. But Skud didn't resolve the debate: "The exact role of the effects of fishing and environmental factors cannot be determined," he wrote. "Until unknowns, particularly about growth and recruitment, are determined, one cannot properly credit the increase in abundance to either the management program or to fishery-induced change or to environmental effects."

In 2014 Jane Sullivan revisited the topic armed with a hundred years of data about the relationship between the size of halibut and their age and based on techniques begun by Thompson to sample and measure lengths and weights of the catch and to read and count growth rings in a halibut otolith, or inner ear bone. She developed a computer model based on fifty years of data on the size and age of halibut harvested off the coasts of Alaska and British Columbia by looking at changes in the average size of a fish at a given age, shortened to the scientific term size-at-age. This statistic reflected the culmination of annual changes in growth over decades before the long-lived halibut had been caught.

Halibut don't really shrink, of course. They either grow more slowly in the environmental bad times, as Burkenroad argued, or fishermen who can keep every halibut over a certain size limit in terms of length catch more of the faster-growing ones because they have more years to try, which gives slower-growing halibut a survival advantage.

Jane used a model that could separate the expected effect of size-selected fishing from other potential variables and so determine whether the change in size-at-age was caused by this type of fishing.

The nature of the Pacific halibut fishery itself changed in the early 1990s. Clem Tillion, then governor Wally Hickel's fish czar, successfully led the charge to manage the commercial halibut fishery with a set number of individual fishery quotas, or IFQs. The commission had responded to the increasingly crowded competition for halibut by making halibut openings shorter and shorter. The 144-day season in 1957 was reduced to 13 days in 1977, and finally to a single twenty-four-hour period in 1993.

Diana Tillion tells the story of Clem's role in *Guardians of the North Pacific Casino*, her romantic version of the rough-and-tumble days of the early halibut fisheries. Although the book is housed in the fiction section of Homer's library, Clem and other real people are its main characters. Diana recounts actual events in the history of fisheries management.

The book begins with young Clem "Red" Tillion, so-named because of his ginger hair, as a near-penniless World War II veteran on his way to Alaska in 1948. On the docks in Seattle, he's told he won't be hired as crew on a halibut fishing boat soon to leave for the Alaska grounds because all the jobs then went to Norwegians. He has only enough money to book steerage, but once on board, he meets Jim Branson, a fisheries biologist who later rose through the ranks to become the first executive director of the North Pacific Fisheries Management Council, one of eight federal regional councils created in 1976. Jim sneaks Clem into a better dining class, which gives Clem the opportunity to meet the wealthy banker Elmer Rasmuson, later longtime chair of the Alaska Fisheries Board and the first chairman of the council. Though Diana wrote in the introduction to her novel that the men were certainly "in the same boat" in terms of managing the fisheries, it's hard to tell fact from fiction in terms of the passenger list for the ship that Clem boarded to go to Alaska.

What is fact is that, just as in the novel, Clem arrived in Homer for the first time by walking 170 miles on a trail from Moose Pass. By the novel's end, Clem has served several terms as a state legislator in the House and the Senate, built his home in Halibut Cove, and served on the Alaska Board of Fisheries and the North Pacific Fisheries Council. In the story of creating the system of IFQs for the halibut fleet, Clem, Branson, Rasmuson, and a handful of other longtime fishermen and processors are, of course, the heroes of Diana's tale. Being the gracious person she was, it's the villain she invents: a man described always as a fish pirate, who speaks in a strong eastern European accent and is eventually exposed as selling Alaska fish illegally to Russia. To further establish his evil nature, she fingers him as responsible for arranging the murder of a female federal government observer on a fishing boat, offed because she checks the catch figures too closely.

Alaskans hate the very idea of overfishing.

Our own late "Uncle Ted" Stevens and Warren G. Magnuson co-authored the Marine Conservation and Management Act, known as the Magnuson-Stevens Act, which passed Congress in 1976 and created regional fisheries management councils. Alaskans pride themselves on participating in the science-based, cautious decision-making of the North Pacific council, considered one of the best in the world. In 1996 the law was reauthorized to place emphasis on the identification and restoration of depleted stocks, which spurred Jane Sullivan's research more than a decade later.

Jane's question was the same one posed by Thompson, Burkenroad, and Skud: were halibut stocks depleted? And if so, what role had fishing played? Jane's overall conclusion was that there was no single answer for the entire Gulf of Alaska.

"In summary, can fishing explain declines in halibut size-at-age?" she asked at the presentation I heard at the 2016 conference. "Based on our results, I think there is strong evidence that the answer is yes, at least partially."

Her regional conclusions were intriguing. When she ran her model for the central Gulf of Alaska fishing area that includes

Cook Inlet and the ocean to the south between Yakutat and Kodiak, selective fishing explained less than one-third of the observed declines in size-at-age. These results meant that factors other than fishing were affecting variability in ocean conditions and growth rates annually. But farther east and south, it was a different story. Her results for the management areas off Southeast Alaska and British Columbia supported Thompson's original conclusion that fishing could control halibut populations, at least in one aspect: up to 100 percent of the change in size-at-age for females and half of the change for males could be attributed to heavy and selective fishing on the fastest-growing fish. So Thompson and Burkenroad were both right, depending on what part of the Gulf of Alaska and intensity of fishing you looked at.

Jane's research was part of a larger research project to look at climate and other ecological factors that might have affected halibut size-at-age. The study was headed up by her major professor and fisheries scientist Gordon Kruse along with NOAA scientists Kerim Aydin and Kirsten Holsman. In the face of increasing evidence of a protracted warming trend for the ocean, they took a holistic "both/and" approach from the outset to the debate posed as fishing *or* the environment during the heyday of the Thompson-Burkenroad debate. In addition to Jane's examination of the top-down effect of fishing, they began with the premise that changes in halibut size-at-age could also arise from climate-driven bottom-up drivers of growth such as changes to the quantity and quality of food availability and competition for prey. Aydin and Holsman analyzed samples of the stomach contents of nearly three thousand halibut and looked for correlations in types of prey available with harvest locations, size, and age.

Quantifying the effects of factors other than fishing has proven more elusive. Water temperature is widely suspected as having a major role in a bottom-up fashion. Late in the twentieth century, scientists detected climate and temperature cycles in the North Pacific Ocean that operated on the scale of several decades throughout the entire century. Warmer-than-average and colder-than-average years came in alternating streaks that lasted several decades, not in random order but in a pattern that also undermined the idea that fishing alone affected fish population dynamics.

The scientists gave the pattern, which stretched from at least 1890 to 1998, a mouthful of a name: Pacific Decadal Oscillation, or PDO. The transitions were particularly abrupt. The pattern switched in specific years: in 1925, from cold to warm; in 1946, back to cold; and in 1977, back to warm again. It was the consequences of the 1977 shift in the Gulf of Alaska that caught the attention of marine ecologists but not until the late 1990s.

Seabird biologists were among the first scientists to notice something strange. I spent the summer of 1976 watching and counting seabirds at the oddly spelled Cape Peirce, in the northwest corner of Bristol Bay. I had no way of knowing that the data I recorded that year about the number of eggs laid, the number of eggs hatched, the number of chicks fledged from each nest, and the timing of all of these events were really the end of a baseline. The entire North Pacific Ocean was on the cusp of a great ecological change of a magnitude I couldn't have imagined as I sat waiting patiently for a kittiwake to stand up so I could count the number of eggs in its nest.

Beginning in 1977, John Piatt, a cheerleader for the notion that seabirds are stellar indicators of the status of Alaska marine ecosystems, began seeing murres and black-legged kittiwakes feeding their chicks something different on Gull Island in Kachemak Bay and other colonies in the Gulf of Alaska. Instead of bringing back one capelin at a time crosswise in their beaks, they switched to pollock. This signaled a major nutritional change for the fast-growing chicks. Capelin were a compact package of fat and protein compared to the leaner pollock, which biologists referred to as marine junk food. Pollock were apparently all that seabirds, and then sea lions, could find to eat. Piatt, who spent many more years studying seabirds than my one summer, accumulated data that showed chicks who were on a steady diet of pollock grew slower, fledged later, and died more often than those raised on capelin before 1977.

Piatt teamed up with another biologist, Paul Anderson, to sift through climate data and fish data from a long-term series of bottom trawl surveys that began in the 1950s. Their correlation of the two datasets connected a shift to warmer waters with the shift away from an abundance of capelin, which explained the change in seabird diets. The abundance of shrimp and crabs also took a dive. As the base of the food web changed, the reorganization of the entire biological community in the Gulf of Alaska was so dramatic the scientists declared it a regime change, the ecological equivalent of a military coup. The leaders turned out to be ranks of voracious predatory fish including not only pollock but also cod and flatfishes, among them halibut. In the 1970s, the total biomass of fish collected with each haul of the trawl net declined precipitously. It continued to decline, eventually by half, throughout the 1980s. Then, in the 1990s, the amount hauled up each time increased explosively. Sea stars, jellyfish, and octopus increased as shrimp and crabs became scarce. The harvestable biomass of halibut and other flatfishes increased during the 1990s by more than two and a half times.

The regime change that transformed the food web took fifteen to twenty years to complete across the entire Gulf of Alaska. It happened first from the bottom up, as warmer water temperatures affected the timing of the great spring photosynthetic event when microscopic phytoplankton burst into a yellow-green bloom of chlorophyll visible from space. Energy rippled upward into the food web to predators in sync with the change in timing. Much later, it happened from the top down as long-lived predators thrived in warmer waters and grew large and abundant enough to gobble up more and more of their prey.

The success of the revolution could only be explained, Piatt and Anderson concluded, if both types of processes were going on in the Gulf of Alaska at the same time.

The discovery of the PDO pattern that persisted from 1925 to the late 1990s has implications for halibut management. It also called into question the success story told by Thompson and the Halibut Commission during the 1930s as the imposition of harvest caps. While the reality of a changing climate can take away some of a fisheries manager's responsibility for declines, it also takes away some of the credit for success of rebuilding stocks.

Jane's model included climate-related variables of summer water temperatures and another variable related to the PDO, but the results were only a weak effect on size-at-age. At first blush, this seems surprising given that one group of fisheries scientists summarized the shift to the warm regime to be the cause of the extensive restructuring of the marine system, particularly the increase of predatory, bottom-dwelling fish like flatfish and groundfish over shrimp and forage fish like capelin. Flatfishes came to dominate the Gulf of Alaska food web by sheer biomass that seemed to indicate a favorable environment for halibut to survive, grow, and reproduce. Scientists William Clark and Stephen Hare had previously analyzed IPHC statistics and concluded that the dominant effect of climate was on the annual production of young fish, which supported Burkenroad's side of the argument for this part of the halibut life cycle and reinforced the origin of strong age classes during the crucial first year. With only a yolk sac for food and high demands for energy for growth, larval halibut drift or swim weakly in currents that can transport them to favorable or unfavorable nursery areas. They're particularly vulnerable, in ways juveniles and adults aren't, to environmental conditions of water temperature, salinity, and turbulence.

Clark and Hare concluded that the environment had virtually no effect on how fast halibut grew except during the earliest stage of their life. After that, the key factor was competition for food. A small population of halibut on the fishing grounds resulted in less competition, a faster growth rate, and a higher biomass—or the mass of halibut in a given area—available for harvest. A higher density of halibut meant more competition, slower growth, and a lower biomass of halibut. This inverse relationship between halibut density and biomass held true through warm and cold phases of the PDO throughout the twentieth century.

The consistency of this relationship seems to support Thompson's side of the argument—that the intensity of fishing and removal of biomass controls population size, at least of older halibut. But while fishing affects the density of halibut, and thus competition for food among halibut, it's not the only factor. Few changes in any part of an ecosystem are the result of a single cause. Halibut compete with arrowtooth flounder, which are halibut predators as well. This flounder also thrived under the conditions that led to higher populations of halibut in the 1990s. Since people prefer the creamy taste of halibut to the coarser arrowtooth flounder that cooks down into mush, Gulf of Alaska fishermen can't be persuaded to remove their entire arrowtooth flounder quota. In some years, they've harvested only 5 percent. Over several decades when the halibut fishery has been regulated with the intent to remove the maximum biomass that could be harvested sustainably, the biomass of arrowtooth flounder increased five hundred times. The super-abundant arrowtooth flounder, along with Pacific cod, now consume more than any other predator in the ecosystem.

With additional modeling, approximately another quarter of the decline in size-at-age in the Gulf of Alaska could be correlated with the ecological factor of competition primarily with arrowtooth flounder and to a lesser degree with other halibut.

The rest of the story is proving to be more complicated. A large part of the cause of Kachemak Bay's shrinking halibut remains unknown. The evidence of the stomach contents in relation to growth rate displayed in otolith rings points to the bottom-up effects of prey, whose abundance and quality in terms of "energy density" varies annually and in different parts of the Gulf of Alaska. The direct effect of warmer water temperatures is an increase in the growth rates of young fish but a slowing in the growth rates of larger, older fish. A higher metabolic rate reduces energy available for growth and reproduction.

As ocean temperatures continue to rise—and they are predicted to continue to do so—halibut and other fish adapted to colder northern waters will become more and more stressed and will likely have even less energy available for growth and reproduction. Halibut, however, are exposed to a variety of water temperatures over the course of their lifetime. Eggs and juvenile halibut float long distances in the currents, and adults make large seasonal migrations every year. Of the potential responses to rapid climate change—move, adapt, or die—halibut may be able to move around during their long lifetime in order to stay in cooler waters. Or fishermen might just need to adapt to a world with fewer and smaller halibut.

The baselines are shifting faster and faster within the lifetime of every manager and fisherman. In such a rapidly changing environment, what will a sustainable harvest possibly mean?

The charter boat fleet are well behind the commercial longline fleet in the amount of halibut their clients catch with hook and line and gaff on their daily forays. The quota they're allowed off the top of the commercial one has grown, however, to 20 percent of the total harvest—a source of annoyance to the commercial fishermen over many years. In 2011 a limited entry permit system capped the growing number of boats in the charter boat fleet.

Leading up to decisions on every year's regulations, however, Homer's newspaper editorials and coffee shop conversations are full of dire warnings about the end of the charter industry or the commercial fishery, or both. Almost everyone is united on the evils of allocating a portion of the catch to *by-catch*, the polite term for the halibut wasted after being scooped up in trawl nets dragged across the bottom for pollock and cod. The trawlers consider them "nuisance fish."

Amid these dire warnings of impending doom for the fishery every year, the fishing tourists keep coming, eager for their chance at seasickness and fishing fame. The charter boats go out every day in summer, and those young men keep trundling halibut up the ramps to their photo ops. Homer remains the Halibut Fishing Capital of the World.

Even after decades of strife among commercial halibut fishermen and the people charged with sustaining them, there's something incurably romantic about the quest for halibut. The gargantuan, ungainly creatures are raised up from the deep with an epic struggle. During the restaurant season on Homer Spit, which lasts only as long as the tourist season, my favorite serves up grilled halibut, halibut and chips, and halibut salads, which I could easily eat every day.

A sepia-toned photograph on the wall shows four men posing with an enormous halibut caught in 1904 "near the Wharf on Homer Spit," so the caption says. The men in the picture are "Messrs. Smith, Stone, Penberthy, and Nicoli." The caption says that Penberthy was Homer's first postmaster. Smith and Stone flank the halibut, hanging head up, as usual. It's longer than they are tall and wider than the two men combined. Stone wears jeans with a halibut hook through his belt loop, a short spiffy vest over his shirt, and a cowboy hat. His arm stretches up to rest on the halibut's flank in a friendly embrace. Penberthy wears a tailored jacket typical of gold miners photographed at their diggings and sports a jaunty fisherman's hat and a mustache reminiscent of Karl Marx. Nicoli sits down a bit away from the others. His round face and black straight hair are those of an Alaska Native. He's the only one smiling faintly.

It's a seriously large fish hanging there.

This is serious business.

Fishermen with their catch of a three-hundred-pound halibut, Homer Spit, 1904. Stone R.W. Collection gypsum Mill, U.S. Geological Survey (srw0069.jpg).

The Silver Horde

Thumps and splashes jerked me out of my slow slide into sleep.

Bear! Bear! My mind shouted, throat closed around my scream. I cautiously raised my head and peered through the summer twilight. The upper half of a gigantic fish seemed to protrude from the ground. Groggy and grumbling, I left my warm sleeping bag to stand on the bank of the narrow stream channel where I had camped. The salmon, so much longer than the channel was wide, twisted, turned, and thrashed its way determinedly upstream. It eyed me, then thrashed again, moving itself a few inches farther.

The channel was close to the braided mouth of the Slug River. I was spending that summer of 1976 counting seabirds in the far northwest corner of Bristol Bay but had hiked to the head of Nanvak Bay for a break from the daily counts at the seabird colonies and to escape the confines of the twelve-by-twelve-foot cabin I shared with another biologist. Still in graduate school, I was only a half-trained biologist, but I knew that salmon migrated from the ocean to the stream where they were hatched to spawn and die. The relentlessness of salmon had never sunk in until I saw that three-foot-long beast of a fish dragging its way up a channel so narrow it could never turn back in water that barely covered its fins. I brought my sleeping bag to the channel and settled in to keep watch. As soon as the first salmon passed, I heard the splashes of another, and when that one struggled by, another; it was a slow-moving parade in the ghostly August twilight.

For millennia of human memory, salmon have been the gift that returns. The first salmon to appear each year was greeted everywhere along the coast with ceremony and gratitude. Stories about how salmon first gifted themselves to people cycle through Alaska Native stories and ancient tales from Japan and Ireland, as the stranger who appeared in the form of a beautiful woman or a young boy. After living among the people, he or she would eventually enter the stream, undergoing a transformation, vowing to return every year. Cornelius Osgood recorded a story about the origin of the first salmon ceremony among the Dena'ina: A chief admonished his daughter not to go near the salmon weir where salmon were trapped. Of course, she did, in the way that children do the very thing forbidden. She slipped into the water and disappeared. Several years later, the chief's grandson appeared in the form of a salmon caught in the same weir. The chief performed a ceremony that became an annual First Salmon ritual to recognize and celebrate the time in their long history that the Dena'ina became salmon people.

One of the creation stories told about fish on Kodiak to the Russian naval officer and explorer Yuri Lisianskii begins differently. At the same time that Raven brought the light, the first woman and first man descended from the sky in a bladder and pushed their way out. The man made trees and forests from his hair, and then the woman made water to create the ocean and then spit into holes to create streams and lakes. Then the woman took out one of her teeth and gave it to the man, who made a knife from it. He cut down trees and the chips that fell into the river became different kinds of fish. Later, when the first-born son of the first couple was playing with a stone, it suddenly turned into the island the storyteller called Cadiack, which floated to its present location presumably bringing along all the streams to which salmon now return.

Raven of the northern regions is an ambiguous creator in the tales of many Alaska Native cultures. He stole the moon and sun before he released them into the world. Although he sometimes appears in stories about the creation of rivers and streams with *his* spit, he figures more rarely in those about the creation of salmon that reflect a rather un-Raven-like spirit of generous sacrifice. Where the salmon run, the connections of birth and death and place are clear. While hooks and nets set down in the ocean can come up empty again and again, the certainty of salmon moving up their home rivers still anchors family groups and complex societies. As people cycle every year to fish camps and favorite fishing spots, salmon cycle back home.

Lacking stories and scant evidence of fish bones in Kachemak middens, the long-term importance of salmon to people is a bit of a conundrum in Kachemak Bay. Bill and Karen Workman pointed to the many, but not particularly productive, salmon streams as a limitation to Kachemak Bay being home to more than a few hundred people at any one time. By modern-day Alaska standards, the number of salmon that run up Kachemak Bay creeks and rivers remains modest but is hard to compare to what might have been available to the Kachemak. The number of fish that return now are a targeted escapement from fisheries in the bay.

The scarcity of salmon bones in Kachemak middens could be a result of poor preservation, but more telling is the absence of winter storage pits for dried fish, even along the Kenai and Kasilof Rivers to the north where different groups of Riverine Kachemak people settled. To the south on Kodiak Island, salmon—their capture, processing, and especially their storage—were the center of Kachemak tradition village life that began a millennium earlier and lasted five hundred years longer. According to the archaeologists who excavated Kachemak campsites on Kodiak, they were "black with the charcoal of ancient fires, riddled with large pits, and contain new varieties of fishing and processing tools." On Kodiak Island, Kachemak villages spread along the banks of rivers like the Karluk, host of massive runs of all five species of salmon, and along lakeshores where sockeye spawned.

With their capability to catch and process large numbers of marine fish, particularly cod, Kachemak people on Kodiak were the first culture in the region with the means to harvest a surplus of fish. At the same time that Kachemak people vanished from Kachemak Bay, settlements expanded on Kodiak Island. The people harvested salmon even more intensively, spreading nets across streams, filleting them with a few well-aimed blows of their ulus, and drying and smoking them in campfires.

Between 650 and 1,000 years ago, Koniag culture emerged seamlessly, archaeologically speaking, from Kachemak. The Koniag leaders, or toions, were an elite class of wealthy traders and raiders. They led their extended families in communal harvests and fought battles that turned their defeated enemies into slaves. A secretive male society possessed the ability to extract poison from monkshood plants, cook it up in the rendered fat from the mummified remains of their whaler ancestors—to add supernatural luck—and then smear it carefully on their slate spear points. The great whales they speared died quickly and their bodies drifted as mountains of meat and blubber into protected coves. Houses grew larger with more and more rooms added on for expanding families. Villages grew. Salmon harvesting became even more intensive with the addition of salmon spears and stone weirs to trap fish in streams. The toions shared food and valuable trade goods during winter feasts that cemented family and political alliances.

When the Russians arrived on Kodiak Island in the late 1700s, some eight to nine thousand people lived there in one of the most complex fishing-hunting-gathering societies in the world, one with extensive trading networks. The toions and their extended family groups occupied a landscape and seascape where every food patch was owned: seabird colonies, seal rookeries, clam beds, berry patches, and above all, the mouths and other fishing spots in streams that yielded salmon, the bulwark of their winter survival and wealth.

The Dena'ina who arrived—or resettled, as some archae-ologists think—in the area around the Kenai and Kasilof Rivers around AD 1000 built weirs. They also dug deep underground storage pits and lined them with birch bark and moss and alter-nated layers of dried fish and grass during the fall when the rivers and ground began freezing. With a surplus of fresh-frozen fish that could be preserved throughout the winter and spring, they too prospered as extended family clans who gathered at summer fish camps. When Captain Cook sailed up the inlet now bearing his name, the Natives who approached his ships in canoes and kayaks offered fresh salmon in exchange for iron.

The Russians replaced the hereditary noble class of toions in Kodiak with village leaders who would obey them and provide sea otter hunters as a commandeered labor force. They treated commoners and slaves equally badly. They demanded a supply of dried fish for the winter. But the amounts required to support the Russian colonies were relatively small, particularly as the Koniag population declined to a few thousand during the rigors of the sea otter harvest and the arrival of European diseases. The Russians sent only small quantities of salted salmon to San Francisco for sale. It was American fishing fleets and processors who transformed the ownership, use, and trade of salmon beginning in the late 1880s.

Congress retained control over the management of salmon fisheries when Alaska became a territory. In short order, the har-vest of salmon was calculated in the millions of cases of salmon shipped. Each case contained twenty-four two-pound cans of salmon. Within five years of building the first cannery, Alaska's salmon packing industry was the largest and most productive in the world.

Salmon went quickly from being the mainstay of Native diets and trading networks to a global commodity. Canneries were established early in Cook Inlet north of Kachemak Bay to target the mighty runs to the Kenai and Kasilof Rivers. Operations began at the mouths of those streams in the late 1880s. The first recorded commercial salmon catch in Kachemak Bay was two decades later in 1911.

In 1912 Fidalgo Island Packing Company opened a cannery in what became Port Graham, where British captain James Portlock had seen a seasonal Sugpiaq camp of thirteen barabaras, the semisubterrean wooden houses that would have stood in the house pits left behind in China Poot Bay 125 years earlier. Portlock also saw another fourteen barabaras "up the bay where the creek was," likely referring to what is now named Port Graham Creek, still a major spawning stream for pink salmon.

As recounted by the Sugpiaq Elders to Henry Huntington in their story about shrinking and vanishing bidarkis, cannery jobs changed the nomadic patterns of the remaining Sugpiat. People from the nearby village of English Bay (now restored to its Sugpiaq name, Nanwalek) began to move seasonally to work at the cannery, a migration that disrupted their annual subsistence round at a critical time of year when they traditionally put up fish for the winter. Some settled and established the permanent village of Port Graham. The new village didn't seem to create fond memories at first; its Sugt'stun name was Paluwik, translated as "where people are sad."

The canneries also provided jobs for people who chose to settle in other Kachemak Bay communities. Tales of gold brought them from all over the world to make their way to the ports of Seattle and San Francisco, with a stop in Seldovia to resupply before heading north to *moil*, as Robert Service put it, for gold. Many returned home broke and no wiser about all that glitters, but others stayed. Fishing brought Scandinavian men—at home with boats, nets, rain, and cold—as well as men who built canneries and tended and guarded fish traps from robbers. It brought the seasonal workers to pack the salmon; they were primarily Chinese men until the Chinese Exclusion Act shut the door on their immigration in 1882 and the bulk of their labor was replaced by a machine blatantly named the "Iron Chink." It brought Henry "China" Poot, who, according to a version of the local story, was the product of an encounter more financial than romantic between a Native woman and a Chinese cannery worker. He eventually bestowed his name on China Poot Bay, China Poot Peak, and China Poot Lake, where he spent his time fishing and trapping. Later, homesteaders like Sam and Vega Pratt settled around Homer and Seldovia and grew gardens and crops and worked the slime line during fishing season.

The Homer Spit Rats came next.

Today, fish—particularly salmon—are at the heart of what we consider local food in Kachemak Bay and are essential to the relatively new environmental issue referred to as "food security." In a state where 95 percent of food purchased is imported and is often costly, Sugpiaq households in Nanwalek and Port Graham rely on hundreds of pounds of salmon and other fish that make up 70–80 percent of their annual subsistence harvests. In Homer and other Kenai Peninsula communities to the north, in almost every household someone fishes. According to the results of a recent survey, salmon caught for subsistence and sport are regularly bartered and traded despite a much-ignored regulation by the State of Alaska deeming this illegal.

I make my own pilgrimages during summer to dip net sockeye salmon returning to China Poot Creek, where the size of the run has varied from around seven hundred to around seven thousand. As a local Alaskan, I can participate in this personal-use fishery. My fishing equipment is a large long-handled net, which is about as much gear as I can manage with my limited mechanical skills. I can even avoid dealing with a boat motor by kayaking from Peterson Bay Field Station to the head of Peterson Bay and then portaging across a narrow isthmus to China Poot Bay and paddling to the opposite shore. When salmon are running, I find an excuse to spend the day at the field station and strap my kayak on the water taxi that drops me off in the morning. At the end of the day, I need to time my departure because the isthmus becomes a channel only at the most extreme high tides of the summer. As the tide ebbs, it's a muddy slog.

I undertake my journey in the long-lived glow of Alaska's summer light. A small crowd, brought by motor boats that threaded through a maze of channels into the shallow bay, converges at the mouth of the creek. I wade into the strong current of the creek as deep as my hip boots allow, where I can see the salmon entering the creek mouth. Some bump against my legs as they move past. Others pass just out of reach. I dip and I dip, missing fish after fish, until finally the weight of muscled silver in motion threatens to pull me down into the water or yank my arms out of their sockets. I keep lifting against the pull, stumbling backward over the rocky bottom until the salmon swings clear. Out of the water on the bank, it quickly succumbs, aided by a sharp rap I inflict with a stone to quicken its death. As I wait and stumble and pull and whack dying salmon a few more times for good measure, I fill plastic bags with my catch and I think of my winter freezer full of fish.

I'd like to cling to the comforting idea that the wild salmon I catch in China Poot Creek are local food, my means to tie myself and my food to the ecosystem's cycles. Yet when I actually trace the lives of those salmon, I find technology, not nature. The sockeye salmon that mill and swarm about the entrance to China Poot Creek can never complete their life journey to a lake to spawn and die. They began their lives as eggs in a high mountain lake many miles away and were reared in a hatchery, far inland from Kachemak Bay, where no predators harried them. Their food arrived on a regular schedule and when they were fry, a slow-flying plane plopped them into China Poot Lake, though the U.S. Geological Survey persists in mapping it as "Leisure Lake."

When the young salmon grew up and were inevitably drawn to the sea, they went downstream and tumbled over falls, caroming over rocks to arrive bruised and battered. Yet many of them evidently made it out to sea, lived there two or three years, and then returned with the taste of China Poot Lake in their memory. Then there were those falls again.

Imagine the confusion in a small fish brain for a moment, like Odysseus milling around with all of Penelope's suitors along with the added problem of a cliff he could not scale. And there I stand with dozens of other human predators ready with our dip nets.

The story of creating a salmon run from China Poot Lake where none existed before is rooted in the culture of federal salmon management during territorial days and its lax or nonexistent harvest regulation. Soon after canneries were established, they built large, wooden fish traps that intercepted salmon bound for their home streams. In Cook Inlet, the traps were well-anchored floating structures, often constructed with pilings that ran on energy from the currents. Migrating salmon were bucketed up and dumped into holding pens.

The efficient traps operated 24-7 when salmon were running. According to one account, a trap near Kasilof to the north of Homer that began operating in 1882 could "furnish fish to keep two filleters busy for 19 consecutive days." Fish were packed into the trap "like sardines," said an observer, so if they were not taken out right away, fifteen to twenty thousand fish might die and be lost to the canneries. In 1896 ten thousand fish piled up at high tide next to two traps on both sides of the river were wasted. By 1901 twenty traps were in place to supply canneries in upper Cook Inlet, the most southerly one at Bluff Point in the northwest corner of Kachemak Bay.

The construction and exclusive use of fish traps by the canneries ignored traditional fishing rights at particular places and for particular salmon runs. Controlling access to fish trap sites was outright illegal, but rights to use the trap sites were eventually bought and sold. In addition, fishing from boats was prohibited within three hundred feet in any direction of the traps. The fish traps became the means by which the harvest and profits were controlled by a few large corporations and a fluctuating number of small independent firms. The fact that the packing industry wasn't a total monopoly led to fierce competition to catch and pack more salmon using well-placed fish traps. While there were some independently owned traps, including some in Kachemak Bay, and fishermen who fished from their own boats, the canneries set the prices.

During the early years of the cannery era, Congress allocated a pittance for Alaska fisheries research and management. The first survey of Alaska salmon fisheries was conducted as part of the 1880 census by fisheries scientists David Starr Jordan and Charles Gilbert, both of whom were ichthyologists, initially on the more academic side of fish science. Although the two scientists returned for surveys in subsequent years onboard the U.S. Fish Commission steamer *Albatross*, little research was done on basic salmon biology. Scientific knowledge about the magnitude and impact of the growing industry on salmon populations quickly fell behind expansion of canneries along the Alaska coast and their rate of exploiting the stocks. The number of millions of cases of salmon shipped each successive year rose.

Complaints by fish biologists about salmon overharvest began early. Tarleton Bean, who had declared Alaska fish resources to be limitless in 1880, changed his tune after he investigated the Karluk fishery in 1889. He reported that year on behalf of the U.S. Fish Commission that Alaska salmon fish populations had already been decimated. In 1892 Livingston Stone, deputy commissioner for fisheries for the Pacific coast, feared that Pacific salmon would go the way of the buffalo. He described Alaska's salmon as "gripped between ... two forces, the murderous greed of the fishermen and the white man's advancing civilization."

The greed, however, was in the cannery system itself. A pattern soon emerged. Reports of the U.S. Fisheries Commission persuaded sympathetic congressmen to introduce bills imposing harvest restrictions or provide additional powers to the commission or the Department of Commerce to regulate fisheries. After great debate and intensive lobbying by the packing industry, a watered-down version of the law might be passed but was then barely or never enforced. An 1899 law made it illegal to completely block off a stream, as was done on the Karluk River. In 1906 no fixed nets or traps were allowed in rivers or narrow bays. Cannery owners merely moved the traps down the beach and extended the wooden corrals out thousands of feet to funnel salmon through corridors whose bottoms and sides were lined with nets.

Alaskans and others concerned about the fate of salmon in Alaska and the Pacific Northwest turned to President Teddy Roosevelt. In 1903 he appointed what was to be the first of several federal salmon commissions to look into the situation in Alaska. He selected Jordan to head up a fact-finding tour more than two decades after his last Alaska fish survey.

"It is pitiful," Jordan told a reporter for the *Morning Oregonian* in Portland on his return, "to see the diminution of the salmon run of today compared to the seemingly inexhaustible supply of two decades ago." He blamed traps and fishwheels "at work incessantly day and night" on the rivers, including those on the Columbia River, for declines in Pacific Northwest salmon runs. Yet he was sanguine about the future of Alaskan salmon populations.

"How does the situation in Alaska impress you?" the reporter asked him. "Are the fish up there in danger of being exterminated?"

"The salmon in all parts of the Coast," answered Jordan, "are too numerous to be exterminated, and the Alaskan situation seems to me to be very hopeful."

The report of the commission to Congress included relatively mild comments on the possible impacts of fish traps. It described them as wasteful, in that they "sometimes take more fish than the canneries can use." It also mentioned that the traps caught and wasted large quantities of "unwanted" fish with no economic value such as Pacific cod, flounder, and pollock.

The report noted some opposition to fish traps by Alaska fishermen but dismissed it in economic terms: "The fact that traps work automatically without the help of laborers is the cause of much of the feeling against them, strong among fishermen."

A few years later, in 1910, local populations of sockeye salmon, the most preferred salmon, were already being depleted.

As early as 1889, a federal Fisheries Act required canneries to establish fish hatcheries near their fishing operations. When the 1903 commission led by Jordan proposed approaches to sustaining large salmon harvests, there were only two possibilities: either the catch could be reduced through regulation to allow salmon populations to recover, or increased artificial propagation would need to be undertaken to meet increasing demand after stocks were depleted. Jordan's choice was clear. "Hatcheries are the key to the situation," he told the *Morning Oregonian*.

Perhaps gauging the unlikelihood of a regulation being passed by a Congress controlled by the salmon packing industry, the commission's report also placed their faith in hatcheries: "It is now evident that this industry can be maintained only by the artificial hatching each year of fry in sufficient numbers to make good those annually used in fisheries and otherwise destroyed." It was time, the commission said, to place Alaska salmon fisheries under the immediate direction of the "trained men" of the Bureau of Fisheries.

Jordan himself was an ardent evolutionist, preoccupied with the "waste of genes." He was a strong supporter of the eugenics movement in America, which helped passed state laws allowing the forced sterilization of disabled people so they wouldn't pass on their "unfit" genes. He promoted world peace and opposed America's entry into World War I because of the potential waste of the "best" genes—those of educated white men who could die in war, eventually diluting the "the blood of the nation." He reasoned that young salmon eaten by predators like bears and bald eagles were essentially a waste as well.

Tarleton Bean was the first fisheries scientist to list the many enemies of the salmon, including sculpins, trout, gulls, terns, and loons as predators on eggs, fry, and juvenile salmon. "The salmon, it appears," he said, "would have been better off had it never been born in fresh-water, where its dangers are cumulative and deadly." The Alaska Territorial Legislature took an equally dim view of salmon predators, setting bounties of fifty cents for the two feet of a bald eagle, three or four dollars for a seal nose, and a bounty even on Dolly Varden trout because they could be observed milling around as salmon spawned, scooping up eggs. Jordan shared Bean's view about wasting young salmon by predation, believing that hatcheries could essentially replace streams with their many dangers and do a much better job of producing salmon.

I first heard of David Starr Jordan, with his memorable middle name, when I was a student at Stanford University, where he had been its first president. A suspicion lingers that he may have poisoned Jane Stanford since she died under suspicious circumstances. His advocacy for world peace had more luster in his university legacy than its racist underside or his scientific fame as an ichthyologist and advisor to Teddy Roosevelt. I learned much later that Stanford had been at the center of fisheries management during Alaska's territorial times under Jordan's leadership. He and his students and protégés were all proponents of hatcheries as a panacea, with the exception of Charles Gilbert. After being placed in charge of the Pacific Fishery Investigations of the U.S. Bureau of Fisheries in 1909, Gilbert warned anyone who would listen that the Alaska salmon resource was in dire jeopardy unless overfishing was curtailed. The composition of the harvest had already shifted as the preferred sockeye and king salmon runs decreased.

The hatchery equation was simple at first. The 1889 Fisheries Act required cannery owners to produce four times as many young salmon as had been removed as adults the previous year. The government paid rebates on fish taxes based on the number of fry planted without regard to their condition or survival rate. Jordan favored government-run hatcheries, as did Congress, who levied a tax on cases of salmon packed to support several hatcheries.

Unfortunately, the idea that hatcheries could be the antidote to overharvest was undercut by the lack of scientific knowledge about salmon life cycles. Some hatcheries were simple affairs, which fisheries historian Patricia Roppel characterized as "sex in a bucket instead of in a stream." Sockeye salmon, the most preferred and valuable species in the harvest, actually required a year or two in fresh water followed by a slow acclimation period for juveniles in estuaries to gradually adapt to life in salt water. But sockeye fry raised in early hatcheries were dumped directly into the ocean, a sure death sentence. Scientists also lacked an understanding of the homing behavior of salmon, which required imprinting juveniles so they could smell their way back. It's impossible to know how many of the millions, possibly billions, of fry dumped into the ocean did manage to return to their home streams.

By 1911 the protests by Alaskans against fish traps became hyperbolic. James Wickersham, then Alaska's territorial representative who was later to become an esteemed territorial judge, made his opposition to the traps plain in the all-caps title of the article he authored in *American Conservation* magazine: "SLAUGHTER OF 'THE SILVER HORDE.'" His subtitle promised to explain "how the salmon are being driven from the waters of

Alaska—huge profits for the packers, not a penny for the people."
Although in hindsight, Alaskans often tout the elimination of fish
traps as the means to save salmon from extinction by a rapacious
industry and lax federal management, the fact that economic
benefits were going mostly to outsiders instead of Alaskans obviously rankled. In 1912 Alaskans lobbied for a transfer of power
to the territorial government to manage their own fish as other
territories did. The salmon industry was able to prevent it.

Livingston Stone's recommendation that only 50 percent
of returning salmon should be harvested became law in 1924.
The Alaska Fisheries Act, which became widely known as the
White Act (after Maine representative Wallace H. White Jr., who
introduced the final compromise bill), attempted "to prevent
further depletion of the salmon runs and of restoring them as
nearly as possible to their former condition of abundance." The
catch was that the 50 percent rule was for streams where the fish
could be counted or reliably estimated. Funds for enforcement
and escapement counts were lacking. The packers counted only
cases of canned salmon shipped. The White Act did, however,
prohibit subsistence fishing by Alaska Natives within streams.
When they pressed for their aboriginal fishing rights with the
Interior Department, they were told they had abandoned their
rights by going to work in the canneries for cash.

Still, despite the vagaries of federal management and the
lack of enforcement of regulations, salmon harvests went up then
down again. The quick ramp-up in the late 1880s peaked in 1918,
when British and American soldiers in World War I trenches dined
on Alaska canned salmon. More ups and downs led to a peak of
136 million salmon harvested in 1938, which wasn't exceeded for
several decades. Just three years before the peak, however, all the
hatcheries in Alaska and Canada ceased operations, having been
declared an utter failure.

The graph of annual harvests took another steep dive in
the late 1950s. Fish traps became a potent symbol for industrial-

scale extraction of Alaska resources transformed into wealth for people Outside. In 1959, the year Alaska became a state, the salmon harvest was at a historic low of twenty-five million fish. Fish traps were finally banned as one of the first acts by Alaska's brand-spanking-new state legislature. The action was widely hailed as the means to reduce the efficiency of the harvest and save Alaska salmon runs from extinction.

In 1969 historian Richard Cooley published *Politics and Conservation: The Decline of the Alaska Salmon*, his scathing analysis of salmon management before statehood. He framed it "as the pathetic history of the ruinous exploitation of one of the nation's important renewable natural resources." Then senator (later governor) Ernest Gruening wrote the foreword, calling federal management of salmon a "tragic and sordid story." In Cooley's detailed history, science was almost a footnote to the long-running economic and political juggernaut between the packing industry and Congress.

Ensconced in a wooden tower overlooking the Wood River in Bristol Bay during the summer of 1977, I saw firsthand how the state of Alaska managed salmon harvests. I'd just finished my master's degree in wildlife management, but wildlife jobs were scarce, so I felt fortunate to be hired by the Alaska Department of Fish and Game's Division of Commercial Fisheries to count salmon.

I was the leader of a crew of biologists hired to count every salmon that had escaped the gauntlet of fishing boats in Bristol Bay to make their way up the Wood River to their spawning grounds. Wood River connected to Lake Alegnagik, the Agulowak River connected Lake Alegnagik to Lake Nerka (*nerka* being the species name for sockeye salmon), and so on up a chain of five long, skinny lakes and short streams of the Lower Wood-Tikchik system.

From the tower, I could tell apart chum salmon by their scarlet slashes on light sides and kings by their bright red sides. Sockeyes share the red sides but have greenish heads. The hooked nose of the male distinguishes them from the females. Jack salmon, which have come back after fewer years in the ocean, are obviously smaller than those that come back after more. In the era before data entry on cell phones and computers, I counted by clicking in each salmon on a handheld tallywhacker and penciled the numbers in each category on a datasheet.

The three of us on the crew split up the twenty-four-hour period. I took the midnight sun shift from 10:00 PM to 6:00 AM, a shift I've never repeated. Each night as I drove a skiff a mile from our cabin to the tower, I prayed the engine wouldn't quit and require some sort of impossible repair that would leave me drifting helplessly out into Bristol Bay. Once I reached the tower, the quiet of the river settled in as the long light of summer began to dim.

After I climbed the wooden ladder to the tower, I watched the ancient salmon pageant unfold beneath me. They came in pulses, in an irregular rhythm syncopated to tides and winds that we in Kachemak Bay call fish winds. Smelling and tasting their way back to the gravels where they first wriggled up toward the light. Pursuing their own breeding imperatives, birds flew at eye level in the spruce trees that surrounded the tower. The singular piercing notes of varied thrushes and the trilling *oh-dear-me* of golden-crowned sparrows reached a crescendo as the sun dropped low, quieted for a time, and started again as it rose a few hours later.

Every day at the same time, I joined the chorus of crews like mine radioing in our counts. Our eyes on the Wood River runs were just one node in a network of watchers and counters. The numbers poured in to managers in Dillingham from counting towers and weirs at knick points in Bristol Bay salmon geography. I felt like part of a well-oiled machine that opened and closed the commercial fishery like a faucet, based on the numbers of spawning salmon that had eluded the fleet to dutifully produce the next generation.

After the managers ran their arcane calculations about the actual numbers against their predictions and models, they made announcements on the marine channel we used and every fishermen tuned into on their boats.

"The Nushagak District purse seine fishery," we would hear, "will be open for twenty-four hours from midnight, July 5, to midnight, July 6." The managers might decide to open the season for forty-eight hours or they might keep it closed for days until they saw the escapement numbers they thought were needed to reach their seasonal target. The equations were complicated; the numbers of spawners was a result of what happened in streams and lakes over several years in the past and the age of return a result of what happened in the ocean. The decisions they made would affect the potential harvest several years into the future.

Escapements, such as the one managed by the elaborate system of counts in the Bristol Bay drainage, were intended to ensure salmon would reproduce. Escapement numbers were also the sweet spot for maximizing the harvest. Allowing too few fish to escape the nets threatened sustainability of the run, but to allow too many, termed *over-escapement*, was just as bad. In their frenzy of digging redds and mating, biologists warned, an overabundance of salmon crowded onto the spawning area could dig up the eggs that had already been fertilized and buried.

Each salmon I counted in the river became an escapement data point. While my view of the run was mostly from the tower, my crew and I also sampled it a couple of times of week. We tied one end of a gill net to a tree on the bank of the river and stretched it across the current, anchoring the other end. When the salmon swam into the invisible net, they pushed their heads through the mesh and their wider bodies caught. It was the flare of their gill covers that caught them, thus the name of the net, but some thrashed and tangled themselves even more. We brought the net onto the bank, untangled the fish and measured them nose to tail and then weighed them.

We kept a few salmon out long enough that they became "trap mortalities," meaning dinner. We released the rest. But if you just put a disoriented, oxygen-starved fish back in the river, more often than not it flips over and hangs, floating downstream in the current and almost sure to die. So each of us waded in and placed salmon one by one in the river. I learned how to hold the salmon upright, nose pointed into the current, so gently I wasn't rubbing off any more of its protective slime and scales. I could see every breath it took as gill covers pulsed and its body shuddered in my hands.

Each salmon I released became more than a data point with a length and weight attached. I could feel that urgent life force again. Each salmon had escaped being caught and eaten by predators all its life. The fishing fleet and my dinner companions were just the last ones to try. The gill net the salmon had nosed into was just one more obstacle to push through, placed there by the entire unwieldy superstructure of Alaska fisheries science and management.

As I slowly released my grasp, the salmon headed home.

What I didn't know was that Alaska salmon management had transformed just before I arrived in the early 1970s. Fewer fishermen were granted the right to fish under a limited entry permit system, while more salmon were slated for production through the revival of the hatchery system. The 1960s had a seen a brief rally in salmon harvests, though not to the level of previous high numbers. Then the numbers descended to another trough of twenty-two million. The efficiency of the fish traps may have ended, one economist later argued, but the purse seine fleet increased rapidly after the trap ban with a single boat able to harvest fifty-five thousand fish in twenty-four hours.

Too many fishermen and too much gear in the water during every opening was an economic problem, James Crutchfield and Guilo Pontecorvo said in their case study *Pacific Salmon Fisheries: A Study in Irrational Conservation* in 1969. The subtitle placed the blame for the declining salmon numbers not solely on overharvest but on what they viewed to be an irrational, and somewhat insane, approach to conservation of fish stocks. That same year, Richard Cooley agreed with them in his critique of the cannery and federal management era.

While more fishermen were joining the "race for fish," fisheries managers raced against the development of more efficient technologies and the savviness of individual fishermen that increased with more fishing experience. The statistics were definitely damning. In 1969 there were twice as many fishermen as there had been in the 1930s, but they were catching about 40 percent as many salmon. The choice to become an Alaska fisherman in the 1960s, like many other choices to do dangerous and adventurous Alaskan things, was apparently more romantic than rational.

Economists argued for limiting entry to fisheries, a most undemocratic approach to the beleaguered system of open access to fugitive resources. Somewhat surprisingly, a majority of Alaskans voted in 1972 to amend the state constitution to allow exclusiveness in the right to pursue fish. Conservation was included as one purpose of the amendment, following the argument that a smaller fleet was easier to manage than hordes racing for fish. But it was joined by another purpose: "avoiding economic distress" for fishermen. The fishermen who qualified for permits had the opportunity to avoid distress by making money off the fish, and those who didn't qualify avoided the stress of going broke trying. Salmon fisheries were the first for which permits were issued.

As Alaskans worked to reduce the number of salmon fishermen through limited entry, Sen. Ted Stevens worked to eliminate foreign fishermen from harvesting Alaska-bound salmon, spurred by the expansion of the Japanese fleet with their large floating processors into Bristol Bay along with increasing harvests by Russian and Korean fleets in Alaska waters.

Congress created an Economic Exclusion Zone, or EEZ, that extended two hundred nautical miles from the nation's coast, ending three hundred years of extractive freedom of the sea.

Despite the early and admitted failure of territorial hatcheries, the State of Alaska decided to try again in the 1970s, banking on more knowledge of salmon biology and improved salmon aquaculture techniques. Salmon harvests were again low at 44 million fish in 1970, but in 1976 the state set an ambitious annual harvest goal of 100 million. By the end of the decade, the harvest had doubled to 88 million. After 1980, salmon harvests continued to soar well past the 100 million goal. It dropped to 96.6 million only once, in 1987.

In the 1970s the Alaska Department of Fish and Game began looking for lakes where eggs raised in hatcheries could be planted. China Poot Lake, the home ground of the salmon I dip net, became a poster child for an ecosystem coaxed into producing salmon. No spawning sockeye had ever ascended from China Poot Bay up the steep outlet of the lake. Undaunted, department biologists added two million salmon fry to the lake every year. Biologists returned to the lake as the juvenile salmon were leaving to catch as many as they could and clip their fins. The biologists showed up at the base of the falls each summer to count the adults that returned. They even tallied up the adults caught by commercial fishermen, using the telltale fin notch as the marker of those spawned in China Poot Lake.

For several years, all went well. Juveniles swam out to sea and returned as adults in two or three years. But then something changed. Biologists noticed the juvenile salmon leaving the lake were smaller in size every year. Adults that were caught or returned became smaller as well.

They had to shift into bottom-up reasoning to realize that in a natural system, while the biological role of spawning salmon was to reproduce, their ecological role meant returning nutrients to the ecosystem via their decaying bodies. Each new load of fry drew on the lake's food web, packing on ounces and nutrients that departed from the lake when they did. When no adults returned, the nutrients were never replenished to support the next year's plant life. With less to graze on, the zooplankton that were the food supply for the fry grew scarcer. When the next load of fry arrived by airplane, fewer found enough food to grow large or even to survive. The circle was clearly broken; the lake had become purely an export economy.

In 1985 biologists decided to try an experiment. They stocked the lake as usual but also added fertilizer—a lot of fertilizer: fifteen tons of nitrogen and phosphorus every year for five years. The result was an astonishing sevenfold increase in the biomass of zooplankton. The survival rate of fry that made it to the smolt stage to leave for the ocean almost doubled, and the smolts went to sea at younger ages. Survival in the ocean by adult salmon increased, and the commercial sockeye salmon harvest received a tremendous boost as well.

The process of stocking the lake with fry fertilizer has continued for forty years. But what if all of this human intervention stopped? Nutrients in the lake would eventually dwindle again, young salmon would grow more slowly and fewer might survive. Fewer, and smaller, adults would return to be caught by Alaskans like me, standing in waders in the current with a long-handled net and proud of her self-sufficiency.

"Alaska's salmon—wild, sustainable, and natural!" is the marketing cry of the State of Alaska in the early twenty-first century. In Kachemak Bay, as elsewhere in the state, this mixed story of salmon origins and destinations has become the new management culture. In the Lower Cook Inlet fishing districts that include Kachemak Bay and Cook Inlet to the west, 60 percent of the sockeyes and just under a third of the pinks caught in 2015 spent at least some portion of their life in a hatchery, as did nearly a third of all salmon caught statewide.

Hatchery managers and the Alaska Department of Fish and Game refer to the practice of raising salmon and releasing them as fry or juveniles as "ocean ranching" to distinguish it from "fish farming," which confines salmon their entire life like other livestock. Leaving aside the questions of whether ranched salmon are truly wild or natural, which border on treasonous in Alaska ("wild and natural for most of their life" doesn't have the same cachet), I think it's fair to question their sustainability. Is a hybrid system—one that relies on science to target escapement numbers for natural runs and hatcheries to produce a lot more salmon—really sustainable? Are salmon a sustainable local food supply for the some ten thousand people who now live around Kachemak Bay?

We've come a long way from Alaska salmon as a resource that Richard Cooley touted in 1969 as requiring "no capital outlay or labor to sow and cultivate." We've created an infrastructure that's a miracle of science and technology, including hatcheries, net pens, float planes, boats, gallons and gallons of fossil fuels, and an army of fish culturists. Billions of salmon fry are released onto the open range of the ocean ranch each year in the hopes that millions will come back. In the circular logic of hatcheries, boats scoop up hundreds of thousands of returning adult salmon to sell to recover the costs of running hatcheries.

Another army of fisheries scientists and managers predict the annual harvest, set escapement goals, and open and close the fisheries. A crew of technicians still spends part of the summer in the counting towers like the ones on Wood River. Other crews count fish at weirs. Others count the fish that escape. Fish tenders and canneries record the harvest on fish tickets. All of the data fed into the process of developing new predictions about future returns.

Still, while the scientific methods for forecasting runs have been steadily improving, it's clearly not an exact science. The predictions can turn out to be not just wrong but spectacularly wrong. In 2016 the actual number of sockeye salmon returning to Upper Cook Inlet was 27 percent lower than predicted. Three years earlier, in 2013, when the statewide salmon harvest was the highest ever, the number of returning pinks (the species most economical to culture with their two-year life cycle) exceeded the statewide forecast by 92 percent.

Alaska salmon harvests in recent years have been off the charts. The 100 million salmon target was exceeded by 172 million in 2013 and by 163 million in 2015. More than 200 million of the more than 360 million salmon in those two years were pinks, returning in odd years when their runs are naturally larger. During even years, the lower numbers of pinks drop the total harvest by as much as 100 million. Compared to historical harvests, this increase is even more dramatic, with half a billion salmon harvested in those two record years compared to 4 billion salmon harvested during the sixty-three years between 1896, when commercial fishing began, and 1959, when federal management ended.

Many fisheries scientists I talk to have utter confidence in Alaska's system of supplementing wild stocks with hatchery fish. They assume the desired larger surplus is a genetic and ecological freebie. They point to Alaska's policies that place the health of wild stocks first and require diligent attention to genetics and the potential for spreading diseases. The State of Alaska's official policy is to enhance wild runs, not replace them or cause them harm. But there's a lively debate in fisheries science literature about whether replacement is what happens after the first flush of increased production occurs.

Evolutionary scientists have always pointed to the effects of relying on only a small number of fish for eggs and sperm to establish hatchery populations. As the gene pool narrows, so do the genetic possibilities. Depending on when they are taken during the spawning season, the timing of the salmon run can become earlier or later for a species already struggling to match their life cycle to a changing seasonal cycle of food abundance for young salmon. Young salmon adapted to survive early life in hatcheries have different genetics than those that survive the stresses in streams and lakes, which can make them more or less fit to survive in the ocean.

Returning salmon do stray and fail to return to the place they imprinted on as home, especially pinks. In the late 1970s, when I sampled Arctic char on the Canning River in the Brooks Range in northeastern Alaska, we caught several pink salmon though we were hundreds of miles from the nearest salmon stream. When hatchery salmon stray, they often enter streams with wild salmon stocks where they compete for spawning habitat and contribute their genes to the next generation.

When biologists surveyed seven streams in Kachemak Bay in 2014, they found that nearly half the spawned-out salmon had hatchery markings. Surprisingly, they didn't all come from hatcheries that release salmon into the bay; nearly a third of those came from hatcheries in Prince William Sound to the east.

In many ways 2015 was a record year in the fishing district that includes Kachemak Bay and stretches westward across Cook Inlet. Compared to the average of the previous ten years, more fishermen who held purse seine or gill net permits fished them and caught more pinks, sockeyes, cohos, and even king salmon. The harvest was still relatively small by Alaska standards: forty-three commercial fishermen caught close to 278,000 salmon. Compared to the previous ten-year average of 95,000, however, the harvest was nearly tripled.

The majority of the harvest, 60 percent, were pinks and nearly a third were sockeyes. Both species have been extensively ocean ranched, although somewhat erratically over the years in Kachemak

Bay due to the vagaries of hatchery operations and salmon prices. That same year, a 3 percent return of more than 1.5 million pinks were expected to return to the bay. They were slated to be harvested to recover hatchery costs and build up the hatchery stock of "green" (fertilized) eggs to rear in the following year.

Instead, the season demonstrated that there could be too many salmon in the wrong place even when they show up at the right time and the desired place. Near Tutka Bay Hatchery, in the shallow lagoon east of Seldovia where salmon had been reared and imprinted as juveniles in net pens, the return was 5 percent, which brought an extra million more pinks than the 1.5 million anticipated. The hatchery operators captured thousands of males and females and stored them in net pens in the lagoon. Still, more than eighty thousand escaped up Tutka Lagoon Creek, where the natural run has generally ranged from five thousand to thirty-eight thousand. The Alaska Department of Fish and Game reported these numbers with only a brief comment that some straying may have occurred.

As the pinks just kept coming, salmon became crowded both inside and outside the net pens. The salmon that made it up the creek spawned and then died as they do at the end of their life cycle. Carcasses began decaying in the creek. The result was a mass die-off and an utter waste of salmon in the lagoon. An anticipated harvest of 124 million green eggs dwindled to only 14 million.

The Cook Inlet Aquaculture Association, the private non-profit organization that operates Tutka Bay Hatchery, has a growth mentality. Even as the events of the summer of 2015 unfolded, they pursued approval of a four-year plan to move the release site to a place with better circulation and increase their releases of juvenile pink salmon in Tutka Bay from around 11 million in even years and 50 million in odd years to 100 million annually. They pegged the predicted return at the same 3 percent, which would mean 3 million pinks returning every year. Homerites came out in numbers to hearings and wrote letters to the editor, stymying the permit process.

In 2016 salmon runs were again unpredictable, but this time the numbers were about 40 percent lower than predicted. At the end of the summer in 2017, people walking their dogs on Bishop's Beach were surprised to see hundreds of pinks crowding up the outlet to Beluga Slough, a biological event that no one seemed to remember witnessing. That same season, the return of sockeye salmon to China Poot Creek, enhanced by the efforts of the same Cook Inlet Aquaculture Association, so far exceeded expectations that the daily harvest limit of dipnetting six salmon increased to twenty-five.

As the aquaculture association pushed forward with their expansion plans and public relations efforts, they admitted in their 2016 newsletter that the baseline was shifting, acknowledging that the ocean conditions over the past few seasons had resulted in returns that didn't follow their predictions based on historical information.

David Starr Jordan, the great proponent of evolution, was eventually proven right that we could build artificial environments and raise more salmon, but he was likely wrong about raising salmon "more fit" to survive and thrive in a changing world. Thousands of genetic lineages in salmon have been honed by survival in thousands of different environments. Each salmon population is a culture; their ability to survive, grow, go to sea, and return is written into their genes.

While a stream may be a dangerous place for young salmon, we've learned that the return of the adults and the recycling of their bodies into nutrients are necessary for the life in the stream and the surrounding forest's roots. Salmon carry the memories of streams and watersheds and the ocean.

I also wonder about the effect of all of those billions of salmon fry and juveniles released into ocean food webs. We have no way to determine a preindustrial baseline to understand if there are limits to how many salmon the ocean can actually pasture, whether they are being ranched or not. Some scientists have suggested we may be approaching a limit, one that could change drastically as the ocean continues warming and acidifying, which might dissolve the shells of animals like pteropods, a translucent marine winged snail favored by juvenile pink salmon.

Others suggest that those billions of chum and pink salmon releases have already shifted marine food webs. Salmon also compete among themselves. Like halibut, sockeye and king salmon have been shrinking in size in recent years, which could be a symptom of increasing competition for food.

As a former habitat biologist, I also fret about habitat. If salmon numbers can be boosted by ocean ranching, someone will surely revive the argument that streams in the way of mines or oil and gas development aren't really all that necessary. After all, what's the loss of a few acres of spawning or rearing habitat or even a few miles of stream habitat when salmon harvests are at record levels and ocean ranchers are standing by?

Hatcheries and salmon ranches are a compromise between wild and tame, between a natural system and one altered by human intervention. They're an application of biology, technology, and economics to the task of creating the largest possible supply for a seemingly insatiable global demand for a tasty, healthy package of protein, fat, and oils. The heavily branded *merroir* of wild Alaska competes in the global market's agricultural mentality.

This compromise in managing Alaska salmon reminds me of the decision I make every day whether to walk to work or drive the mile and a half. I know that walking is the better thing for my health and the health of the planet, but despite a friend's mocking advice—"don't use your car as a raincoat!"—the decision is harder on days when it's pouring rain. When I've spent an extra fifteen minutes in bed and am already late on a winter day, the temperature well below freezing, the sidewalks unplowed and those people who get to work on time have already made the roads drivable, the scales tip further. On those days, I often rationalize that it's actually safer to drive on icy roads with studded snow tires than to risk a fall on icy sidewalks.

The compromise I made to relieve my environmental guilt was to trade in my gas-guzzling Subaru for the first new car I've ever owned: a Prius. Its hybrid nature reeks of compromise like my bargain for salmon in the freezer. The amount of fossil fuels I consume with a single trip is small, which tips the balance of the argument as long as I ignore the resources that went into building the car and what's required to keeping it and a road system operating.

And of course I worry about the resilience of Alaska salmon in a rapidly warming world since they have to navigate the warming ocean with its shifting food web as well as warmer streams and lakes. Streams that flow from melting glaciers, while cooler, carry more silt that can make it harder for salmon to see and catch their prey.

The oldest ancestor of every species in the salmon family on both coasts of North America was named *Eosalmo driftwoodensis* (after Driftwood Canyon Provincial Park in British Columbia, where its fossil was found). It lived fifty million years ago and only in fresh water. The salmon lineage has thus had a remarkable duration, with its capability of contracting its range during ice ages and expanding by navigating the coastline after thaws. According to the salmon bones found in the hearth of an archaeological site, salmon have survived 11,500 years of warm and cold periods deep in Interior Alaska.

On Kodiak Island, people have been catching and eating salmon for at least six thousand years. The sediment on the bottom of lakes there record twenty-two hundred years of fluctuating but prolific sockeye salmon returns through Kachemak and Koniag times. Around 100 BC, the Karluk River run estimated at three million crashed dramatically when presumably environmental conditions changed. The run stayed low for 350 years and then increased for nearly 1,000 years, most steeply beginning in AD 800. It peaked in AD 1200, perhaps not coincidentally during the Medieval Warm Period and the emergence of the class society of the Koniag, with the means to capture large numbers of salmon and preserve and store them. The expansion of the Dena'ina eastward and southward on the Kenai Peninsula around AD 1000 may also have been tied to an increasing abundance of salmon in addition to their innovative technology of weirs and underground storage pits.

For seven hundred more years, even as the climate cooled and glaciers advanced, the runs stayed consistently high, estimated to have reached three million again by the end of the Little Ice Age only a few decades before American commercial harvests began. In 1880, before any canneries had begun operations at the mouth of the Karluk River, Tarleton Bean described the salmon run as "so great as to interfere seriously with the movement of canoes in crossing the stream." For several years in the 1890s, more than three million salmon were harvested and canned—about half of the entire Alaska salmon harvest—and in 1901, four million. By 1955, however, the unmanaged harvest had declined to fewer than thirty thousand.

Bruce Finney, one of the scientists who cored and analyzed the mucky bottom of Karluk Lake, points to the cycles of marine-derived nutrients from salmon carcasses as occurring before people had any real impact on salmon population numbers. He settled on the side of bottom-up forces controlling salmon numbers until commercial harvesting began. In 2003 he joined with Milo Adkison to foretell the long-term prospects for commercial harvests of Alaska salmon. They could see the pattern of overharvest driving some salmon populations in the early decades of the twentieth century but concluded that environmental change has controlled the size of salmon runs ever since. So, they reasoned, if the management of escapements truly works to preserve the spawners and hatchery salmon are truly gravy over and above natural production, the only culprit left as the cause of declines is environmental conditions.

Others read strong trends in Alaska salmon numbers during the twentieth century related to the surface temperature of the ocean. The PDO shifts seemed also to affect Alaska salmon. The effects of colder or warmer waters are sure to be complex on the five salmon species that spend different lengths of their life cycles in fresh water and in the ocean, but sockeye, pink, and chum salmon generally thrived in decades of a warmer-than-average ocean and did less well in cold ones. King salmon were just the opposite, possibly related to the longer time they spend in streams during their life cycle.

When waters warm, oxygen levels drop, especially in shallow estuaries that salmon pass through as smolts and spawning adults. The fish that crowded into Tutka Bay Lagoon during the summer of 2015 died of suffocation.

Two very different stories have emerged about Alaskans long-term relationship with salmon. The first is of successful top-down fisheries management after the steep decline wrought by a lack and then by ineffective regulation of fish traps and harvests during the cannery era. Statehood brought the shift to a scientific approach of counting and managing escapements. In this version of the story, a limited entry system and the shift to ocean ranching of pinks and chums accompanied the dramatically increasing trend in harvests that began in the 1970s and that have recently reached record levels.

The second is a bottom-up story, told by scientists who see patterns and trends in ocean temperatures and measure fluctuations in abundance on the scale of decades or centuries. Despite natural ups and downs of sockeye runs on Kodiak Island, they provided an undiminished abundance to populations of people that grew into the thousands on a relatively isolated island. While overharvesting did occur for half a century or so, nature has batted last ever since.

Of course, what happens at the top and at the bottom is happening simultaneously, making the patterns inextricable. Perhaps the end result can never be predicted but interpreted only in hindsight, like the surprise ending of a murder mystery with a multitude of clues and an equal number of statistical red herrings.

I take some comfort that past predictions of the imminent extinction of Alaska salmon by fishing have been proven wrong, not once, but twice by what managers claim as the success of regulation of the harvest and clever intervention. But my hope is with salmon lineages whose fidelity to the scent of home is not completely without a penchant for moving up or down the coast and spawning somewhere else. When I pulled a salmon out of a net in the Canning River on Alaska's North Slope, I was looking at the future.

For now, salmon remain a gift—to me in Kachemak Bay, to Alaskans, to the world. Alaska Natives say salmon give themselves to people wily enough to learn their ways and persistent enough to catch them. Like all gifts, they're best when they keep circulating—from people who catch them and gift them first to their family, their neighbors, and community potlucks and regift the scraps to their dogs and to the soil microbes in their gardens. I'm thankful from the first one I catch in my net to the last one in the freezer.

Salmon are the gift that returns. As they come back to the streams where they were born, they weave the abundance of the ocean back into the land. The next generation returns the favor. But the circle of the gift can be broken; salmon come back to hatcheries and even push on valiantly toward lakes they'll never reach.

When the sockeyes run strong in China Poot Creek, I can scoop up my daily limit of six in an hour or so. I load them into the storage compartment of my kayak and paddle back to the field station. I clean my catch on the beach well into dawn. I'm as tired and as rich as I'll ever be.

A Meditation on the Ecosystem

Reductive science is concentration, but to comprehend ideas like eco-
system health . . . we need something more like meditation.
　　—Sarah Gaichas, computer modeler for marine ecosystems

My beach walks took place that winter of 2015–16 amid a carnage
of common murres, seabirds I rarely saw close to shore during
my winter trudges. Dead bodies were arrayed along the wrack
line with dirty white breasts torn open, exposing the keel murres
balance on so gracefully in flight. Dark, comic feet jutted out
from rounded bellies. Bloodied clumps of feathers were strewn
about and tangled in the seaweed.

Arrayed in crisp black-and-white patterns of their breeding
plumage, murres were part of the fabric of the bay in the summer.
Gull Island, the huge rocky island that juts up in the middle of
the bay where they gathered by the hundreds to breed, was a
waypoint on my boat trips between Homer and the field station.
We circled it either going or coming from May until mid-August
just to view the spectacle. Murres were always leaving or returning in squadrons. Parents exchanged nest duties with courteous
butler-like bows before the stay-at-home mom or dad flew off to
forage along the north shore. When we approached large rafts
of birds on the water near the colony, they dove like cork lines
being pulled from below.

I learned their ways during my summer at Cape Peirce in
1976. Most of the year, they roamed the open ocean, homing in
on cliffy shorelines and islands with ledges. They tolerated an

apartment-building density, crowding together a few wing-lengths apart on bare rock to claim a nest site. I watched mating take place, compactly and somewhat precariously. A short while later, a single greenish-brownish egg appeared. A downy black chick with a gaping bill was next. Returning birds began carrying a single silvery fish crosswise in their bills.

It had been my job to count them. Sitting for hours every day above areas enclosed by imaginary plot lines, I waited to see what lay under the warm belly of each murre. At the end of the season, we tallied up the numbers: pairs of birds in the plot, eggs laid, chicks hatched, and chicks fledged.

Gull Island became mildly famous in seabird biology circles later as a control site for a seabird study after the unplanned experiment in 1989 that spilled eleven million gallons of crude oil into the Gulf of Alaska. John Piatt headed up a five-year post-spill study that began in the late 1990s and was nearing its end when I moved to Homer in 1998. The results of the study demonstrated the advantage of the location of Gull Island as a seabird breeding colony. In contrast to the Barren Islands' location close to a vortex of ocean currents, Gull Island had been spared the brunt of the oil. And compared to the murky banquet around an island that served as another study site at the head of Cook Inlet in the path of a massive outflow of glacial rivers, Kachemak Bay's currents and gyres made it into a place of continuous feasting during the summer.

John Piatt joined a team of biologists during the winter of 2015–16. They were charged with counting the dead, the same duty seabird biologists were assigned after the oil spill. The U.S. Fish and Wildlife Service declared an unusual mortality event, or UME, but seabird biologists typically call piles of dead birds on beaches a *wreck*. Applying their scientific methods for quantifying doom, the biologist counted forty-six thousand dead on the beaches they flew over or walked, and then expanded their total estimate to half a million to take into account the ones that died, sank, and never washed up on shore. The number was twice as high as the estimated death toll for the oil spill and established a new, grim baseline for the Gulf of Alaska, and the highest wreck ever counted.

It had been a strange fall. Humpback whales showed up in the bay by the dozens, in numbers never seen before at that time of year. Fishermen began catching plenty of king salmon and noticed their stomachs were stuffed full of small herring that had hatched only that year. People who had lived and fished in Kachemak Bay for decades reported seeing schools of small herring in numbers they'd never seen in their entire life.

While unusual, some of these changes in typical patterns among the fish and wildlife didn't seem bad. Who didn't want to spend a beautiful fall day watching whales on the bay or catching king salmon? An abundance of young herring seemed like good news.

But the dying had already begun. The first seabird carcasses on beaches were noticed in July by citizen scientists, people dedicated to regular surveys for beached birds that were just plain dead. Their baseline of the occasional dead bird was exceeded week after week. The dead were almost always murres. Live ones also came in to shore or wandered dazedly on the beach, too weak to return to the water. By the end of the summer of 2015, every murre chick on Gull Island had died.

The sea otters also began dying in July and developed into another unusual mortality event. Ninety-seven washed up in September and the death toll topped three hundred by December.

The humpbacks stayed well into November, leaving late to begin their usual migration to Hawaii. Whale watchers identified individuals in the bay by the patterns on their tail flukes but heard from whale watchers in Hawaii that the individuals never showed up there. During the spring, a third unusual mortality event was declared for highly endangered fin whales. Most of the whale carcasses eventually drifted onto beaches much as they had after being hunted by the Koniag.

Just when we thought it couldn't get much worse the following summer, sea stars, those keystone predators, developed white patches or appeared with gaping lesions. Their arms fell off, and then their bodies dissolved into piles of goo. Murres that survived the winter returned to Gull Island to breed, but again all the chicks died.

The dead were the climax of an ecosystem story, eventually told by scientists, both professional and citizen. Unlike the Sugpiaq Elders who connected the beads of the ecosystem on a string that stretched backward through time and generations, the scientists connected the beads on the string of energy that moved through the food web.

I was taught that the structure of an ecosystem is a pyramid of life, and so I teach kids. Ecologists call it a trophic pyramid, a fancy word for who-eats-whom. There's a collection of species at each step. The organisms that live on sunlight and air and minerals occupy the lowest, largest tier and support the narrowing tiers of animals that graze or prey. In my own long, slow slide from biologist to ecologist, I learned to see that image of the pyramid for the imperfect model that it is. The two-dimensional shape of the pyramid floating in the white space of a page or computer screen is nothing like the reality in the ocean. Under the surface of the water, the pyramid is alive and three-dimensional, spread out through a column of water that is itself in motion from tides and currents over a bottom with its own architecture. The fourth dimension is the cyclical time of seasons and years and regime shifts.

The ecosystem story began with the seabird and marine mammal biologists who counted and examined their dead. The way the murres died was obvious by their empty stomachs and lack of any trace of fat on their bodies. The pile-up of dead otters coincided with the local branch of the University of Alaska's semester-by-the-sea program for undergraduates. They got a real and smelly science experience of dissecting otters to search for the cause of each death. The majority of the otters died from infections that indicated a stressed immune system, but a small number had traces of toxins.

The story moved to scientists who tow fine nets through the water to detect the beginnings of toxic phytoplankton blooms. They detected a massive one with the scientific name of *Pseudo-nitzchia* in China Poot and Peterson Bays among other locations. Domoic acid, the toxin it was capable of producing, caused its own kind of food web horror by affecting the nervous system of big-brained predators like birds and mammals, including humans, who became amnesiacs with little memory of anything they had learned about finding food. While high concentrations of the toxin moving up the food chain might explain the strange behaviors of the murres, only very low amounts of domoic acid were ever measured in the bay.

Since the murres were fish-eaters, the story moved to the biologists who study the fish whose fate is to be foraged on by seabirds, whales, and bigger fish. The summer of 2015 had been a strange one for the biologists during their routine survey of the Gulf of Alaska waters over the continental shelf. Their trawl nets came up nearly or totally empty of young capelin and walleye pollock in places where they usually congregated in large schools. Since these were the same places the murres usually foraged during winter, this seemed to explain their empty stomachs and their unusual appearance close to shore and even far inland. In December and January, while I was seeing dead and dying murres on Bishop's Beach, other Alaskans spotted live ones waddling weakly across their backyards. Dog mushers and skiers encountered them on trails. They ranged as far from the ocean as Denali National Park and Fairbanks.

When more plankton scientists joined the conversation, they reported other oddities. During the spring of 2015, the composition of the phytoplankton bloom had shifted from a preponderance of species that were round and fat in shape to ones that were long and skinny. In the zooplankton community, the next major link in the food web was a species of copepod with the scientific name of *Neocalanus flemingeri*—this copepod was large, fat, and important enough in the food web to be considered a keystone species. They hatched out right on schedule that year but began growing on a faster timetable than usual. This meant each one stored a smaller amount of fat before it reached the stage where it went into its winter mode of sinking into dormancy in deeper waters. The copepod basically disappeared from the community at the time that pink salmon and other fish needed them most to capture enough energy to grow and fatten up for winter. Next, the fat shrimp-like krill that were the food of choice of juvenile fish in late summer never showed up at all. The nutritional differences were substantial. It was like the difference between eating bread sticks while waiting for the next course of rolls with a dab—or, in the case of the copepods and krill, a pat—of butter. The dabs and pats were smaller than usual, left the table early, or never came at all.

It was the absence of capelin in the beaks of seabirds returning to feed their chicks in the early 1990s that alerted Piatt to the regime shift from colder to warmer ocean temperatures that had begun the winter 1976–77. After the die-offs during the winter of 2015–16, the biologists looked to the oceanographers who were documenting their own unusual oceanographic event. They first noticed unusually warm temperatures in Alaska waters in the fall of 2014 on a research cruise along the Seward Line, a series of oceanographic stations over the continental shelf south of Seward. Temperatures in the upper 300 meters (328 feet) of the ocean were 1 to 5 degrees Fahrenheit warmer that fall than the average over the previous seventeen years. Fall water temperatures were even higher in 2015, up to 8 degrees Fahrenheit above average.

The northern Gulf of Alaska remained unusually warm during the winters as well, according to continuous temperature measurements at a sentinel buoy moored at the seaward end of the Seward Line. It wasn't just that the temperature averaged over the entire year was warmer than that of previous years, but every month was warmer than average for more than two years, which meant the ocean never cooled over the winter, a shocking turn of events in the seasonal pattern in the North. Although there have been other warm ocean years recorded in Alaska waters in the twentieth century, most notably in 1926, the magnitude and duration of the warming was unprecedented.

The abnormal ocean pattern occurred not only in Kachemak Bay and the Gulf of Alaska but over a large area of the North Pacific Ocean stretching from southern Alaska to California. The oceanographers called it a "sea surface temperature anomaly" in their nonjudgmental scientific descriptions, until Nick Bond, Washington's state meteorologist, seeing the sprawling presence of a gigantic pool of warm water on the map of the Pacific Ocean, gave it the nickname of the main character in the 1950s' horror movie *The Blob* that engulfed everything in its path. Later, he and other scientists began referring to the event as a "marine heat wave."

The unusually warm, deep mass of water eventually expanded across one million square kilometers, which sounds a bit more impressive than the square-mile equivalent of 386,000 square miles. But if the Blob at its peak was superimposed on a map of the state of Alaska, it would completely cover it with 25,000 square miles to spare.

During the first winter of the Blob, only the surface of the ocean warmed. The next winter the ocean wasn't only warmer at the surface, but the Blob engulfed the entire water column over the continental shelf in the central gulf. By April, 2016, the upper 250 meters (more than 800 feet) of the Gulf of Alaska was 1 degree warmer (measured on a Centigrade scale, equivalent to 1.75 degrees on a Fahrenheit scale) than average. While this doesn't sound like a very large increase, oceanographer Seth Danielson equated the amount of heat added to the gulf as about equal to an extra hundred days of solar heating.

"If you prefer to think in terms of electrical appliances," he wrote in a blog post, "the excess heat contained in one square mile of ocean having the same depth is equivalent to the power needed to operate 50,000 toaster ovens over 24 hours a day for a year."

It had been eerily calm the fall of 2015 and on into the winter, seasons that are normally stormy. When there was precipitation, more of it fell as rain, which ran off the mountains rapidly, than as snow that would take much of the summer to melt. The result was an ocean stratified into a layer cake with colder and saltier, thus denser, water at its base and a thick layer of warmer, fresher water above. In Kachemak Bay the pattern was similar. The persistent upwelling of nutrient-rich oceanic water squeezed up through the passages between islands at the entrance to Cook Inlet onto the shallower shelf and drove the water into the bay along its southern shore where it sank beneath a lens of fresh water fed by melting glaciers, streams, and winter rains. The bottom-up processes that swirl nutrients and energy up the food web to phytoplankton, and thus to zooplankton and forage fish, require wind as its churn.

Of all of the effects of a warming ocean, the changing patterns of the flow of energy and matter through the food web remain the most unpredictable. Every animal in the Gulf of Alaska, from the zooplankton to the seabirds to the whales, use the energy they accumulate from their food first to run the machinery of staying alive and then to grow and reproduce. Warmer waters increase the metabolic rate for all but the smallest animals and youngest life stages of larger animals adapted to live in cold waters. While the summer system runs on light and wind, the winter system runs on fat—both for animals that stay and even some that leave, like the humpback whales that feed only during the summer. Murres range hundreds of miles offshore and can swim down through the water for hundreds of feet. All of this takes tremendous amounts of energy.

John Piatt once calculated that an adult murre feeding on sand lance (a long skinny fish it seems to prefer in the nearshore waters of Kachemak Bay) needs to eat nearly half of its body weight each day just to stay alive. If the prey available offshore is walleye pollock, the requirement jumps to three-quarters, which is what places them in the junk food category. Raising a chick requires additional energy. Each member of a breeding pair needs to find and deliver two oil-rich fish every day to the chick. Although it seemed like they were staying longer at the feast, the humpback whales in the bay in December may have, instead, been trying to recover from a skinny summer and accumulate enough fat to make their long migration and survive the winter. The stress and death of so many animals at the top of their food chains was a symptom of an entire food web starved of energy. The murres who returned to Kachemak Bay from the empty continental shelf waters would have had those young herring to feed on, but apparently they gained too little energy too late to survive. Those that survived and returned to Gull Island the next summer were failures as parents. The circle was broken two years in a row.

Fisheries managers think more about ecosystems now than they did in the heyday of managing for maximum sustainable yield of individual stocks of fish or the days when they insisted that fishing controlled fish populations. Scientists talk regularly across disciplines, from physics to fish to human societies, to piece together complex narratives of connections that explain the consequences of the PDO and the Blob. Some fisheries managers, however, have gone a bit overboard with the assumption that entire ecosystems, in which we are but one predator, are inherently manageable. Some think we are smart enough to manage them. But really, we're the only the super-predator in the system—armed with rapidly and constantly improving technology, the capability of learning, and the power of language to share information about where and how to fish. We move fish products around the world at a rate that could barely be imagined in the late nineteenth century, when glacial ice was used for cold storage and railroads first connected Alaska seafood to East Coast markets. Unlike other predators, we're not limited to the energy from the sun in real time to grow and harvest and eat our food; we reach back through millions of years of life and death to fuel our fishing boats, processing plants, refrigeration, and global transportation systems. Without much thought or intention, we've altered the temperature and chemistry of the entire ocean.

Sarah Gaichas's PhD dissertation in fisheries was full of the usual data tables, graphs, and outputs of runs of computer models. Yet at one point, she stepped away from her talk of science to plead that the North Pacific marine ecosystem was the type of place that required a meditation.

"Unfortunately for us," she said, "the marine ecosystem is not one we can inhabit or even walk through briefly and experience like a forest. We sense it by the remotest of means."

When I walk the forest trail winding away from Peterson Bay Field Station, the sun filtering through the trees warms my skin. Their shade cools me. The plump, sweet taste of blueberries explodes on my tongue as a red squirrel gnaws a spruce cone and a sundew traps a mosquito. I see dead things—logs crumbling into sawdust, leaves turning brown, fallen blossoms from plants visible without the aid of a microscope. I feel sheltered. With every walk, I build my understanding of the forest as a place, the less scientific way of saying a "system." The connections are visceral, and the changes I notice are personal, even those that originate far away.

Sarah Gaichas is certainly right about the insubstantial nature of the ocean, where full immersion requires at least an oxygen supply and, in cold water, considerably more than that to remain for even a few minutes. I can barely imagine the ocean as a place despite underwater snapshots and films, images of plankton blooms taken by satellites from space, graphs of temperatures collected by instruments festooned on buoys, the boxes-and-arrows diagrams of marine food webs, or the bleached, dead specimens brought up from the depths.

Understanding the dynamics of the North Pacific Ocean requires confronting the inescapable truths of northern seasons—the harshness of winters, the lushness of summers, and the abruptness of the transitions. Life in this ocean is governed by its cycles of light and darkness interacting with water—both salt and fresh—and wind. A great recycling of life takes place on the bottom but can only take place in the light through the forces and patterns of the winds. The temperature of the water and the air above it matter, but in ways we are only beginning to discern as the patterns change again.

The scientists term the Blob a "weather event," too short by decades to be any kind of a climate pattern. Science also can't say whether humans can be blamed for the extra heat in the system; it could just as easily have been an odd run of meteorological luck. By the time a man who said climate change was a Chinese hoax had been sworn in as president of the United States, the Blob began to dissipate, at least at the surface.

At a meeting of Alaska's marine scientists just a week after the inauguration, Nick Bond asked if the Blob had been a dress rehearsal for what to expect if the trend in ocean warming continues. If it is, it's not a play I want to stand in line to buy tickets to watch. Even the scientists who usually speak in cool tones about their research are convinced the ocean and planet are changing dramatically. Like Cassandra, however, they've become prophets who seem doomed to be disbelieved, as least by half of the people much of the time.

It's hard to imagine what all of the impacts of natural and human-caused changes to the ocean will be or all the ways its living web will be tweaked. Murres will likely be confounded again by the fickleness of winds and currents. My winter travels will be along bleak windrows on their carcasses on the beach or perhaps I'll meet them as earnest travelers on my ski trail. My Cape Peirce summer among them will remain as my baseline of their abundance.

"We have never lived through this kind of death," Chief Walter Meganak Sr. said after the oil spill killed a quarter million seabirds, most of them murres that time as well. "But we have lived through other kinds of death. We will learn from the past, will learn from each other, and we will live."

Beyond any calculation of tons of biomass extracted, of the slope of graphs that go upward and downward, amid battles among fishermen who troll or seine or trawl for fish, the ocean—while not limitless or filled with resources free for the taking—is still astonishingly abundant.

Abundance is a remarkable gift on this planet; it's one that the earliest people in this place never took for granted. It's mercurial, shape-shifting in response to our taking, then taking some more, until one form of abundance has yielded its very nature to us.

Combining the two perspectives of science and meditation is daunting, even for Kachemak Bay, just one small pocket of the part of the ocean called the North Pacific. It's different than a shifting of baselines from a single viewpoint. From our perch as a species on the top of the food web, we would need to learn to see simultaneously from the top down and the bottom up, sideways, backward and forward, and to look both outward and inward.

Maybe it's something that can only be done over the course of a lifetime, like the migration of halibut eyes. Or maybe it's just a way to describe ecological thinking: the apprehension of ecosystems as webs of energy and matter, with every knot in the web in relationship to every other knot. I can at least aspire to be such a knot.

Science does well in its focus on one thing at a time—one species, one hypothesis, one variable. Scientists are understandably wary of stories and argue hard and long about what can be said with certainty. Correlation, they say often, is not causation. Things are always more complex than can be described and certainly more complex than can ever be told. Meditation, on the other hand, focuses on all things at once, on the parts and the whole—on the story, the many ways it can be told, and the silence.

Part IV

THE ECOLOGY OF DESIRE

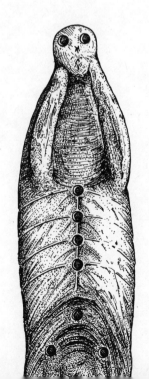

Tidepooling to the Stars

Chasing low tides is part of the rhythm of my life in Kachemak Bay. I study the tide book missal, looking for the minus fours and fives, when the narrowed slot of Cook Inlet's shoreline squeezes the incoming North Pacific into a mound rising as high as twenty-five feet at flood tide. When it ebbs from the rocky beaches, it exposes a wide world of seaweeds and animals draped over and clinging to every surface.

The tidal pattern in the bay is approximately two tidal cycles every day. It's approximately because a single cycle lasts a bit more than twelve hours in sync with the length of a lunar day. Despite our precise understanding of the effect of gravity on the ocean as the moon and sun move around the Earth, the math of future tide cycles never quite computes. The geography of water comes into it such as that of the narrowing inlet, as do changes in atmospheric pressure. The cycle knocks my life off-kilter a notch from one ruled neatly by the clock to one ruled by the interactions of forces.

Still, I find that the more I pay attention to the cycle, the less attention I have to pay. The tide cycle becomes my cycle. I ebb and flow right along with it, chasing it to exhaustion during the extreme lows and resting in between. Consulting the tide book is just a fine calibration. I wander the intertidal zone at the maximum extent of its cycle.

Constantly in transition from land to water and back again, the intertidal zone is no place and no kind of baseline. Yet it's a place of patterns as constant and as variable as movements of the Earth, moon, and sun. Earth turns, its ocean sloshes in large gyres and currents. Life on the beach is a reflection of those patterns, a mosaic stitched together with salt and rock and flesh. As the world warms and the seas rise, the stitches start to loosen.

Bishop's Beach is my favorite beach on the north side of the bay. It's Homer's tame portal into the rowdier Pacific Ocean. People live along the north shore as far as the road goes, some thirty more miles. It ends at the head of the bay with an abrupt dive down dizzying switchbacks to two communities of Russian Old Believers. Most Homerites live away and upward from the shoreline in tiers of homes that capture sweeping views of the bay and mountains. Homes on the edge of the thousand-foot bluff have the best views, but at any elevation there is a mish-mash of shacks, cabins sprouting unwieldy add-ons, and trophy retirement homes fronted with heat-losing glass.

Bishop's Beach is a short walk from "downtown" Homer, a compact area no larger than ten square blocks. The route from the Sterling Highway down Main Street passes the Mermaid Café and Old Inlet Bookstore, Bunnell Street Art Center with glazed sculptures peering out through its windows, and the wafting scents of savories and espresso from Two Sisters Bakery. A blaze of fireweed and lupine lines the road during summer, but in winter, the snow in Bishop's Beach Park can be thigh deep. Some years lately though, there's been no snow at all for most of the winter.

The road ends in a parking lot, recently paved and marked with actual parking spaces. Whenever you arrive, someone is always sitting in a Subaru, SUV, or pick-up truck, just gazing outward. Bishop's Beach is Homer's relief valve; it opens out from the town into the bay like a sigh.

Everyone shares the beach—alone, in pairs, in swarms of kids, moms, dads, and dogs. Roaming kids and dogs are called back occasionally. During summer we greet familiar faces among the throngs of tourists, but in winter, we bundle up beyond recognition in whatever combination of less-than-stylish clothes will keep us warm and dry.

Dogs rule this beach. I used to walk it with Kiana, my Samoyed who went blind in the last years of her life. I miss her doggy joy at the first hit of salty air. In her earlier days, she would have run off immediately to sniff the tall grass that flanks either side of the path down to the beach to read the arcane language of dogs who had recently passed by. In her last year, she was too weak to jump in and out of the car and stayed huddled in the back.

When I walk the beach, the alive and the dead and the dying become the real news. Barnacles, mussels, and tangles of seaweeds wash up or live in woven patches on rocks in the lower reaches. Storms bring the occasional dead bird or soft spongy spheres called sea pork that are really colonies of animals called tunicates. Acorn barnacles, their hinged shells waving at the tops of gelatinous stalks, wash in on pieces of rotting wood.

Once, Kiana flipped a small halibut out of a pool with her paw, surprising us both, and no doubt, the halibut.

The wet rocks shine.

My obsession with beaches began long ago in California the day I first saw the ocean. I was twelve, on a family vacation in Los Angeles with my parents and two brothers, visiting relatives who, like my father, had once lived on homesteads in eastern Montana. Unlike my father and grandparents who moved only ninety miles westward after a string of wet years turned to drought, these great-aunts and great-uncles had kept moving west until they could go no farther and settled in a place where they could gaze out on a horizon of water instead of the wind-beaten plains.

I was more interested in the ocean than the stories they told each other of that time of leaving behind their dreams, though my interest had nothing to do with science. I'd never heard the word *ecology*. The smooth sandy beaches were crowded with tan, blond boys who paddled their enormous surfboards seaward.

As teenagers imprisoned in landlocked Billings, Montana, every slumber party had sing-alongs to the Beach Boys, when we fervently wished we all could be California girls.

The next time I visited a California beach, it was a straight-shot night drive from Stanford University, where I was an incoming freshman. I was tipsy from California wine that flowed at every party and grappling with the information provided by my self-proclaimed Maoist RA: I could walk across the street from my dorm to the health center and ask for birth control pills. At San Gregorio Beach, the same RA howled and scampered across the sand to the surf ahead of us.

As often as I could, I'd cadge a ride to San Gregorio and south to Pescadero Beach, the place a young man claimed he fell in love with my backside that year. Farther south at Bean Hollow, rocks emerged from the sand like giant ribs. Next along Highway 101 was Año Nuevo, "New Year's Point," as the Spanish explorer Sebastian Vizcaino proclaimed it when he sighted the dangerous point and its fangs of rocks from far offshore. It was the wildest and best place of them all. A narrow trail wound along the cliff's top, where coastal oaks thrust their way skyward. The trail plunged to the base of cliffs where rocks tumbled out, interlaced with white fossil shells of the Purisima Formation—"the most pure."

Back in Stanford biology classes I peered into microscopes and learned about classic laboratory experiments. My student lab jobs involved collecting data on the circadian rhythms of caged mice as they ran on wheels in the dark. I fed captive butterflies for Paul Ehrlich, who was already famous for announcing an imminent human "population bomb." It wasn't until my senior year that I went on an official field trip to the beach. Having spent most of my time at beaches blissing out, I never even looked for beach animals until I took an invertebrate biology class from Charles Baxter. I learned that it was the intertidal zone I'd been most drawn to, a place patterned in bands of life, all sorted by their distance above the lowest tides.

Mr. Baxter was a curiously unlettered man among the PhDs who taught undergraduate courses and had million-dollar grants to run labs populated by tight phalanxes of graduate students. Mr. Baxter had only a couple of nerdy male graduate students, who seemed to live in the lab room amid jars and petri dishes holding all manner of wet or pickled creatures. He looked and dressed something like my father on a fishing trip, in khakis and flannel shirts. There was nothing cool about Mr. Baxter. Even worse were his responses to my questions about marine invertebrates that were intended to impress him with my intelligence. He usually answered that no one knew, then handed me a jar or a petri dish and a microscope to find out for myself.

On Mr. Baxter's field trips I first entered the edge of the ocean to look for its hidden life. Before each trip, he assigned sections of *Between Pacific Tides* by Edward F. Ricketts and Jack Calvin, the book that soon became my beach bible. All the forms of life I could expect to find in the intertidal zone from California to southern Alaska were laid out in an orderly, scientific fashion, in a way focused not so much on their classification into families, orders, and phyla but on the types of places where I could expect to find them. It was a view of life in biological communities as a locus of the beach surfaces and tides that created their mutual habitat, the types of places where they found food and often had interesting ways of avoiding becoming food for another member of their community. Mr. Baxter and his graduate students showed us this intricate world as we staggered about in our hip boots.

I read John Steinbeck's *Cannery Row* that same year after I learned that Ricketts had been a great friend of Steinbeck. They were young together in Monterey Bay in the 1930s and stayed lifelong friends. It was obvious to everyone literary that the main character in *Cannery Row*, the director of a collecting business for biological specimens from the intertidal zone, was based on Ricketts. Sometimes I had trouble separating Edward F. Ricketts, the serious scientist who had written *Between Pacific Tides*, from the romantic fictional Doc created by Steinbeck, himself a failed Stanford biology student. Steinbeck's version of peregrinations in tide pools was equally romantic. I fashioned myself like Doc in the tide pools, collecting marine invertebrates in a golden California haze of youth and friendship. I imagined Ricketts's Pacific Biological Laboratory in Monterey as a place of science and philosophy intertwined with epic parties that were the place to go, as one biographer described it, for "Gregorian chants, jugs of wine, and arty women."

In Steinbeck's telling, Monterey in the 1930s was a place permeated by the stink of the sardine industry and populated by soulful bums and whores. Collecting tide pool specimens and stray cats had, in fact, been a viable means of support for Ricketts throughout the Depression and the beginning of World War II. I was so inspired by this lifestyle that after I moved to Alaska, I quit my biologist job for several impecunious years to run my own collecting business that I named Scavengers.

In 1932, in the midst of writing *Between Pacific Tides*, Ricketts came to Alaska on a collecting trip aboard Jack Calvin's boat *Grampus*. He sought to catalog all the marine invertebrates along the western coast of North America and to seek an explanation about their patterns of distribution. Also onboard the *Grampus* was young Joseph Campbell, Ricketts's Monterey neighbor. Along with Steinbeck, Campbell accompanied Ricketts to the tide pools, engaged in extended philosophical discussions, and attended the epic parties memorialized in *Cannery Row*. (The three men had complicated relationships with women and sometimes with the same woman; Steinbeck had declined to come along on the Alaska trip after Campbell had become involved into a reportedly platonic but deeply emotional affair with Steinbeck's wife, Carol.) During low tide, Ricketts and Campbell explored the places exposed to collect shiny and slimy figments of life; onboard, they sorted and drank and talked, searching for patterns and deeper meaning.

Ricketts's great scientific questions, the impetus for the organization of *Between Pacific Tides*, are variations on a single question, of the type that I pose to kids on the beach: Why do you find this animal *here*?

Here, out of the water, not in it?

Here, not higher or lower in the intertidal zone?

Here, under a rock not on top of it?

Here, on the rocky beach, not on a sandy beach?

Here, clustered with a group of animals of its kind, not alone?

Here, eating or avoiding being eaten?

Ricketts's idea of unifying physical drivers, or factors, that were made manifest as biological communities in the intertidal zone was new in the 1930s.

Other biologists who studied marine invertebrates were taxonomists and systematists, who were busy classifying animals into related groups and staking out territory as experts in the relatedness of chitons or snails. Charles Darwin himself spent eight years peering through a microscope at the structures of barnacles, beginning with one strange specimen he named Mr. Cyptobalanus that he found on his voyage on the *Beagle*. He wrote four volumes about the classification of barnacles to establish his credibility before he put forth his radical theory of evolution.

At times Darwin despaired. "My cirripedal task is an eternal one; I make no perceptible progress . . . and I groan under my task," he wrote. In the miniscule structures of the barnacle feet that swept the water for food, in the penises that turned out to be the longest proportionate to size of any animal in the world, in the twists and turns of digestive systems, he found his evidence of adaptation to a variety of environments through variations that supported his theory of descent from common ancestors.

For Ricketts to take on the explanation for distribution of all marine invertebrates found along the Pacific coast was simply unthinkable, particularly coming from another unlettered man who only had access to Stanford's Hopkins Library by sneaking in at night. As arduous as Darwin's work on barnacles had been, he contemplated them in the comfort of his laboratory attached to his home. Biologists and amateur naturalists from all over the world sent their specimens to him by mail so he could make global comparisons of variations in their form with his only technology, a microscope. Ricketts instead went out in the world— studying it inch by inch, low tide by low tide—and kept copious notes about what might influence the distribution and survival of every creature he saw.

The patterns Ricketts finally described were based on looking sideways, gathering painstaking physical data that cut across the biological groupings required as evidence of the theory of evolution, to see the greater ecological whole. He described an environmental calculus rather than a hierarchy of species. The calculus was one of environmental factors interacting in patterns of stress and response that resulted in community. Beginning with communities he observed, he sought the "what" to which the community members had adapted.

The same question was taken up in a slightly different form by Robert Paine and Anne Salomon, who looked at the internal dynamics of relative abundance of prey with high stakes predators in the community but within the context set by Ricketts. Just as Darwin's theory had established a new baseline in biology, Ricketts established a new ecological baseline of biological communities sorted in intertidal zones: lower, middle, and upper.

At the same time that Ricketts, Steinbeck, and Campbell saw the animals in the tide pools for what they were and classified them precisely, they saw echoes of human societies in the interrelationships. Ricketts saw "kind, sane, little societies" in the tide pools. For the rest of his life, he wrote philosophical essays that were never published. One, about "the philosophy of breaking through," refers to breaking through "the crust of humanity," in the words of poet Robinson Jeffers, to something beyond and whole. Campbell referred to "these little intertidal societies and the great human societies" as "manifestations of common principles." He later claimed his time with Ricketts in Alaska set him on his journey to contemplate and catalog great mythical themes as unifying factors that cut across cultures, much like the environmental factors that cut across species and phyla.

In his autobiography, *A Hero's Journey*, he described his time in the tide pools, of being among "all those strange forms, cormorants and little worms of different kinds and all. You'd hear, my gosh, this generation of life was a great battle going on, life consuming life, everything learning how to eat the other one, the whole mystery, and then from there they crawl up on land."

Steinbeck found the greater human whole in labor movements. *The Grapes of Wrath* was published in 1939, the same year as *Between Pacific Tides*. One of Steinbeck's masterpieces, it tells the story of the cause and consequences of the Dust Bowl, that great ecological event that began in the Northern Plains and spurred my relatives to head west and south, leaving the lifeless Plains behind. When it spread to the Central Plains, it eventually displaced thousands of people westward to California, where they could only find dignity by organizing against California's greedy agribusiness owners.

The Grapes of Wrath won the Pulitzer Prize for literature. There was, of course, no Pulitzer for *Between Pacific Tides*, considered by many marine scientists as no more or less a quirky field guide for beachcombers. Yet it became a classic in its own way and a baseline of understanding intertidal ecology due to the "organizing factors" Ricketts summed up in the introduction: "On the Pacific coast . . . the three coordinates and interlocking factors that determine the distribution of shore invertebrates are: (a) the degree of wave shock, (b) the type of bottom (whether rock, sand, mud, or some combination of these), and (c) the tidal exposure."

This characterization was true in China Poot Bay. I could use *Between Pacific Tides* to predict the intertidal animals I would find on a beach anywhere on the West Coast of North America from Southern California to southern Alaska. Like the scarcity of katy chitons that Anne Salomon noticed on the beach in front of Nanwalek and Port Graham, degrees of absence became a signal of a changing ecology.

In 1940 Steinbeck and Ricketts set off to the south on a six-week-long collecting trip on the *Western Flyer*, chronicled in *The Log from the Sea of Cortez* as a unique combination of travel, science, male bonding (despite the fact that Carol Steinbeck was onboard and seemingly invisible), and philosophizing. A section of the book referred to as an "Easter Sunday Sermon" is an excerpt from one of Ricketts's essays, although the authorship of the book was eventually attributed to Steinbeck alone. "It is a strange thing that most of the feeling we call religious," begins one pronouncement of the sermon, "most of the mystical out crying which is one of the most prized and used and desired reactions of our species, is really the understanding and the attempt to say that man is related to the whole thing, related inextricably to all reality, known and unknowable . . . the knowledge that all things are one thing and that one thing is all things . . . all bound together by the elastic string of time. It is advisable to look from the tide pool to the stars and then back to the tide pool again."

In the winter of 1970, the first time I walked along the shore of Monterey Bay, the signs next to the derelict sardine cannery cautioned me not to enter the water at risk of getting sick from teeming bacteria. The sardine canneries no longer contributed to Steinbeck's *Cannery Row* description of Monterey as "a poem, a stink, a grating noise, a quality of light, a tone, a habit, nostalgia, and a dream." The sardine populations had crashed in the mid-1940s and hadn't recovered.

I was there for a meeting of a Stanford seminar called Peak Experiences, my own flirtation with breaking through. On our weekends in Monterey, we listened to Gregorian chants and Baba Ram Das, drank from jugs of cheap wine, drummed, wrote in our journals, and walked the beaches, all more or less for credit. In the 1930s America had been in the depths of an economic depression and on its way to a world war; in the 1970s, my own time in California was dire in other ways. Although we were children and teenagers during one of the most affluent periods in American history, the Vietnam War and the specter of rivers so polluted by oil they could catch on fire defined those years for us. The lure of dropping out or transcending that society was as strong as that of striving together, like Steinbeck's characters, for social justice or for peace.

In the fall of 1969 I marched against the war. By spring, I found myself at the heart of the first Earth Day at Stanford. It was merely a diversion, some said, from the anti-war protests that had yet to stop the war. But it accomplished something else. Thirty years after Ricketts, Steinbeck, and Campbell had begun to see that the patterns of interrelationships in the intertidal zone had something to do with patterns in human societies, ecology became politics. We humans were all implicated in the destruction and salvation of a natural order.

Even in 1939 Ricketts saw signs of human impact on intertidal communities. In the introduction to *Between Pacific Tides*, he raised the alarm: "We are, alas, no longer in the halcyon days of carefree collecting and unspoiled abundance of life on our seashores." School field trips were the particular subject of his ire: "There is probably no hope for those teachers and counselors who stand placidly by while robust, undirected adolescents throw sea urchins at each other or stamp the gumboot chiton to death." He noted the places on the central California coast that once abounded with urchins were barren of them, and abalone, once the dominant animal of the intertidal regions, were "now common only on inaccessible offshore rocks or islands" and the rock scallop, also once common in the lower intertidal, had become rare.

Steinbeck said it a bit differently. "Let us go," he wrote as he and Ricketts embarked on their journey to the Sea of Cortez, "realizing that we become forever a part of it ... that the rocks we turn over in a tidepool, make us truly and permanently a factor in the ecology of the region. We shall take something away from it, but we will leave something too."

In Kachemak Bay we preach an elaborate beach etiquette to schoolchildren on beach field trips, which is rooted in Ricketts's observations of over-collecting in the 1930s and various means by which overzealous children torture marine invertebrates. "How would you like it if a monster came stomping around and ripped the stone roof off your house?" I asked kids on the field trips I led, who were as eager as I was to look under rocks. "What if the monster picked you up and put you down miles away from your home? Or dropped you from very high up because you were so squishy and slimy?" Then I asked the kids to make up their own rules for how they wanted to behave on the beach. They walked more carefully after that, and there were sometimes tears when they inevitably stepped on what they now saw as living things.

Today, exhorting unruly children to handle marine invertebrates gently feels almost quaint. The threats to survival are now on the scale of the driving environmental factors that shape communities—warmer ocean temperatures and water so acidic that it melts the shells of clams and bidarkis.

Kachemak Bay is a place of edges, of meetings of different intermingling communities. To live along its edges and on its beaches requires fitting in over centuries and millennia of attunement to the shape of the beach and its cycles while clinging and grasping for succor in the tidal soup. Slime rules. The tidal zone is a place of settlement, of attaching and shutting down within defensive shells, of hunting and hiding—sometimes in plain sight—and of relationships millions of years old. But it's also a zone of displacement. The denizens of any particular place shift with the tides and the currents. They communicate more often in the language of scents than that of sight or sound.

Washed up on the Alaska shore, I'm many generations into my family's displacements, of leaving places, pushed or pulled by invisible currents. My great-grandparents left the village now known as Zagare in Lithuania. They were pushed out by waves of pogroms and hatred for Jews toward a more tolerant Ireland. My grandparents left Ireland: my grandfather to join the homesteaders who followed the railroad as it extended across the western United States like a tentacle and my grandmother in search of a nice Jewish spouse in America. Later, they left Vananda, in eastern Montana, when the Great Plains dried up and crops withered. Both my grandfathers were immigrants to America. They became shopkeepers, fathered children, and died of heart attacks in their forties, long before I was born. My grandmothers were immigrants who raised their children as long-lived widows in the midst of cultures and places far from the ones in which they were born. I left Montana when college and, later, the greater wilderness of Alaska beckoned.

My family history teaches me nothing about what sustains human communities. Like me, my ancestors abandoned places. Behind them, communities vanished. My father's family landed in eastern Montana during a time when the weather was briefly, but as it turned out, uncommonly favorable. As my father remembers being told, at first the springs were wet, the summers were cool, and the winters were mild. A few years later, the more usual pattern of heat and drought during growing seasons resumed. Deadly winter blizzards followed, blizzards that swallowed up starving cattle and children trying to make it home from school. People hung on as long as they could, but all but a few families eventually gave up homesteading and moved away. The stories of the shopkeepers in my family who settled briefly in seven Montana communities always end with them leaving later than most, with their ledgers full of accounts payable.

But they fared better than the Jews who stayed in Zagare, Rhodes, or Smyrna. Much of Smyrna burned to the ground in 1922, just months after my grandmother left for her New York City wedding day. Near the town square in Zagare, 2,402 Jews were killed on October 2, 1941, by a tsunami of bullets. Their remains lie several soil layers down in a mass grave in the woods next to the town square. On June 24, 1945, 1,820 Jews left Rhodes on their way to Auschwitz where all but 179 were transformed into ash. Thanks to the precise accounting by the Nazis, the family names of my ancestors can be found among the rolls of those who never returned.

The only choices in a changing environment are leave, adapt, or die. But when the global environment is changing, where can you move? I've already abandoned Montana, often touted as the "last, best place." I don't want to abandon Kachemak Bay. It's my last place, the only one I can imagine as home. I have two choices left.

During my time as a naturalist in Kachemak Bay I journeyed across the bay from Homer, disembarked onto a dock in Peterson Bay, ferried myself to shore on a hand-pulled raft, and trekked across the narrow peninsula between Peterson and China Poot Bays. For eleven springs and summers, I led groups of schoolchildren on field trips and tourists on natural history excursions. Although I was responsible for maintaining the field station—the barely functional volunteer-built cabin where the school groups stayed overnight—and quelling the dramas of the twenty-something seasonal naturalists I supervised, those muddy visits to China Poot Bay at minus tide were my calling.

In China Poot Bay, the schoolchildren followed me around as I once followed Mr. Baxter as we explored the tidy array of intertidal zones explicated by Ricketts. The upper intertidal zone is a desert, I would say, a place too dry too often for the creatures of the sea and too salty from high tides and ocean spray for the creatures of the land. The soil of the land ends. The first sign of life as we march seaward are the barnacles, ensconced in their tiny, dry castles. Next the limpets, occupying low ground, tucked into their single streamlined shells and clinging to rocks with their single foot. Periwinkle snails the size of thumbtacks cluster in large, black masses of closed shells where any trace of dampness remains.

I portrayed the middle intertidal zone as a forest, one that is drowned about half of the time. On a rocky beach like China Poot, it's a seething, living architecture. Dense, shaggy bands of blue-black mussels hang like limp castanets on the wall, trussed up in the shiny golden threads binding them to the rocks and each other. Limpets, dogwinkle snails, and hermit crabs become ensnared in these nets as they climb slowly over the shells to search for food. Tiny barnacle larvae settle on every hard-shell surface. Mussels rule this zone, along with the tough yellow-green seaweed called rockweed, or popweed, whose common name I always demonstrate with the satisfying "pop!" of my rubber boots stepping hard on air-filled floats that keep the algae upright in the sunlit zone when the tide submerges them. At low tide, the animals that live in this zone are closed up or shriveled. They're waiting, like a still life, for the next broad strokes of water to animate them.

We'd walk carefully down to the most exciting lower intertidal zone, a slick rock jungle emerging from the water only briefly at the lowest minus tides. I asked the kids to think about the flooding tides delivering chunky, nutritious soup to the animals that feed by filtering, or sifting, the ocean through their bodies. At this extreme trough of the low tide, sea stars were high and dry. They were draped across the rocks, without the hydraulic power to move up the beach or back to the water's edge.

I scanned the ranks of sea stars. A true star whose midsection was hunched up was a sure thing because it meant it was wrapped around a clam or mussel. I picked up the dinner-plate-sized animal and flipped it over to expose what it was holding tight in its rows of the sticky linguini-like feet along five, tapering arms.

"So," I said, "this is how the sea star gets its dinner. When the mussel feels the sea star trying to eat it, it closes its shell tight." I held the base of my palms together and clapped my two hands together.

"Then the sea star uses its tube feet and starts pulling on both shells." I let my hands bulge out. Then I asked the most distracted, and distracting, kid to help me demonstrate what happens next. "Hold your arm out and try to resist what I do next," I said, and I pushed down on the kid's arm as long as it took to at least engage in the physical struggle I could easily always win. The arm dropped. "Eventually, what happens? Even if you're a mussel, your muscle would get tired, right? The sea star just needs to get the shell open a crack and then it turns its stomach inside out." I'd point to the clear jelly-like blob in the center of the star. "It pours out its digestive juices and starts digesting. What's it making? Clam chowder!"

Turning your stomach inside out on your dinner plate was something most kids, especially the boys, could see as a great strategy to gross out their siblings and parents. They looked more closely at each sea star after that for the hidden drama of slow attacks and death by stomach acid. After they figured out the purpose of the tube feet, sea star flipping became a competitive sport, so we could time how long it took them to right themselves, foot by foot.

That was just the beginning. Everyone began turning over rocks, shouting out over what they found so everyone would gather round. Most kids lowered the rocks back down gently, following a rule nearly every group came up with. We saw barnacles in pools flicking their comb-like feet outward to rake for food, the waving crown of sea cucumber tentacles, sculpins so well camouflaged with counter shading that we saw them only when they darted after their prey. I poked worms gently until they shot out a proboscis that could stab and poison a smaller worm. It was always good for a squeal or two even though they were too big to feel the stab or keel over from the poison.

We saw what the anemones had caught on their sticky tentacles. On silly days, I dared them to touch the tentacles and try the sticky stuff as hair gel. We visited octopus dens that were usually cavities at the base of larger rocks far enough down that at least one entrance was submerged most of the time for a quick exit. Most times, you could only spot a pale tentacle that couldn't be pulled out of view. When we didn't find the octopus at home and receiving guests in a place I knew to be a den, we sorted through crab shells and urchin parts thrown out in the octopus's front yard.

With animal after animal, and even the seaweeds, we played the guessing games of What does it eat, How does it protect itself from being eaten, and What ends up eating it anyway? Adaptations abounded.

When we returned to the field station, we took off our muddy boots and rain gear, warmed up with hot chocolate and cookies, sprawled on the floor, and listed all the species of seaweeds and animals we'd seen. And then we constructed a food web, from the sun to phytoplankton and seaweeds to zooplankton and grazers to predators. We chanted the words *producer* and *consumer* and *decomposer* together, like a mantra. If we weren't all too tired, or the kids weren't tired enough, we played the food web game. We each became one part of the web, receiving a ball of yarn from what we ate, passing the ball of yarn to what ate us, until we were all tied together, our connections into a community as tangible as the strands of yarn that wound throughout the room.

We saw how diverse and complicated it all was—that some animals ate several different kinds of plants and animals, and everything depended on plants, and the plants depended on the sun. I asked one kid to tug on a connection and we passed the tug around until everyone got tugged as the dance of interconnection filled the room.

"Some he taught how to think, others how to see or hear," John Steinbeck said about Ricketts in a eulogy that became the foreword to *The Log from the Sea of Cortez*. "Children on the beach, he taught how to look for and find beautiful animals in worlds they had not suspected were there at all."

I can think of no better benediction.

In the novel *Sweet Thursday*, Steinbeck's sequel to *Cannery Row*, the fictional Doc is a depressed and lonely middle-aged man who has returned to a failed laboratory and a changed Monterey after World War II. He begins studying octopus emotions and writing a scientific paper he can't complete.

The book ends with Doc driving off into the sunset toward La Jolla on another collecting trip with a woman he's been set up with by the entire town. The real-life Ricketts died in 1948, six years before *Sweet Thursday* was published, in a collision between his car and a train. He and Steinbeck had been planning another collecting expedition to cover the area from Sitka out to the Aleutian Islands that would have begun one week after the day Ricketts was killed. He had already collected notes for a book he planned to title "The Outer Shores."

Surely he would have stopped in Kachemak Bay to explore its world-class tidal range and ponder something profound.

I visited Vananda a century after my grandfather opened the doors of Vananda Mercantile and forty-five years after I left Billings for Stanford. Just north of Forsythe, the green strip along the Yellowstone River ended abruptly at the extent of irrigation, like the upper edge of the intertidal zone. Beyond the reach of the water, clumps of dull sage and bitter scrawny bushes rose from the flats glistening with white alkali that floated up with the groundwater. The temperature was in the nineties and the air was filled with haze from wildfires burning across eastern Washington and Canada. My air-conditioned rental car felt like a spaceship floating through the postnuclear nightmares I'd trained for as a child. All that remained from my father's childhood were falling-down wooden structures and a few dazed cattle. The big blue Montana sky I always remembered from my youth was brownish and wan. A single hawk moved through it. When I got out of the car, the heat pressed on me like an iron.

That same year, 2014, I returned to the California beaches. Like all beaches, they remain liminal, defined by in-betweeness and transformations. It was a good place to be during my own protracted transition between the low and high tides of childhood and adulthood. Returning in middle age, I could still feel my seventeen-year-old self in my bones, although the flesh hung heavier on them.

At seventeen my mind had been a chaotic tangle of biology lectures and chemistry equations and the anxiety of trying to fit in as a Montana girl with the seemingly laid-back but actually cutthroat California girls that freshman year at Stanford. At the beach, though, I'd felt the invisible currents that blew under and through it all—the football games, the drugs, the philosophy lectures, the chem labs, the drumming and dancing, marches for peace, booths for the Earth, the Vietnam War protests with the sounds of glass breaking as policeman marched like armored cockroaches across the campus in riot gear, rock concerts, symphonies, sunsets.

I watched the ranks of endless waves come in and curl and crash against the rocks in a frenzy of force and change with the sand sucking away beneath my feet in the cold and wet and foam and sparkle of it all.

Perhaps I broke through, if only for a moment. With the storm tide of old age in sight, I again sensed a driving rhythm.

Some thought Ricketts's death might have been a suicide because the daily train was, predictably, right on time and Ricketts was, if anything, a great discerner of patterns.

He was rarely appreciated as a scientist during his lifetime. The original publication of *Between Pacific Tides* was delayed by Stanford University for nine years due to the eccentricity of his science for its time. In 1947 he was also the first to try to explain the cause of the sardine population crash, the change that turned Monterey into the diminished town of polluted beaches I saw in the 1970s. He turned his thoughts back to the notion of driving environmental factors and again proved himself to be ahead of the scientific thinking of his time by entertaining the possibility that water temperature patterns might affect fish growth and survival. He analyzed several decades of temperature data and documented that periods with lower sardine harvests correlated with warmer years. A few scientists agreed with his analysis in 1955, but it was too late for the California sardine fishery. It ended, not to resume for forty years. The fishery managers had ignored his caution against fishing hard as the population graph was falling during the warm years of the 1950s. They clung to a belief that the sardines had moved somewhere else in the Pacific Ocean.

Ricketts wrote an epitaph for the sardines in answer to a reporter who asked him "Where are the sardines?"

"They're in the cans!" he replied. "The parents of the sardines we need so badly now were being ground up then into fish meal, were extracted for oil, were being canned; too many of them, far too many."

Sardines eventually rebounded and the fishery reopened. Ironically, sardines became so scarce off the coast of California during the warm winter of the Blob that the fishery was shut down again. Some scientists now hail Ricketts as a prophet who got it right the first time.

As the California that's as tangible as a tide pool dries out and burns in the warm years and is drowned during the wet years, the California-esque myth of something total and whole and invisible remains, hovering just beyond our fingertips. Ecology, that science of connections and relationships that Ricketts described in the tide pools, is the remembering of something ancient. Every living thing is no thing at all but a node of energy in motion. Sunlight and minerals swoosh through water into whirling protoplasm and floating seaweeds, connecting, transforming. Mineral to plant, plant to flesh, flesh to flesh, flesh to rot, and mold to mineral. Reincarnation is just a fact. In perpetual motion, the intertidal zone is never a stable place.

Still, standing hip deep in the Pacific Ocean one day on a California beach, the taciturn Mr. Baxter showed me a perfectly round white circle of a bryozoan colony at the base of a frond of a forest of kelp. The sun-shot intricacy of life, awash and cycling in the exuberance and excess of energy transforming, shimmered.

Tangles

Trips across the bay were different after Oscar disappeared.

I knew I shouldn't have named the wildlife; disdainful Fish and Game guys drummed that into me when I followed moose around. Fraternizing with individual moose, particularly cows and calves, was too much like crying over a deer named Bambi and her dying mother. The collective horde of a population was the thing, swelling like any crop after it reproduced and shrinking back down after being harvested.

But Oscar just looked like an Oscar, his squashed sea otter face bristling with muttonchop whiskers, white with age. He was a solitary but constant inhabitant of the small bight off Peterson Bay, right below the field station. An old male, he was past his days of chasing females and biting their noses in the throes of passion. He seemed to have this territory to himself. No other males appeared to challenge him, and females with pups spent their time in other parts of the bay.

Every day as the tide rose, he would swim in at a leisurely pace and flip over on his back to float like a brown, furry log, raising his back paws like flippers in the air to cool himself off. During the spring, he was impervious to the chaos of school groups visiting the station, the quasi-military drill of thirty kids coming and going on a fifty-five-foot boat that tied up to a thirty-foot dock. It involved a lot of yelling about where to stack gear and where to stand. He stayed close, like he knew it was his job to show up and be part of field trip memories.

During summer, he was in place most late afternoons when kayak groups rounded the point in the last half hour of their tour. The guides put on a show—circling the kayaks and cautioning their clients to approach quietly so as not to scare him as he craned his short neck to regard their slow approach. He never startled, but on a timetable known only to him, he would do his otter roll or somersault over and over before diving deep and popping up well away from the kayaks. The crowd went wild.

I would sit on the stairs leading to the beach, hidden from the field station, as the high tide lapped to within feet of the first landing. As Oscar floated by, marbled murrelets would come in to dive for sand lance around the dock. Pigeon guillemots would make swooping flights from their nesting ledge on the shore. Some days the kingfisher that nested farther down the beach would emerge from a hole in the cliff, chattering, to perch on a spruce branch. Occasionally, it would make a sudden fluttering plunge into the water after a fish. But often it was just Oscar and me.

The absence of the solitary old otter didn't sink in until I'd made several trips to the field station one spring without seeing him. My sightings of Oscar—and our sharing of space in that bight— had been part of what was right with my world. His presence was reliable, like my first annual sighting of whirling shorebirds each spring, returning north after their perilous travels from bustling California beaches, or the first murres who swarmed yet again around Gull Island and stayed to raise their chicks, or the orderly procession of purple-striped faces of violets followed by pink urns of blueberry flowers and reddish-green shoots and flowered spikes of fireweed that eventually burst into cotton. When Oscar disappeared, he left something behind like a wake in the water and the air that lingered as an otter-shaped hole in the world.

Now when I go sit out on the stairs, I miss Oscar, which is perhaps a peculiarly human thing. Oscar didn't even acknowledge my existence; I was part of the background that moved once in a while. Since I didn't scare him or threaten him, he slept and rocked on the waves. He's part of my shifting baseline—one of my favorite places with Oscar and the same place without. It's part of being human to be able to think in terms of shifting baselines. I can look back and feel what is missing now in comparison to what existed in the past. I can wax nostalgic in a way that no other species can.

But can the way I think about one otter's death help me understand the relationship of the Sugpiat to sea otters? The relationship of hunter to hunted in Kachemak Bay began thousands of years ago when people first threw otter bones into their middens. When I began to move in a widening circle around the bidarki story, I saw that there were holes in it, ones left by otters and others by people that had both vanished and returned.

The presence of otters around bidarki harvesting sites weaves them into the changing food web. They tie the bidarki story into a nice tight bow of scientific logic and significance and wrap the villagers up as well in a cultural logic that points the way to harvesting more otters. This, however, places them on a collision course with another point of view that sea otters are too recently endangered and too cute to kill. What do I think is the right thing to do? I'm in an otter dilemma—well, really, a human dilemma. If otters and the Sugpiat have been racing each other down the food chain and facing off over bidarkis on the beaches of Port Graham and Nanwalek, the obvious solution, for the Sugpiat, is to eliminate their competition. And yet, even to put the word *kill* in front of *sea otters* gives me a twinge in the Oscar part of my heart.

When I arrived in Alaska in 1974, wolves were the predators that it seemed rational to control, according to my professors in the Department of Wildlife Management. Coming from California after celebrating the first Earth Day, I had my doubts, but I kept them to myself. After all, wolves ate moose, my soon-to-be study animals.

As I switched my Stanford brain over from Jane Goodall's chimpanzees and Paul Ehrlich's butterflies to the principles of wildlife management, I soon realized that the concepts I was learning, like harvestable surpluses and compensatory mortality, were about humans killing as many animals as possible by assuming that a number of animals was destined to die by the cruel hand of winter or starvation anyway.

Lured by the wildness of Alaska, I had stumbled into a Goldilocks world, where there are usually too many or too few of the animals people want to kill and use. I learned all the statistical methods of getting it just right for moose. The wolf was our enemy in this, I learned, rapaciously eating moose and caribou that people wanted—and deserved—to have.

Right after graduate school I went to work at Fish and Game in Fairbanks, where everyone presumed to know what I must think about killing animals, particularly wolves. I was widely suspected of being a wolf lover, which was equivalent to the term used for liberals during the civil rights era. I was female. I'd come from California. I'd grown up in Montana, but in a city, not on a ranch. I watched birds. I'd worked for a greenie environmental group on the lock-up of federal lands from everyone who wanted access for hunting by any means possible. I knew what vegetarians ate. I was sure to be "soft" on predators—and anti-hunting and anti-trapping to boot.

One day I walked out the front door of the Fairbanks Fish and Game building to see several dead caribou laid out on the lawn in a neat, but bloody, row. They'd be measured for their body condition and have their organs decanted into sample jars. I looked into their blank faces and must have had what could be interpreted as a sympathetic expression on my face because suddenly Joe Want, the legendary big game hunting guide who worked for the department in winter, was staring me right in the face. Joe was famous for bringing a string of pack mules on his hunts. He wore hip boots year-round and stuffed the toes with straw when the temperatures dropped below zero.

"You wear leather shoes, don't you?" was the opening line of his diatribe, of the type that everyone in Fairbanks honed over each long winter on the subject of their choice. He delivered his—the gist of which was that cowardly hippie women like me who thought we were smart were too stupid to know that anything we ate required killing something—without pause.

I didn't really know what I thought then, wanting desperately to fit it with the guys and be a tough Alaska woman while continuing my yoga practice secretly in my log cabin. It was like the heady days of Vietnam War protests at college, where the thing to do during the spring when protests shut down the university was to play cat and mouse with riot police and listen to the sounds of glass being broken by students cursing loudly and throwing rocks.

But I never threw a rock then, and I never stuck up for wolves at Fish and Game. I stayed silent, churning away at it all, trying to see both sides, trying to be a team player. The rationality of the numbers game was hard to resist. I didn't really like thinking about moose being torn to pieces by a pack of wolves. But then I didn't like to think about a wolf being shot from an airplane or strafed from a helicopter either.

The history of humans and wolves in Alaska and the history of humans and otters are tangles, like the windrows of bull kelp on the beach. Balls of kelp strand themselves after being ripped away from their beds by the large swells following storms brewed up in the Gulf of Alaska gyre of wind and water. Huge knotted strands and streamers of fronds wash up on the beach. Rolling around in the surf, they entangle and glue together their own shell middens, stuffed with crab molts, mussel and clamshells, fragments of sea urchin, and a confetti of the other seaweeds on the beach. Sometimes there are bones. Now there are often the more permanent leavings of our human ways—pieces of lumber, boat parts, fine pellets of Styrofoam. The tangle of otters and humans has everything to do with kelp and human consumption.

"Otters eat urchins, and urchins eat kelp," I told children on the beach as the tide crept toward us, a classic example of the mysterious science of ecology. During the winter, I took the lessons I taught on the beach and turned them into written lesson plans and units that eventually lived on the Internet.

The otter-urchin-kelp mantra became the centerpiece of an ecology unit for fourth graders called The Case of the Missing Sea Otters. It begins as a mystery story about James Estes, a sea otter biologist who began studying sea otters in the Aleutian Islands in the 1970s. On a summer day in the early 1990s, he cruises around Shemya Island and is surprised to find very few otters where he expected to see large numbers. He alerts the authorities—in this case, the U.S. Fish and Wildlife Service—who marshal their mini air force to make a proper scientific count. No full survey of the Aleutian Islands had been made since 1965 when biologists counted ninety-seven hundred otters. When they counted around eight thousand in 1992, they weren't unduly alarmed, but when they flew again twenty years later, they found only about twenty-four hundred. The graph, in fact, had been pointing steeply downward. The translation into the estimated total population of fewer than nine thousand in 2002 was a 75 percent decline since 1965, one that was, in hindsight, apparently underway in 1992.

The science story is about what happened after sea otters were removed from the food web, at least what had happened in the waters around the Aleutians. It was like the experiment carried out by Bob Paine on sea stars. But where Paine's experiment was conducted on the scale of square-meter plots, the removal of sea otters that began in the late 1700s for their pelts in the fur trade took place on the scale of thousands of miles of coastline: from Hokkaido, Japan, to midway down Baja California. By the time the inadvertent experiment was completed, sea otters were absent from 99 percent of their former range. Some of the remaining

1 percent of occupied range was in the Aleutians, where small groups of several hundred otters survived, and their population slowly began to expand.

In the 1970s some islands had otters and some didn't, which gave Estes and other scientists their own experimental set-up to compare the ecosystems of haves and have-nots. Their research produced one of the loveliest data graphs in the history of ecology. I say lovely because it's among few in which the data is actually so clean and the trend so clear, without error bars or a spaghetti of trend lines required to connect the data points. A fourth grader can easily read the story the graph tells. Take away otters from an ecosystem and the number of sea urchins increase, so the graph of sea urchin density is a straight line upward. As these data points climb, the data points for the number of kelp beds go straight down to zero. With otters in the system, sea urchin densities remain low and the number of kelp beds remains stable.

The data, said James Estes and John Palmisano, revealed an Aleutian marine ecosystem existing in "alternate stable states." The presence or absence of sea otters, they concluded, was responsible for which state persisted.

In this story of sea otter ecology, the nearshore ecosystem with otters is a lush three-dimensional habitat, manic with life, from mussels to crabs to juvenile fish with inelegant names like lumpsuckers. In the absence of otters, it's a one-dimensional, monocultural desert of a place, swarmed by hordes of slow-moving pincushion urchins. The scientists themselves call the first state a *forest* and the other a *barrens*, not particularly precise scientific terms. The urchins, of course, prefer the barrens, where they gnaw on the base of towering kelps until they crash down like old-growth trees. If the rampaging otters return, the urchins are reduced to hiding out in rocky crevices.

This study and its simple storyline made sea otters another ecological rock star, with the keystone status of sea stars in Paine's studies. Estes thought the story had a moral as well. Since a forest is better than a barrens, the health of ecosystem, he would say, depends on the presence of sea otters.

Before humans arrived on the scene, sea otters had their own lineage and a baseline of a million-year history of foraging on prey animals that coevolved to survive their predation. The kelps in the North Pacific Ocean also coevolved with their urchin predators, but they seem to have coexisted with sea otters' hearty appetites for just as long. With otters to hold the urchins and other grazers in check, the kelps never evolved an abundance of toxins to defend themselves from hordes of hungry grazers, which make them relatively defenseless when otters are removed from the system. Normally, red sea urchins stay on the floor of the kelp forest, feeding on bits of kelp that drift down to them. In the absence of otters, however, the growing mass of urchins eventually begins to starve. An order is given, in the chemical language of urchins, to join forces and march across the kelp bed in a wave, chewing up the bases of the kelps.

Urchins also evolved longevity, allowing them to grow very slowly. They can survive and reproduce for up to two hundred years, provided they escape being crushed in the strong teeth of otters.

When Ocean Bay people arrived in Kachemak Bay eight thousand years ago, they were already hunting otters, although not in the numbers they harvested seals. Ancient pictographs on rock walls tucked under cliffs in the bay depict sea otters, some of them pierced by lances. The Kachemak people harvested more otters early on, but in later years, they clearly preferred to hunt harbor seal and porpoise.

I can't imagine they didn't make use of otter furs, but otter meat is considered particularly unpalatable, according to every Alaska Native person I've asked. The otters' evolutionary trade-off for keeping warm in cold North Pacific waters made then much more attractive for their dense fur than their scant fat.

The only positive culinary review of otter meat in modern times came from the German naturalist Georg Steller, shipwrecked on Bering Island in 1741. Sea otters saved the crew from starvation; their meat was eaten half-raw daily. Steller declared the flesh of adult otters to be more tender and savory than that of seals, the female being best (pregnant ones fattest), and the flesh of the young otter most delicious, "like that of an unweaned lamb." Sven Waxell, an officer of the ship and a survivor of the shipwreck, described it differently in his journal: "Even if you can perhaps endure the smell of otter meat, it is extremely hard and as tough as sole-leather and full of sinews, so much that you have to swallow it in large lumps."

Archaeological evidence that aboriginal people ate otters, and didn't just skin them for their furs, comes from Sanak Island south of the Alaska Peninsula, where the zooarchaeologists found telltale cut marks on otter bones that indicate they had been butchered. They also saw a pattern over the course of the last two thousand years: an abundance of sea otter bones in middens alternating with an abundance of sea lion bones.

The cause of the pattern wasn't apparent until they looked at climate records for the same period. Both sea lion bones in the middens and people, as was evident in the size of their settlements, were more abundant during cold periods. Otter bones were more abundant in warm ones. The anthropologists also learned that the local Native word for cod meant "the fish that stopped," and the pattern fell into place. As cod populations dwindled during warm periods so did sea lions and the availability of sea lion skins to cover hunters' kayaks. Fewer kayaks meant fewer hunters who survived by eating otters they could harvest close to shore.

There's a long-standing debate among scientists about whether ancient people intentionally killed sea otters because they were so similar to humans in their eating habits. Charles "Si" Simenstad, a fish biologist who worked with sea otter biologists

James Estes and Karl Kenyon, tried to read Aleutian middens for clues. When the team of scientists found the same alternation between otter bones and red urchin remains in middens, they interpreted it as evidence that the otters had been killed because they preyed on the urchins and thus the hunters kept them in check around villages.

But another group of archaeologists and biologists headed up by Debra Corbett looked at the same pattern in the context of the Aleutian Island ecosystem. They saw how easily otters could be eliminated locally as people settled down and their numbers increased, and they saw how slowly otters recolonized a place. In the absence of otters, urchins would have flourished and provided a new abundant source of food. All the scientists agreed, however, that the pattern was one of otters and kelp beds being scarce only in small circles around villages during the thousands of years that people lived in the Aleutians. These small absences, the second group claimed, would have had no effect on the vast, stable system of the Aleutian Archipelago in which people, otters, urchins, and kelp beds coexisted.

The elimination of sea otters around settlements as the human population grew larger could also explain the smaller number of otter bones in Late Kachemak middens. The question about whether or not otters were killed intentionally as competitors or for the warmth and prestige of their fur, however, is one that can't be answered by reading the bones.

Anthropologists have also suggested that an absence of otter bones from middens may have been a result of disposal in the water, or away from the village. The cultural experts for the Alutiiq Museum say a traditional ritual was performed for otters after they were killed: they were brought to shore and skinned, and fresh water was poured over the mouth to quench the thirst of an animal that had lived in salt water. The bones, they say, were cast back into the sea or buried if the otter had been killed on land.

By the time of European contact, sea otter fur had clearly come to be considered a luxury in many Native cultures. On Kodiak the families of chiefs wore otter parkas and robes, not the commoner class that worked to procure and process salmon and marine fish nor the slaves that were taken in warfare. Otherwise, the cultural importance of sea otters is somewhat ambiguous. In the few surviving Native stories about sea otters, they seem to lack the spiritual power of many animals that humans also compete with for food, like wolves and bears. Perhaps it's because they're relatively small and lack anything fearsome, like slashing teeth and claws. There's a duality to their appearance—their front half more like the animals of the terrestrial weasel clan but with arms and handlike paws, while their rear half has legs like paddles on either side of a short, rudderlike tail.

For thousands of years, people made similar stylized carvings of sea otters to the one found near Halibut Cove. They're small, ivory amulets or charms, with the ribs and spine incised and the paws held up around the face, as if in surprise. They remind me of Oscar, my own amulet, for a time, against change and loss.

The Sugpiat tell a story that says the sea otter was originally a man who, while collecting chitons to eat, was trapped by an incoming tide. To save himself, he wished to become a sea otter. His desire transformed him, and he swam away as the first sea otter, creating all the others of his kind. It was widely believed that sea otters were transformed ancestors, imparting an eeriness to their killing. In these stories, sea otters, it seems, are too close to humans to be wholly other. When their fur has been removed, their skinned out body is thought to look uncomfortably humanlike. The relationship of people and sea otters is built on this strange closeness and ecology of human desire. Our desire tugs the web of relations strongly, but the sea otter also tugs on the food web with its own type of strength. The tugs can break the connecting strands.

The story told in the Aleutians by the Unangan people is more complex, as recounted by the Reverend Michael Oleksa, in the tradition of Russian Orthodox priests transforming oral tradition to writing. The story begins with an incestuous relationship. A brother visits his sister at night when she's secluded for her first menstrual period and rapes her. Although it's too dark for her to identify her attacker, she grabs a sharp rock and cuts him, severing the tendons in the backs of his knees as he escapes. The next morning, the girl's parents send word of a tragic accident that has befallen her brother, who bled to death after falling on rocks and cutting his tendons. Hearing this, the sister goes mad and dresses herself in all of the fine clothes and jewelry she planned to wear when emerging from seclusion to be presented to the community as a woman. She goes to the place where her parents and community members have laid out the corpse of the brother. Her desire for her parents and relatives to know what he did—the rule he broke—is so strong that she's able to bring him back to life. As soon as he revives, he begins to pursue her. She runs, he follows, and her entire family follows both of them. She reaches the brink of a cliff and, with nowhere to escape, jumps into the ocean. The brother follows. The parents lament, speaking of shame and disgrace their children have brought to the family.

Then the children reappear as the first sea otters. They move away from the land, one to the east and one to the west, for as Reverend Oleksa explains, "Even marine mammals do not mate with their own family members." But "because they both dove in wearing their most beautiful regalia—hers designed to celebrate life-giving powers and his to be worn in death—the sea otters sport the finest coats of the animals who swim in the sea."

Father Veniamov, Russian Orthodox priest to the Unangans in the early 1800s, observed in his journal that hunters went out in their finest clothes and adornments because they believed otters were attracted to human beauty and finery. They fastened their otter amulets to their kayaks as decorations to please the otters and their throwing sticks were carved in the form of an otter. Sea otters were also believed to abhor anything relating to human sexual relations. Women were never allowed to step over a hunter's kayak and it was the hunter who sewed the last kayak seam lest his luck seep out through one sewn by a woman.

Regardless of the relative importance of sea otters to diet, clothing, or mythology, the people who lived in the sea otter's realm from the Aleutian Islands to Prince William Sound developed an efficient technology to launch stone-point harpoons from the decks of their kayaks. This single aspect of their culture, at first contact with Russian fur traders, entangled their souls, just as it sealed the fate of sea otters.

Fur

As to the beauty of the animal, and particularly of its skin, this sea otter is alone incomparable, without a peer; it surpasses all other inhabitants of the vast ocean, and holds the first rank in point of beauty and softness of its fur. . . . The gloss of their hair surpasses the blackest velvet . . . . The Natives of Kamchatka and the Kurile Islands . . . straighten out the hairs with the bones of wings of gulls, and sleep upon them naked, to make them glossier, nicer, more beautiful.
    —Georg Steller, naturalist, 1751

Next to a beautiful woman and a lovely infant, a sea otter's skin is the finest natural object in the world.
    —William Sturgis, American fur trader, 1846

The first dark spill of sea otter fur drew me close. My friend Steve, who collects all manner of mammals for a living, offered it to me like a secret he kept in a huge flat drawer in the university museum. I stroked it, felt the deep nap of it, and saw the tone of it change from deep brown to a lighter bronze, its texture in windrows. The long guard hairs glinted silver. My fingers, and then my palm, sunk into it. In the center of that Fairbanks winter, I might have done anything for the caress of that fur on my flesh, to curl up under a robe of it and dream the winter away. If I had a coat of it to slip into every stone cold, dark morning, it would be my cocoon.

Steve explained that it was among the densest fur of any mammal—hundreds of thousands of hairs per square inch—but that explained nothing of its feel against my palm. Surrounded by its luxuriant beauty, I would never be cold again. As I watched him close the drawer and lock it, I felt like he had thrown ice water on my lust, leaving behind unrequited desire for the thing that would change all that might grow cold in my life.

> *We killed them on Bering Island with spears, and nets, and, when they were lying asleep or in the act of copulating, with clubs. . . . They were found there in so great abundance that from the beginning our numbers did not suffice to kill them. . . . Nevertheless, we killed upwards of 800 of them, and if the narrow limits of the craft we constructed had permitted we should have killed three times as many.*
> —Georg Steller, 1751

The entry of sea otter pelts from Alaska waters into the global fur market began in 1743 in Kamchatka, when Steller and the shipwrecked sailors from Vitus Bering's voyage of discovery to America finally reached home. The furs could be traded to China for a fortune at the fur-trading center of Kiakhta on the Russo-Chinese border. Winters were cold in northern China, and it turned out that sea otter fur was the perfect lining for jackets and robes, creating an insatiable demand.

A rush for "soft" gold began. The Russian fur traders, or *promyshlenniki*, island-hopped eastward to the Aleutian Islands. No one is sure how many sea otters there were before the fur trade began, but estimates range from one hundred thousand to three hundred thousand, spread out in a continuous band along six thousand miles of coastline.

By 1755 six thousand otter pelts had been taken from the Commander Islands, off Japan. By 1756 no otters were to be found there or around Bering Island. Between 1745 and 1762, eighteen thousand were taken from the Near Islands, the group farthest west of the Aleutian Islands, followed by sixty-five hundred from the Pribilofs. But it wasn't just sea otters that were removed from the ecosystem.

> As the little sable had enticed the Cossack from the Black Sea and the Volga across the Ural Mountains and the vast plains of Siberia to the shores of the Okhotsk Sea and the Pacific, so now the sea otter lures the same venturesome race out among the islands, and ice, and fog-banks of ocean. . . . The Ioann Oustioushki, owned by Ivan Popof, made two voyages between 1767 and 1770, returning the second time with 3,000 sea-otters, 1,663 black foxes, 230 cross foxes, 1,025 red foxes, and 1,162 blue foxes.
> —Hubert Bancroft, American historian

Several decades after the launch of the *promyshlenniki* eastward, the journals of Captain Cook's fateful third voyage were published in England in 1784. It had been six years since he had sailed up the inlet now named after him in search of the Northwest Passage and declared possession of Alaska by England. British fur traders learned about Nootka Sound, along the British Columbia coast, where Cook's crewmen had traded iron nails for sea otter furs and sold them for enough in Canton to buy their own ship.

Another rush began westward from England and eventually Spain and Boston. The two rushes converged in Cook Inlet in 1786, when Nathaniel Portlock and James Dixon, who had been crewmen on Cook's voyage, anchored their ships in Kachemak Bay. A group of Russians and Aleut sea otter hunters were already camped on the south shore. The Russians built an outpost there the same year, which they named Alexandrovsk (later the site of Nanwalek), not only the first Russian trading post on the mainland of Alaska but also on the North American continent. The British traded for a while in Prince William Sound and then retreated to Nootka Sound. For the next eighty years, Kachemak Bay was part of Russian America and the Dena'ina unwittingly became subjects of the tsar, as did the Unegkurmiut on the outer coast of the Kenai Peninsula.

The Dena'ina living in Kachemak Bay, the sea otters, and the ecosystem were swept into change—the transition from hunter-gatherer societies enmeshed in local ecologies to participation in a relentless, global industry focused on killing one single species desired by people a continent away. I can't really see it as malice toward sea otters, or even toward the Dena'ina. Both were merely the means to the end of fortunes to be made in distant markets. At first the Dena'ina resisted the Russians; they banded together with the Alutiit to attack and destroy a Russian outpost on Shuyak Island in 1785 and later attacked and burned others in Iliamna, Tyonek, and Kenai. Eventually, however, Native men of all ages living in Cook Inlet and along the outer coast of the Kenai Peninsula left their families behind and joined the armadas of hundreds of kayaks that gathered each year to hunt sea otters from spring to fall.

On Kodiak Island their participation wasn't voluntary, and in both areas, otter pelts were compensated only by scant trade goods. Gedeon, a Russian Orthodox monk, described the early system on Kodiak: "A father is sent to hunt birds, the son to hunt sea otters . . . having taken from everyone all the bird skins, the men's wives, mothers, or sisters processed the skins and finished the parkas [which were then] issued to the men . . . against the sea otters they take." It became nearly impossible to get out of debt to the company that demanded labor.

> Besides beads, tobacco, and other European trifles, they are paid for their catch with parkas of birdskin, squirrel, and marmot. The trade is most profitable to the Company, because it costs almost nothing.
> — Yuri Lisianskii, Russian ship captain and explorer, 1814

I can't help but wonder how the Natives regarded sea otters after they became part of an industrial-scale killing machine. Many Native women married Russians, voluntarily or not, and were tasked with sewing kayak covers and bird skin parkas for little more than a package of steel needles. Everyone was forbidden to keep any otter skins for their own use. Perhaps the ambiguity in tales told now and in the oral histories about sea otters has to do with an animal that, through no fault of its own, brought so much suffering and loss.

Lisianskii's accounts depict the methodical nature of the sea otter hunt: a group of ten to fifteen hunters in kayaks moved forward until one hunter raised his paddle to signal he'd spotted an otter, the group of hunters formed a semicircle (about "100 sazhens" wide, Lisianskii recorded for posterity, the equivalent of sixty yards). The hunters flung their light harpoons from throwing boards or shot arrows from bows, aiming to strike the otter with the detachable tip of the harpoon or arrow.

Then there was the dive of a struck otter, the wait for it to come up, the new circle, again and again, the otter staying under a shorter duration each time until it finally tired itself out or lost strength from blood loss, the retrieval of the dead otter and determination of whose spear point was closest to the head.

A slow sea otter apparently weakened after five wounds, an agile one receiving up to ten. Sometimes twenty kayaks fought with a single sea otter for half a day. Lisianskii said there were some animals that pulled arrows out of themselves with their paws, but "for the most part after the lapse of several hours they become the hunter's prey."

Georg Steller was the first to complete scientific descriptions of both sea otters and the now-extinct Steller's sea cow while he was on Bering Island. He noted that when hunters "press" upon female otters with pups, "they seize their young with their mouths and never let go of them except when compelled by extreme necessity or death itself. And so they are

killed often when they might have got away themselves." Ever
the scientist, he experimented: "I have sometimes deprived
females of their young on purpose, sparing the mothers
themselves, and they would weep over their affliction just
like a human being."

The only account of the hunt I found that departed from
describing it mechanically or with a cold scientific regard was
one by Alphonse Pinart, an aristocratic French man who traveled
by kayak to collect Native masks. He remarked on the "heart-
rending cries" of a dying otter "that almost resemble the moans
of humans."

> When Shelikhov's party first visited Cook Inlet, they first
> secured three thousand, during the second year 2,000, in the
> third only 800, the season following, they obtained 600.
> —Henry Elliott, Report Upon the Condition of Affairs
> in the Territory of Alaska, 1875

The records from Alexandrovsk have been lost, but other Russian
accounts seem to point to a relatively short period of heavy exploitation of otters in Kachemak Bay and Cook Inlet by several different
fur trading companies vying for dominance. Gregorii Shelikhov,
who brutally established the Russian American Company (RAC)
headquarters in Kodiak in 1784, brought Aleut hunters to Cook
Inlet the next year where other companies were also operating
before the RAC became a monopoly. One report claims that 5,500
otter pelts came out of Cook Inlet in 1788 and 1789, in addition to
Shelikhov's 6,400. So at least 11,900 otters were killed in six years,
most of which likely came from the rich shallows of Kachemak
Bay and Kamishak Bay across Cook Inlet, nearly 1,000 more than
were estimated to live in the same areas in 2008.

In 1792 Alexander Baranof, manager of the RAC, wrote in
a letter that otters were already extinct around Kodiak, Cook
Inlet, and Prince William Sound. In 1794 hunters from the Kenai

Peninsula assembled with others from Kodiak and the Alaska Peninsula in Kenai to form a flotilla of five hundred bidarkas (a thousand hunters) to push on to new grounds around Yakutat in the territory of the warlike Tlingit. The following year, two thousand pelts were shipped from Yakutat.

By 1800 Baranof had moved his headquarters to Sitka, and the bulk of the sea otter pelts were shipped from there back to Russia. The Russians joined the British and Americans in the hunt for more sea otters by sending Aleut, Sugpiaq, and even Dena'ina hunters all the way down to California and, illegally, into Mexico off the Baja California coast.

Sea otter hunting didn't cease around Kodiak and Cook Inlet as the Russians moved Native hunters to new areas. Populations actually began to recover from the first rapid wave of Russian fur traders who forced the Unangan people, residents of the Aleutian Islands, and Sugpiat, and Dena'ina people to relocate eastward and southward down the West Coast. The "surround system" of hunting otters was probably fairly inefficient, since it required a group of hunters to kill a single otter. Along the stormy Gulf of Alaska coast, groups of kayaks were likely pinned down for days by wind, waves, and fog. Without any supplies from the Russians, the men had to hunt and fish for their own food.

The hardships of the hunt took an incredible toll; historian Lydia Black calculated that the number of able-bodied Native men on Kodiak who died in seven years from a combination of drowning, being killed or captured in warfare by the Tlingit in Southeast Alaska who were their enemies, illness, or being poisoned by toxic shellfish totaled 10 percent of the whole population on Kodiak Island and one-third of the adult men. "The social dislocation," Black wrote, "can hardly be imagined."

With all the forced movements of Alaska Natives, parts of the Aleutian Islands were nearly depopulated of people as well as otters, and the human population on Kodiak Island was greatly reduced. Less is known about how well the Dena'ina in Kachemak

Bay or Natives on the outer coast of the Kenai Peninsula fared, but compared to the indentured Koniag on Kodiak they retained some independence—the Dena'ina, by their ability to fade back into the forest and by uniting, at times, to fight back, and the Unegkurmiut by the ruggedness of their coastal homeland. In 1812 fewer than a hundred pelts were shipped from Cook Inlet, and after that it dwindled to a tenth of that.

Cal Lensink, a biologist who spent his career studying sea otters and birds for the U.S. Fish and Wildlife Service, was the only scientist to try to figure out exactly how many otters had been killed during the fur trade. He pored over trading companies' shipping records, including those for nearly one hundred Russian voyages between 1742 and 1867, the year Alaska became an American territory. He calculated a total of 264,800 pelts returning to Kamchatka during the 125 years of Russian colonization, but he also saw patterns in the harvest. The Russian harvests slowed after 1825 as both otters and Native hunters became scarce.

In 1850 human desires shifted. Trade with China, where sea otter fur had been the most prized, collapsed after the country opened its ports to trade in opium. The Russians switched their efforts to whaling, and the American and British traders began sending pelts to Europe and New York for shipment to London, where they were often purchased by Russian noblemen, who favored sea otter collars for their overcoats.

Another part of the pattern that Lensink's numbers revealed was at odds with the picture of rapacious Russians slaughtering sea otters that American historians, like Hubert Bancroft, painted. The numbers of pelts shipped show the effect of conservation measures that the Russian government imposed beginning in the 1830s. They may have been aware of the problem of depletion; they certainly wanted to keep the flow of pelts coming. They divided the Russian colony into districts, imposed quotas and a rotation system that opened districts for a number of years then closed them for an equal number like fields allowed to go fallow and regenerate.

British, American, Spanish, and French traders also took their share of pelts in Southeast Alaska where the Russian American Company didn't have a monopoly. Lensink calculated the total number of otters taken and shipped by 1867 by all traders to be more than 360,000.

But there were still otters to be hunted when the United States purchased Alaska.

When the Territory came into our possession, the Russians were taking from four to five hundred otters from the Aleutian Islands and south of the Alaskan Peninsula and perhaps 250 from the Kenai, Yakutat, and the Sitkan District [each year].
—Henry Wood Elliott, 1875

Territorial rule was the final disaster for the remaining sea otters. Killing otters in territorial waters within three miles of the shore was prohibited in 1868 but soon reopened by regulation, and neither the closure nor the regulations were enforced. The Russian American Company sold its trading posts to the U.S. government–supported American Commercial Company, still known today as "the AC" in Alaska villages where it's often the only store in town. The AC had a more efficient system for killing otters than the Russian company men, who sat in the third hole of a kayak as foremen while Native men hunted. AC traders purchased large schooners and loaded the Natives and their kayaks onboard to move them around to the remaining pockets of otters.

In the 1880s the Americans started trading rifles to the Aleuts, something the Russians had avoided, along with the trade in alcohol, which meant that rifles became the weapon of choice to kill otters everywhere in their range. The U.S. government eventually restricted hunting to Natives and the husbands of Native women, which spurred more intermarriage by men who had come to Alaska as gold seekers and cod fishermen. As the gene pool of the sea otters narrowed, Native gene pools became more of a swirl. Even as numbers dwindled in Cook Inlet, the hunt continued.

> [In Alexandrovsk] seven skins of sea otter recently killed were stretched on drying frames. The sea-otter are said to feed largely on chitons and clams. The abundance of fine clams near Alexandrovsk makes it a good otter-ground. From Alexandrovsk due northward is a settlement called Seldovia, consisting of sixty-eight Kodiak natives and Creoles, who are devoted to sea otter hunting. . . . On the opposite site . . . near Anchor Point, is the settlement of Laida, with seventy-eight Kenai people, who are also sea-otter hunters, but with indifferent success.
> —Tarleton Bean, Report to the U.S. Fisheries Commission, 1880

When Adrian Jacobsen visited Kachemak Bay in 1881 and found Soonroodna, the mysterious archaeological site that has never been found again, he recorded in his journal that "the entire population of Fort Alexander [the former Alexandrovsk] was occupied with sea otter hunting."

Because of the Russian quotas, only twelve thousand pelts were shipped during the last ten years of the Russian colony. The Americans and the British ramped up hunting in the few areas where otters could still be found—along the Aleutians, the Alaska Peninsula, Kodiak, and west on the Kuril Islands off Japan—and began shipping five thousand pelts every year. In the first four years of the Alaska Territory, the Americans traded more than the Russians had in the last ten years of their colonization. In the forty years after Alaska became a territory, Lensink calculated, Americans traded more than 107,000 pelts, to add to the 360,000 traded earlier by the Russians.

The U.S. government made back its $7.2 million purchase price of Alaska on sea otter pelts alone. Prices became higher as the otters became more scarce. By 1900 a pelt could go for as much as $2,300, although $300 was the portion that went to the Native hunter. The British, French, and Spanish also continued to trade in sea otter pelts. When Lensink added up all the pelts he could account for from Russian, British, American, and Spanish traders, the total was more than seven hundred thousand, but considering shipwrecks and gaps in the reporting, he thought it could have been even higher—more than nine hundred thousand. The Russian fur trade accounted for only about half.

It seems important to me, somehow, that it was *us*, the Americans, not *them*, the Russians, who we can blame for the near demise of sea otters. The Russians are our recurring enemies, after all, almost like wolves—if not over the killing of otters, then over the killing of their own people in a various cruel ways or threatening to kill us through mutually assured destruction by nuclear weapons. But it was *us* and our civilized European allies who almost did in the otters before the next generation brought them back from the brink.

It wasn't even the sheer numbers harvested that reduced the otter population to between two and five hundred animals (less than 1 percent of their original population) in thirteen scattered, inaccessible pockets of shoreline. Scientists looking at the slaughter from a wildlife management perspective calculated that the population might have withstood the rate of killing, spread as it was over 170 years. But that required thinking that the global desire for luxury fur that sent traders six thousand miles into new territory and enslaved and ended in the death of thousands of indigenous people was a rational pursuit. It was the pattern of the hunt—if it can be called that—the relentless killing of otters until they were all gone in one area and then moving on, that caused a serial depletion similar to that of the different marine invertebrates on the reefs near Port Graham and Nanwalek in recent times. But this one took place serially both in space and in time. The pattern of the harvest reduced what had been an ocean of otters to just a few small and isolated pools.

In 1898 only six sea otter furs were recorded in the Seldovia trading post. In 1899, zero. One lone otter was sighted in 1900. It was immediately surrounded by eight baidarkas, but it somehow escaped a killing blow. The species was not extinct in Kachemak Bay. The correct term is extirpated, that murmuring word for their loss from one particular area of the planet.

No sea otter was seen in Kachemak Bay for sixty years.

RETURNING

The sea otter has practically disappeared. . . . It has disappeared like the buffalo and other animals. . . . [But] civilization went on before the advent of the fur seal; it will go on if it should turn out, and we would be sorry if it so happened, that the fur seal should cease to exist.
  —Sir Charles Russell, testifying on behalf of England at an arbitration over the fur seal treaty, 1895

In 1911 the killing and commercial trade in sea otter pelts was finally banned by the International Fur Seal Treaty signed by the United States, Russia, Britain (for Canada), and Japan. The treaty's focus on fur seals reflected the general opinion voiced by Sir Charles Russell that sea otters had nearly vanished. Others thought they had been added to the treaty as more of an after-thought or obituary. But a few small groups remained scattered over their vast former territory, including two within a few hundred miles of Kachemak Bay.

Otters reproduce quickly—each female can usually raise a pup every year—and have few predators other than humans. With only the occasional attack on a pup by a killer whale or a bald eagle snatching a pup to feed its own young in the nest, most pups survive, and otters live as long as twenty years. But sea otters are locals, not long-distance migrants like the great whales. They occupy territories along a few miles of beach. Because of their need to feed nearly constantly to stay warm, they would starve trying to move great distances over deep water. All of these factors combined meant that although otter populations expanded rapidly after the fur trade ceased, they took decades to reach Kachemak Bay.

The Sugpiaq Elders in Port Graham and Nanwalek say they caught sight of solitary otters off their villages in the early 1960s. In 1973 the Alaska Department of Fish and Game recorded a sighting of a mother and pup, one year before the report on Kachemak Bay resources came out with its treasure map showing a bay with an abundance of crab, shrimp, and clams, which were typical prey of otters.

Sea otters returning to Kachemak Bay entered an entirely different ecosystem than the one where the last otter had been killed in 1900. As far back as the Sugpiaq Elders who are in their seventies and eighties now can remember about their childhood, the reefs and beaches near the villages were rich, in the ways that beaches are rich when otters are absent. As Sugpiaq Elder Nick Tanape Sr. put it: "Years ago, people didn't only go for bidarkis, everything was available. Why would they want to just hit the bidarkis? They had crab, mussels, and urchins."

In the absence of otters, the ecosystem had shape-shifted to one dominated by another predator gathering hundreds of pounds of shellfish from its beaches and harvesting millions of pounds of shrimp and crab every year.

But even in their absence, the remembered abundance and diversity didn't last. The bidarki story was not only about urchins, although green sea urchins were the first to go missing in the late 1960s. It was also about the disappearance of gumboot chitons, crab, shrimp, clams, and cockles, in that order. Sea otters were only one part of a story shaped by the desires of people hundreds and thousands of miles away, particularly those with a taste for shrimp and crab, and an ecosystem prone to temperature shifts and regime changes. Then, in 1989, that massive amount of oil spilled and spread across the region.

Despite all of the changes in the ecology of the bay, if the treasure map drawn in the early 1970s is compared with the resource map that could be drawn today, the location of kelp beds stand out as a feature that hasn't changed in the way the pattern in the Aleutian Islands might have predicted. In 1975 scientists described a seaweed zone in the bay that extended from the highest reach of the tide to about ninety feet deep, but their map of major kelp beds shows them in some of the exact same places they are found today. If anything, there are fewer kelp beds now, even with otters. Their persistence seems to have more to do with light levels through glacial water, salinity, and currents that reseed the annual plants. In terms of grazers, kelps in Kachemak Bay are more likely to be beset by swarms of snails than pods of urchins. One of the largest kelp beds in the bay—one that extended for one mile along Homer Spit—disappeared a few years ago when it was smothered by a bed of sand. In short, the distribution and abundance of kelp beds in the bay doesn't depend entirely on the presence of otters as the research in the Aleutians predicted. Another indicator is required to define the health of the ecosystem.

In 2008 scientists surveyed the bay and estimated a population of thirty-six hundred sea otters. They calculated their rate of increase over the previous six years to be 26 percent each year; in other words doubling in four years. Because this rate was biologically impossible in terms of births, it meant that new otters were still arriving from the south, filling up otter-shaped holes and munching their way into the food web one urchin and bidarki at a time.

The explosion of otter numbers between 2002 and 2008 was a solid indicator of the bay's diversity and abundance that attracted otters from other areas, in addition to those that were born here. The bottom of the bay that supports such a high density of otters is a smorgasbord of marine invertebrates—mussels, small crabs, clams, urchins, snails, and the occasional octopus—that live in and on a shifting patchwork of rocks, sand, and mud. Scientists who have studied other areas along the Alaska coast that also have "soft bottom habitats" intermixed with rocky bottoms have described the otters' regional cuisines as dependent on what's available, with an initial preference for urchins or sea cucumbers, followed by clams and eventually broadening out to more than a hundred types of prey when their favorite food begins to run out. They are efficient foragers, choosing the largest and the ones with the highest concentrations of calories as well as the most accessible animals first.

By 2012, the population had grown to six thousand. Signs that the otter numbers were approaching a limit began to increase. They appeared to subsist on prey that were less nutritious or that took more energy to find and consume. The large numbers that died during the winters of the Blob were another indication of the otters' vulnerability to sudden changes in the environment.

In 2010, on my first springtime visit of the year to the beach in China Poot Bay and just upstream from the ancient house site, I had an inkling of how it might feel to the Sugpiat to see their shellfish disappear to otters. Where there had been a dense carpet of urchins and sea cucumbers, there was only an empty stretch of beach. It had been one of my favorite spots for school groups and tours, an example of life so abundant and jam-packed that everyone had to walk carefully. Under every rock, brittle stars and six-rayed stars humped up to brood their eggs during spring, and I knew under which rock I might find an octopus den. While scientists would have called it an urchin barrens that had developed during the long absence of otter predation, it seemed considerably more barren to me after the otters had cleaned out the patch. While otters had returned to the beaches around Port Graham and Nanwalek sixty years after being extirpated, it had taken them fifty more years to find my particularly favorite beach midway up the bay. Then it took them only one season to eliminate the diversity in the intertidal community that had thrived there.

Sea otters are protected now in a different way than they were in 1911 when the international ban on otter hunting allowed

Alaska Natives to continue hunting them, as they had for thousands of years, provided they did so with rather ill-defined "aboriginal means." The 1972 Marine Mammal Protection Act placed a moratorium on killing all marine mammals, including sea otters. But it continued an exemption for Alaska Natives. It's a rather schizophrenic conservation law. Natives are allowed to take as many otters as they want up to the brink of extinction; the government can't impose bag limits or seasons or regulate the hunt in any way.

But there's a major catch: the animals can't be wasted, which means, for otters, the furs must be used. Everyone seems to agree that no one should be required to eat otter meat. But Natives can only sell the furs to non-Natives by producing "traditional handicrafts." These last two words have spawned endless legal challenges and controversy, especially as applied to otter furs, which Alaska Natives were not allowed to keep for themselves during the several hundred years of the fur trade. Consequently, the transmission of skin-sewing skills nearly ceased. The law positions Alaska Natives as the only people who can legally extirpate otters because they're a predator—one that feeds on the shellfish they've come to depend upon.

The Sugpiat aren't clamoring loudly for predator control of otters, which they could accomplish by harvesting more of them as long as they use the skins in some way. But in Southeast Alaska, where otters were transplanted to speed the recovery of the species, Alaska Natives became inadvertent political allies with commercial fishermen who developed markets for sea cucumbers, sea urchins, and crab, which are now being overtaken by expanding populations of otters.

I shouldn't have been surprised, I guess, in 2013 when a legislator from Southeast Alaska introduced a bill in the state legislature to create a $100 bounty on otters. Bounties are an Alaskan tradition, from those paid for eagle feet and seal noses during territorial days and on wolves in Southeast Alaska until the 1970s. Then governor Sarah Palin briefly revived the tradition in 2007, allowing the Department of Fish and Game to pay what she called a $150 "incentive" to hunters and trappers who turned in the left front leg of wolves. A judge quickly ruled it a bounty and halted the program. The move in 2013 was entirely political. A bounty on marine mammal parts would have been illegal under federal law, but that's never stopped an Alaskan legislator before. One fisherman shared his point of view with the *Anchorage Daily News*: "What strikes me funny: I'm fishing crab right now, and if a crab stock gets low or something, . . . any fishery, they shut us off or close us down to protect a crab or a fish. Yet when a sea otter comes in and absolutely decimates an area, they don't do anything about it. . . . They just say, 'Oh, they're warm and fuzzy and cute.' Well, I'm pretty warm and fuzzy and cute, too, but I don't totally wipe anything out."

Sea otters seem always to be described as "voracious" these days. Six thousand otters require tons of seafood to survive for a year in the bay. But so do a variety of other predators, like the arrowtooth flounder, the top predator in the Gulf of Alaska ecosystem, which dines on the bottom of the ocean out of sight. The eventual fate of sea otters has as much to do with what they eat—the same species we desire to harvest at the rate of maximum sustained yield—as the way they do it, which is just offshore, in plain sight. Otters can't really share, and we don't seem to want to. There's more than a hint of the too-close relationship that Native tales hint at for humans and otters. Otters seem to be a mirror we don't much like looking into.

The day I made my mind up about wolves was a hot sunny day in June at the Fairbanks Fish and Game office, where beer drinking on Friday afternoons was a tradition. We partied with the wolves that day. Following a crackdown from "those bureaucrats in Juneau," we could no longer lock the doors to the public and begin drinking at noon, so the keg had been stashed in the shed where Joe Want skinned out the dead wolves the biologists had shot after spotting them from airplanes. No one seemed to mind their inside-out skins and dead bodies hanging meat-locker style as the décor for our clandestine gathering. The low temperature in the skinning shed kept the beer cold and the smell down.

I drank with the boys. I smiled and laughed appropriately at alpha-male tales about killing the largest moose, fighting and landing the biggest grayling, and clashing their large antlers and wits against their pitiful political bosses. But I concealed a growing unease. I felt like the only person at a wake who noticed the dead bodies and the lack of even off-key mourning. I knew that killing those wolves had been perfectly legal and encouraged by the Board of Game and the State of Alaska for whom we worked. I knew the bodies of the wolves had yielded scientific data. I knew the furs would be sold at auction and the money plowed back into wildlife management. This was our business. I didn't hate wolves as a predator on *my* moose. I didn't love them either, in the New Agey, quasi-mystical way that my fellow environmentalists and I were always accused of. But the dead wolves were a presence I couldn't ignore. They exuded energy I could feel. Something of their wolfness was still present. In their deaths as in their lives, they were due respect missing from the desire that had brought them to their demise and to that uncaring place.

I didn't leave the party except in spirit, as I watched the goings-on as if from afar and heard what was being said as if it was being spoken in a foreign language. The wolves spoke to me in the only language I understood.

I didn't come to Alaska as a hunter, and I never became one. But after my first winter of observing moose for science, I was hooked on hunting for wild animals just to catch a glimpse of their lives. I spent enormous amounts of time and energy, to say nothing of dollars spent on gear, to pursue them. In terms of optimal foraging expected of predators, I was a dud. I invested large amounts of energy where the pay-off was not a single calorie. The long-term relationships I began then with moose and birds and bears didn't fit into boxes and arrows like the one used to track the flows of energy and the who-eats-whom of food chains and food webs. They had nothing to do with the hunger that would put bones and shells into garbage piles for the zooarchaeologists of the future to sort out. Yet I eagerly sought out ways to entangle my life with those of wild animals.

We are entangled with wild animals by our many uses of them, some of them not even tangible. It's a greater ecology constructed by human desires that have always coexisted with our need to fill our bellies. In the greater ecology of desire, the earliest people to live in Kachemak Bay killed not only for food but for clothing and shelter, to make tools, to have something to trade, to make art. The greater ecology also involves luxury and prestige, trade and wealth. Today, we also kill animals for science, money, and our desire for what money can buy. Our world feels like one in which "it might be true," as the writer Jonathan Franzen grimly contemplated, "that nothing can stop the logic of human priority." Killing the competition is just one part of the greater ecology.

In the ecology of my desire, wild creatures feed me with beauty and wildness. Moose bed down in my yard and become my winter neighbors, whales surface just where my eye is placed, and otters rock in the same quiet pool of water as my kayak. Every boat trip across Kachemak Bay feeds my desire to see puffins and whales. Cormorants fly past, their long legs and necks like the strokes of hieroglyphics in an ancient language I can almost read.

Otters remain wild to me—other, and yet so entangled with everything good and bad about our history in this place. A pure, canny instinct for return to their territory lies behind that cute baby face and beady eyes. But so is the culture of the Sugpiat due respect, as they continue to eat what lies at their feet and sustain their hunter-gatherer way of life. Their culture is the one closer to extinction, and if the people lose their connection to the sea and the land, some essence of the place will fade away. I trust them not to take too many and be content with what is left. The restored ocean of otters can withstand a few pools of absence around the villages.

I think of myself as a conservationist, and even an un-repentant greenie, yet I'm scornful of the endless gloom and pessimistic self-righteousness that we're often aptly accused of promoting. There's a part of me that cringes when I think my aim in reconstructing baselines may be to make the degradation of the environment more real as I bask in the sepia tones of times past. Seeing the loss, if only in my mind, of a Kachemak Bay that might have had billions of shrimp and millions of crab doesn't make me any happier. The perception of shifting baselines is as much about terrible knowledge as it is about a soothing ignorance.

The bidarki story and the story of my place leave me with a mixture of longings. I miss Oscar. I miss the sea stars recently hit by a disease aptly named sea star wasting disease. I miss the sandy beaches in China Poot Bay with clams that squirted in the rhythm of a symphony. I miss the reef I've never seen, the one the Sugpiaq Elders describe, with its abundance of sea urchins, sea cucumbers, and bidarkis. I miss the Kenai wolf, that great carnivore that stood shoulder-high to a lion and roamed the Kenai Peninsula until 1915, and the giant Kenai moose, whose antlers are all gone to walls and dusty attics. And even though I can never really know the spiritual depths of Sugpiaq culture in relation to the sea otter and the furthest extent of what they may have conceived as the living, constantly regenerating world, I would miss communities of people who care fiercely about sustaining both their place and their traditions.

I try to step back to see the larger ecology of culture and nature intertwined. Out of the corner of my eye, I see something coming: the shallow waters around Alaska becoming more acidic and threatening bidarkis, clams, and everything else that sea otters eat, with dissolution. I see the reports of the diseases favored by warmer waters that weaken otters and make them susceptible to infections, or to blooms of toxic algae, like those that accompanied the Blob. I witness the federal government planning to offer a gigantic swath of Cook Inlet west and north of Kachemak Bay for oil and gas leasing. These are changes that sea otters can't see approaching, like everything else in their history—the circling kayaks, the Russians traders and American bureaucrats, the skiff bearing down on them as they paddle backward, spilled oil floating in with the tide.

The strands of kelp draw tighter as we are all rolled in and out with the tides. It's hard to find the place I can plant myself and hold fast.

Humans have always had better powers of prediction than the other animals, and we have better powers now than the Kachemak, the Dena'ina, and the Russian and American fur traders.

Yet I'm beginning to believe we will collectively ignore the changes in the atmosphere and the ocean until we are again at the brink of unsustainable losses and holes in our ecosystems that will never be filled in the time of our species on the planet.

One of my friends who lived his dream of becoming a commercial fishing captain said it true one day. "Someone has to be the one to catch the last fish," he told me as I lamented about yet another environmental issue over beers. "It might as well as be me."

A year later, he went down with his boat.

EPILOGUE

We were a motley crew assembled on the beach in Peterson Bay across from the field station. It's the one we call Outside Beach, steep gravel turned over and over again by the winds and waves. At the top was a flat, clean-washed strand of shells and rocks and wood. We had assembled a shrine, each of us carrying something we'd found as we'd walked from the field station to the beach for the ceremony. I brought a slick dark case with the whimsical name of a "mermaid's purse" that had carried the eggs of a shark. Its chocolate-colored tissue covering made it look as if it was dressed up for the wedding. I piled it with the rest of the treasures in a heap within a circle of flat, gray stones.

The bride's mother wore a wool cape over a crepe skirt; the groom's mother wore plum-colored slacks and tunic, set off by a silk scarf in swirls of lavender and silver. The bride's stepfather wore fleece, as did half the people around me. Women dressed in layers ranging from crocheted dresses to spangled tops to crazy-striped tights to camo. Knee-high rubber boots were de rigueur, although the bride and bridesmaids wore leather.

It was mid-September, the first partly cloudy day in weeks of rain, and we weren't taking any chances, our rain gear draped over our shoulders. Rubber boots in conservative black stood next to shiny Xtratufs—reddish, pink, and polka-dotted. There were down jackets over beaded tops, full-length London Fog raincoats over silk, and in honor of Texas, the groom's home state, a cowboy hat.

A long solid rock, aptly named Otter Rock, stretched out into the water in front of where we stood. If you squinted and the tide was right, you could see its resemblance to an otter lying flat on its back with paws stretched upward above a head and long, flat tail. The bride, who was as close to being a mermaid in spirit as anyone I've ever known, emerged from the tall beach grass in a long confection of white panels and lace on the arm of her father. He had rowed her across a small slough to honor a Scandinavian tradition of fathers and daughters and coastlines. Her blonde hair was plaited in neat side braids and done up in a twist that draped a loop held in place by a lone burgundy daisy. The groom, in an uncommon suit and tie, wiped away tears when the pastor said, "Dearly Beloved."

The Episcopal pastor, a Texan himself, performed the ceremony, with entirely too many references to Jesus Christ for my distant Jewish upbringing. But I wished the bride and groom so well that I doubted it mattered that I was a nonbeliever or that my amens were not entirely heartfelt. They met on this beach, the bride then a naturalist, the groom on vacation with his father. The bride taught me what it meant to mentor someone from intern to professional. As I stood beside her mother, I empathized with my own motherly pangs of launching her into the big, bad world and letting go.

As they joined their lives and ways of survival together in a place that meant something special to both of them, I thought of other human events that might have happened on this beach— on the same rocks and shifting shoals of gravel and sand as the glaciers advanced and retreated to the west of us. But this was the twenty-first century after all; the bride and groom had been living together for five years in Homer, then California, now in Baltimore. It was almost quaint that they chose to marry. But the ceremony seemed to be about just what was being said—vows of giving to each other and truly seeing each other and, yes, loving each other. Their chosen passage from Corinthians seemed to say something about all the people who have come together in this place and cared about it: "Love is patient; love is kind. . . . It always protects, always trusts, always hopes, always perseveres."

The pastor spoke of love in the sense of love between people, not the lubricious rubbings of mollusks we used to snare the attention of ten-year-olds and peevish tourists on the same beach. The Athabascans, he told us, have hundreds of words for snow, and I doubted his cultural accuracy but granted him poetic license. "We, in our culture," he said, "have only one for love. Sanskrit has ninety-six. Greek has three."

"*Eros. Agape. Philia.*" The Greek words rolled around in his mouth like hard kernels.

He didn't speak of the love of place or dogs or spineless animals or moose. But I counted five former naturalists among the wedding guests. One summer in this place was apparently enough to bond people to it. More than that and it became *your* place, the one to which you could always return to be comforted by its enduring beauty and vitality. What would it be like to be born into a place where your ancestors had lived for a thousand years?

The looks that the bride and groom gave each other charged the air with a kind of warm energy, the reality of their love and their lives moving between them. The bride was incandescent; every step of her life seemed to lead her to this beach where she gazed into the groom's eyes before us all. I was a witness to their joining in the midst of that time-bound place. In witnessing, I felt part of it.

On Bishop's Beach flakes and chunks of coal, whose discovery led to Homer's first industry, lie in patterns that trace the forces of the currents. They tumble down from seams that thread through the crumbling sandstone, siltstone, and mudstone cliffs above the beach. The coal is ancient, formed from peaty wetlands buried by sediments after the warm Triassic two hundred million years ago. Clams bore into the coal and take up residence there, leaving behind their cylindrical holes.

I find and collect things from Bishop's Beach: a beer can, a bottle, a memory of Kiana running, a shell, a gleaming patterned rock, sand in the treads of my shoes, an insight. I lose things: an earring, a glove, my worries, the collected treasures in my pocket that crumble into shards by the time I return to the parking lot. My feet almost always get wet.

The day of the wedding, I walked down the beach to be alone at low tide in China Poot Bay, where we collect nothing except the seaweeds and animals we bring back to keep in live tanks at the field station. After so many journeys to that beach with a group of people in tow, talking loudly and frantic to show them something marvelous, I was strangely silent. In the low tide community, everything alive was clinging or creeping to a sweet spot of wetness. Moving down the beach toward the water's edge, the going was rough. Even in my rubber boots, I lurched and wobbled over the barnacle-encrusted cobble. Lower down a glistening tangle of seaweed covered the rocks. Barnacles unfurled their whispering feet to comb the water, a dull red crab waved its black-tipped pincers, a mottled fish appeared suddenly in a shape that had been hidden in camouflage to lunge for its prey. The true stars were nearly all humped up and wrapped around their meals of clams and mussels.

Outward toward the mouth of China Poot Bay, the sun lingered just above the horizon. The cliffs, the far shore, the surface of the bay, and the thickening air sheltered me in the silence broken by a sound like castanets coming from the beaks of gulls testing mussel shells for meat. Indignant crow babies squawked against the urgent, mournful chorus of gulls, receiving their twice-daily surprise of the tide coming in.

It was the end of the summer season and my last trip across Kachemak Bay before the fall and winter storms began and pinned me down, snug in Homer. The beach beckoned me to sit but not as a bed of sand that would yield and fit itself to me. Instead, the angular rocks made a poor chair as I squirmed and tried to ignore the edges that cut painfully into my back and bottom. Those ancient stones were no sanctuary welcoming me to linger and settle into a timeless stillness. The relentless tide was already rising. I could never be at home in that low tide place teeming with life.

An eagle called a whistling vibrato. High walls of twisted rocks topped by the thinnest frosting of soil and grass and an enormous spruce tree with its roots wrapped over the cliff's edge rose above me.

During my natural history tours, I told the geological story of those rocks, called cherts, many times—how they had accreted from radiolarian zooplankton with shells of silica raining down for millions of years somewhere near the equator until their weight and the weight of the water slowly turned them into the crystalline seafloor. How the rocks were moved slowly northward by the world's tectonic heart, which oozed lava at the edge of massive oceanic plates. How the cherts crossed the deep abyss of the Aleutian Trench that lay south of Alaska, and how they finally piled up along this shoreline that had emerged during its slow-motion collision with the North American Plate.

To look at them was to gaze through 180 million years of the history of rock below the frail-looking skim of life at the top of the cliff, the place where I fit in. I lived atop that narrow band of soil that had accumulated in ten thousand years after the last glacier melted. The Kachemak people had dug fifteen feet into that layer to bury their shells and bones. The Dena'ina had lived their lives in houses dug down into the top six feet. I had dug no deeper than my garden rows.

My whole life had happened in that topmost layer of thin skin and yet, at eighteen, I had wanted to save the world. At twenty-one, I had wanted to save Alaska wilderness, at twenty-five to save habitat for all of Alaska's fish and wildlife, at thirty to save the wild terrain in the minds of children. I had thought science was the way, then education. Finally, in my sixties, I was realizing that not everything could be saved because change was the true way of nature. But nature could be savored and its beauty and integrity defended as long as possible and then savored again and mourned in memory if it vanished bit by bit. Time and the weaving and unweaving of the web could not be stopped. Life— voracious for more life—clung and defended its territory. Need and desire expanded until vanquished by the death that honed it all.

My search for a baseline—a search for a point from which I could trace the trajectory backward to the time when the path forked—had consumed me. But it was all forking paths, all the way back, from the radiolarians who floated for their brief moment of time, their shells now frozen into chert, to the people who settled here and shaped blades from that chert and sent them whirling into seals and sea otters, to the whirling plankton that bloomed again every spring. The ecosystem was a process of constantly shifting relationships, not a destination. It had no true reference point, except in human memory and desire. All its participants, including me, were striving toward life and health, while redefining it, together, again and again.

I wish it could have been as simple as the Alutiiq tale that the sea otter is a magical creature who brings wealth through its death and returns to be hunted again if treated respectfully. I wish I knew what the Kachemak people thought about beauty and the afterlife as the volcanoes on the horizon sent forth plumes of smoke and they walked a frozen beach searching for mussels. I wish, like the Dena'ina, I could have found not beggesh, but comfort in the relative mercy of the Russian Orthodox priests and their teachings.

But these are not my beliefs. Instead I believe the forecasts of scientists, of looming ecological end times, even in a place where humans have been entangled with nature for thousands of years.

That thin top wedge of soil that makes it possible for us to inhabit this place was shaped by maelstroms of air and water, by deep cold winters and short dazzling summers. Like the cherts, I was brought to Kachemak Bay by forces that battered and shaped me, carrying me in an inescapable direction even as I was so merged into the flow I thought I was propelling myself. I'd become rounded in some places, sharp-edged and jagged in others, with crystalline knots of experience. The cherts were like frozen whorls of memory, twisting and turning through their intertwining relationships.

Something enormous released within me on the beach. I perched on a fluttery edge of laughter and grief as the knowledge about the past I had so laboriously accumulated dissolved. I had a glimpse of how it really is: that we always live within a thin and vibrant wedge of life, a labyrinth of branches and leaves and flowers and people and other animals, supported by the trunk of our imagined solid self, rooted in the layers and layers of turbulent and unfathomable history—deeper than any bedrock we can imagine—that wells up into the stories of our lives. Just like this place we call Kachemak Bay and the people who lived there before me, I had been shaped by sea, wind, rain, snow, long and short seasons, volcanoes, and earthquakes. But I had shaped something too in the people who walked alongside me, inhabiting this place, however briefly, and learning something about it in our human way, however scant. Something to savor, like the scent of seal oil and smoke.

When I returned to the lodge, the fog had rolled up off the bay and shaken itself from the shoulders of the mountains. Between the hors d'oeuvres and dinner, we danced—the bride, the groom, the parents and stepparents of the bride, cousins, sisters, friends from childhood, college roommates, naturalists, the flower girl. Sunlight shafted into the bay and spangled the peaks with clean, precise light.

We danced along the shore where people have lived for so many years—impressing their desires and intentions, eyeing the surface of China Poot Bay for ripples that preceded a surfacing sea otter or porpoise, watching for the kayaks that might signal enemies and danger or approaching kin and friends. From where we stood on the deck, eye level with the house site on the cliff, we had the bay in front of us. Two otters made waves in the bay below.

On the beach, the pastor had blessed us and spoken last about mystery: "May you have it every day of your life."

Acknowledgments

At the center of this book is my time among the family of staff and supporters of the Center for Alaskan Coastal Studies (CACS) in Homer, Alaska. My thanks go to Beth Trowbridge for making it possible for CACS to continue to be my home away from home during the writing of the book. My writing was also nurtured by my time among the University of Alaska Fairbanks faculty and staff of Alaska Sea Grant in Anchorage and the value they place on science and traditional knowledge for sustaining Alaska coastal communities. They indulged and accommodated my work schedule arranged around researching and writing the book over the course of seven years.

I'm grateful to all who shared their knowledge and insights into aspects of the natural and cultural history of Kachemak Bay, especially Daisy Lee Bitter; the late Carmen Field and her husband, Conrad; Scott Burbank and Susan Aramovich; Bree Murphy; Gretchen Bersch and her family on Yukon Island and the lineage of naturalists they mentored. I thank Conrad and also Kim McNett for providing their illustrations. The Dena'ina and Sugpiat and Kodiak Alutiit have generously shared their stories, their histories, and their hard-earned environmental knowledge through written accounts, films, and exhibits at the Anchorage, Pratt, Alutiiq, and other museums. I pestered too many scientists to name with questions and emails as I waded through the scientific literature and attended science conferences. I'm especially thankful for reviews of draft chapters by Anne Salomon for her bidarki research, Jane Sullivan and Gordon Kruse for their halibut research, Janet Klein for Kachemak Bay archaeology and anthropology, Angela Doroff for sea otter ecology, and Charlie Trowbridge for fish science and fisheries management. The work of scientists involved in the Gulf Watch Alaska long-term monitoring program was the source of much of what I learned about the complex dynamics of the Gulf of Alaska ecosystem. Scientific knowledge itself is a shifting baseline, so it's highly likely that new methods and evidence will cast a different light on the past. Any inaccuracies or misinterpretations of the science or traditional knowledge are, of course, my own.

The University of Alaska Anchorage Creative Writing and Literary Arts program provided the supportive and demanding writing environment and community that kept me on track for writing this book. I feel very fortunate to have had outstanding natural history writers as teachers and mentors in Craig Childs, Sherry Simpson, and Nancy Lord, as well as being blessed with the late, great writer Eva Saulitis as a mentor who showed me the way to the poetry in the sciences. I'm grateful to all of my fellow nonfictionistas in the UAA program for their companionship and critiques of early drafts of chapters of this book. Particular thanks go to Margaret Williams, my writing buddy, who joined me in writing sessions on many cold winter mornings, and to Mary Kudenov and Teresa Sundmark for additional reviews. Erica Watson did a heroic and excellent job of editing the next-to-last draft of the manuscript. Daryl Farmer and Jan DeBlieu provided very helpful manuscript reviews.

I owe another debt of gratitude to University of Alaska Press editor Peggy Shumaker, who afforded me the great honor of being included in the Alaska Literary Series and to Nate Bauer, Dawn Montano, Amy Simpson, Laura Walker, Krista West, Elizabeth Laska, and Joeth Zucco at the University of Alaska Press for shepherding me through the mysterious book publishing process.

Peggy Cowan shared many walks and conversations about the book over the years that its writing dominated my life. I also thank Don Williamson with whom I shared much of my life and experiences in Alaska along with Kiana, the Samoyed—who was to me the best dog in the world during her long dog life.

Sources

A full list of citations, by chapter, for all sources referenced directly or indirectly in the book can be found at www.ShiftingAlaskaBaselines.com.

The following sources provide overviews, syntheses, collections of articles, or proceedings of symposia or conferences in specific fields or topics.

Part I. Shifting Baselines

Jackson, Jeremy B. C., Karen E. Alexander, and Enric Sala, eds. *Shifting Baselines: The Past and Future of Ocean Fisheries*. Washington, DC: Island Press, 2011.

Mann, Daniel H., Aron L. Crowell, Thomas D. Hamilton, and Bruce P. Finney. "Holocene Geologic and Climatic History around the Gulf of Alaska." *Arctic Anthropology* 35.1 (1998): 112–31.

Salomon, Anne K., Nick M. Tanape Sr., and Henry H. Huntington. *Imam Cimiucia: Our Changing Sea*. Fairbanks: Alaska Sea Grant Program, University of Alaska Press, 2011.

Torben, C. Rick, and John M. Erlandson, eds. *Human Impacts on Ancient Marine Ecosystems: A Global Perspective*. Berkeley: University of California Press, 2008.

Part II. Artifacts

Crowell, Aron L., Amy F. Steffian, and Gordon L. Pullar, eds. *Looking Both Ways: Heritage and Identity of the Alutiiq People*. Fairbanks: University of Alaska Press, 2001.

Dixon, E. James. *Arrows and Atl Atls: A Guide to the Archaeology of Beringia*. Washington, DC: Government Printing Office, 2013.

Drabek, Alisha S. "Liitutkut Sugpiat'stun We Are Learning How to Be Real People: Exploring Kodiak Alutiiq Literature through Core Values." PhD diss. Fairbanks: University of Alaska, 2012.

Fagan, Brian. *Where We Found a Whale: A History of the Lake Clark National Park and Preserve*. Washington, DC: USDI National Park Service, 2008.

Friesen, T. Max, and Owen K. Mason, eds. *The Oxford Handbook of the Prehistoric Arctic*. New York: Oxford University Press, 2016.

Graf, Kelly E., Caroline V. Ketron, and Michael R. Waters, eds. *Paleoamerican Odyssey*. College Station: Texas A&M University Press, 2014.

Jones, Suzi, James A. Fall, and Aaron Leggett, ed. *Dena'ina Huch'ulyesh: The Dena'ina Way of Living*. Fairbanks: University of Alaska Press, 2013.

Kalifornsky, Peter. *A Dena'ina Legacy K'tl'egh'I Sukdu: The Collected Writings of Peter Kalifornsky*. Edited by James Kari and Alan Boraas. Fairbanks: Alaska Native Language Center, 1991.

Klein, Janet R. *Archaeology of Kachemak Bay, Alaska*. Homer, AK: Kachemak Country Publications, 2002.

————. *Kachemak Bay Communities: Their Histories, Their Mysteries.* Homer, AK: Kachemak Country Publications, 2008.

Korsun, S. A., and Y. E. Berezkin, eds. *The Alutiit/Sugpiat: A Catalog of the Collections of the Kunstkamera.* Fairbanks: University of Alaska Press, 2012.

Lantis, Margaret. *Alaskan Eskimo Ceremonialism.* New York: American Ethnological Society, 1947.

Stanek, Ronald T. "Sugpiat of the Lower Kenai Peninsula Coast." *Alaska Park Science* 3.2 (1998): 17–21.

Steffian, Amy, and April Laktonen Counceller. *Alutiiq Word of the Week: Fifteen Year Compilation.* Kodiak: Alutiiq Museum & Archaeological Repository, 2012.

Workman, William B. "Continuity and Change in the Prehistoric Record from Southern Alaska." *Senri Ethnological Series* 4 (1980): 49–101.

————. "Archaeology of the Southern Kenai Peninsula." *Arctic Anthropology* 35.1 (1998): 146–59.

Workman, William B., and Karen W. Workman. "The End of the Kachemak Tradition on the Kenai Peninsula, Southcentral Alaska." *Arctic Anthropology* 47.2 (2010): 90–96.

Yaw, Nancy Davis, and William E. Davis, eds. *Adventures through Time: Readings in the Anthropology of Cook Inlet, Alaska.* Anchorage: Cook Inlet Historical Society, 1996.

Yesner David R. "Evolution of Subsistence in the Kachemak Tradition: Evaluating the North Pacific Maritime Stability Model." *Arctic Anthropology* 29.2 (1992): 167–81.

————. "Origins and Development of Maritime Adaptations in the Northwest Pacific Region of North America: A Zooarchaeological Perspective." *Arctic Anthropology* 35.1 (1998): 204–22.

PART III. FUGITIVE RESOURCES

Atkinson, Clinton, E. "Fisheries Management: An Historical Overview." *Marine Fisheries Review* 50.4 (1988): 111–23.

Colt, Steve. *Salmon Fish Traps in Alaska: An Economic History Perspective.* ISER Working Paper 2000.2. 2000.

Cooley, Richard. *Politics and Conservation: The Decline of Alaska Salmon.* New York: Harper & Row, 1963.

Crutchfield, James A., and Giulio Pontecorvo. *The Pacific Salmon Fisheries: A Study of Irrational Conservation.* Baltimore: John Hopkins Press, 1969.

Dunn, J. Richard. "William Francis Thompson (1888–1965) and His Pioneering Studies of the Pacific Halibut, *Hippoglossus stenolepis.*" *Marine Fisheries Review* 63.2 (2001): 5–14.

Finley, Carmel. *All the Fish in the Sea: Maximum Sustainable Yield and the Failure of Fisheries Management*. Chicago: University of Chicago Press, 2011.

Gaichas, Sarah, Kerim Y. Aydin, and Robert C. Francis. "What Drives Dynamics in the Gulf of Alaska? Integrating Hypotheses of Species, Fishing, and Climate Relationships Using Ecosystem Modeling." *Canadian Journal of Fisheries and Aquatic Sciences*. 68.9 (August, 2011): 1553–78. doi: 10.1139 /f2011-080.

Glavin, Terry. *The Last Great Sea: A Voyage through the Human and Natural History of the North Pacific Ocean*. Vancouver, BC: Greystone Books, 2000.

Hollowell, G., E. O. Otis, and E. Ford. *2016 Lower Cook Inlet Area Finfish Management Report*. Anchorage: Alaska Department of Fish and Game, Fishery Management Report No. 17-26, 2017.

Johnson, Terry. *Climate Change and Alaska Fisheries*. Fairbanks: Alaska Sea Grant, 2016. http://doi.org/10.4027/ccaf.2016.

King, Robert W. *Sustaining Alaska's Fisheries: Fifty Years of Statehood*. Juneau: Alaska Department of Fish and Game, 2009.

Mundy, Phillip R., ed. *The Gulf of Alaska: Biology and Oceanography*. Fairbanks: Alaska Sea Grant, 2005.

Spies, Robert B., ed. *Long-Term Ecological Change in the Northern Gulf of Alaska*. Amsterdam: Elsevier, 2007.

Springer, Susan Woodward. *Seldovia, Alaska: An Historical Portrait of Life in Zaliv Seldevoe-Herring Bay*. Littleton, CO: Blue Willow Press, 1998.

Thoman, Rick. "The Pacific Ocean and Alaska's climate." *Alaska Climate Dispatch* (Winter, 2015–16), 9–11. https://accap.uaf.edu/dispatches.

Wennekens, M. P., Lance L. Trasky, David C. Burbank, F. F. Wright, and Richard J. Rosenthal. *Kachemak Bay: A Status Report*. Anchorage: Alaska Department of Fish and Game, Habitat Division, 1975.

Part IV. The Ecology of Desire

Bancroft, Hubert Howe. *The Works of Hubert Howe Bancroft: History of Alaska: 1730–1885*. San Francisco: A. L. Bancroft, 1886.

Black, Lydia T. *Russians in Alaska: 1732–1867*. Fairbanks: University of Alaska Press, 2004.

Bodkin, J. L., and B. E. Ballachey. *Sea Otter: Enhydra lutris*. Restoration Notebook series. Anchorage: *Exxon Valdez* Oil Spill Trustee Council, 1997.

Braje, Todd J., and Torben C. Rick, eds. *Human Impacts on Seals, Sea Lions, and Sea Otters: Integrating Archaeology and Ecology in the Northeast Pacific*. Berkeley: University of California Press, 2011.

Donlin, Eric J. *Fur, Fortune, and Empire: The Epic History of the Fur Trade in America*. New York: W. W. Norton, 2010.

Jones, Robert D. *Traditional Use of Sea Otters by Alaskan Natives: A Literature Review*. Anchorage: U.S. Fish and Wildlife Service, 1985.

Larson, Shawn E., James L. Bodkin, and Glenn R. Blaricom. *Sea Otter Conservation*. San Diego: Academic Press, 2015.

Lensink, Calvin J. "Status and Distribution of Sea Otters in Alaska." *Journal of Mammalogy*. 41.2 (1960): 172–82.

Luehrmann, Sonja. *Alutiiq Villages Under Russian and U.S. Rule*. Fairbanks: University of Alaska Press, 2008.

INDEX